The Digital Literary Sphere

THE DIGITAL LITERARY SPHERE

Reading, Writing, and Selling Books in the Internet Era

Simone Murray

JOHNS HOPKINS UNIVERSITY PRESS   Baltimore

Johns Hopkins University Press
2715 North Charles Street
Baltimore, Maryland 21218-4363
www.press.jhu.edu

Library of Congress Cataloging-in-Publication data is available.

ISBN-13: 978-1-4214-2609-9 (hc)
ISBN-10: 1-4214-2609-9 (hc)
ISBN-13: 978-1-4214-2610-5 (electronic)
ISBN-10: 1-4214-2610-2 (electronic)

A catalog record for this book is available from the British Library.

Special discounts are available for bulk purchases of this book. For more information, please contact Special Sales at 410-516-6936 or specialsales@press.jhu.edu.

Johns Hopkins University Press uses environmentally friendly book materials, including recycled text paper that is composed of at least 30 percent post-consumer waste, whenever possible.

This book belongs to
Elliot

Thus the act of recognising literature is not constrained by something in the text, nor does it issue from an independent and arbitrary will; rather, it proceeds from a collective decision as to what will count as literature, a decision that will be in force only so long as a community of readers or believers continues to abide by it.

STANLEY FISH (1980: 11)

So, does this mean that literature is dying on the Web? On the contrary. If anything, true to the nature of silver ages, we are into a miniboom as electronic magazines and prizes proliferate, new electronic publishers emerge, organizations spring up to develop online readerships and bring them into contact with the new writers. No . . . the new literary mainstream is being carved here.

ROBERT COOVER (1999)

Exploring how these connections [between book, reader, and other readers] are formed and what readers draw from them is crucial to the future of literary culture, particularly as literature itself increasingly becomes part of the mediated world from which it historically held itself apart.

KATHLEEN FITZPATRICK (2012: 202)

CONTENTS

TABLE

The bulk of the research comprising this book was made possible by a three-year Australian Research Council Discovery Projects grant (DP120100815: *Performing Authorship in the Digital Literary Sphere*). A further 2014 grant from Monash University's well-designed Advancing Women's Research Success scheme made possible attendance at that year's Society for the History of Authorship, Reading and Publishing (SHARP) conference, hiring of a research assistant, and a beneficial course of professional mentoring. As significantly, this grant gave my research career a crucial post-maternity-leave psychological fillip.

Sections of this book have assumed various guises during the course of the project and have benefited from the constructive criticism of editors and reviewers at several journals. Specifically, an earlier version of this volume's introduction appeared as "Charting the Digital Literary Sphere" in *Contemporary Literature* 56.2 (2015) Summer: 311–39. I am grateful for then editor Professor John Marx's enthusiastic championing of the rather unorthodox (for a literary studies journal) material at a crucial early stage. Work in chapter 2 previously appeared as "'Selling' Literature: The Cultivation of Book Buzz in the Digital Literary Sphere" in *Logos* "Independent Publishing Conference" special issue 27.1 (2016): 11–21. It was a new pleasure coauthoring an article with my then PhD student Millicent Weber: "'Live and Local?': The Significance of Digital Media for Writers' Festivals," *Convergence: The International Journal of Research into New Media Technologies,* "Writing Digital" special issue 23.1 (2017): 61–78. Some of the material in chapter 3 had its first print iteration in that guise. I am grateful to Millicent for illuminating discussions of the theatrical concept of liveness, derived from her own doctoral research, which informed and improved the theoretical scope of chapter 3. Most recently, portions of chapter 5 appear in *Book History* 21 (2018) under the title "Reading Online: Updating the State of the Discipline." Finally, early draft ideas for the conclusion's discussion of digital paratext were workshopped in an invited contribution to the special relaunch issue of *Literature / Film Quarterly,* now rebadged online as *LFQ:* "Three Key Questions for Adaptation Studies in the Digital Age," *LFQ* 45.2 (2017), "Adaptation Today" special issue (http://www.salisbury.edu/lfq/_issues/first/three_key_questions_for_adaptation _studies_in_the_digital_age.html).

Over the course of the preceding five years, I have undertaken the work of thinking through the nature of the digital literary sphere in a range of keynote addresses, conference papers, and workshops that were immensely stimulating. My fellow attendees' intelligent and occasionally uncomfortably probing questions prompted me to simultaneously sharpen and deepen my analysis. I give them my performative thanks here. These events included the Association for the Study of Australian Literature (ASAL) "Road Ahead" conference, Macquarie University, Sydney, 2013; the Literature and Affect: Australasian Association for Literature (AAL) annual conference, University of Melbourne, 2014; Religions of the Book: SHARP annual conference, University of Antwerp, Belgium, 2014; the Small Press Network Independent Publishing Conference, Sydney, 2014; Critical Matters: Book Reviewing Now symposium, Wheeler Centre for Books, Writing and Ideas, Melbourne, 2015; the inaugural Literary Studies Convention, University of Wollongong, Australia, 2015; The End(s) of Electronic Literature: Electronic Literature Organization (ELO) annual conference, University of Bergen, Norway, 2015; Between Texts and Readers: Book and Literature Promotion in the 20th and 21st Centuries, International Book Studies Society (Internationale Buchwissenschaftliche Gesellschaft) Young Scholars Conference, Johannes Gutenberg-University, Mainz, Germany, 2015; the AAL annual conference, Western Sydney University, 2016; Languages of the Book: SHARP annual conference, Bibliothèque Nationale de France, Paris, 2016; and the Technologies of the Book: SHARP annual conference, University of Victoria, British Columbia, Canada, 2017.

Additionally, I gave in-house seminars based on the material in this book on multiple occasions in my hometown of Melbourne, both at my home institution Monash University (2013, 2016, 2017) and across town at the University of Melbourne (2016). I also discussed my evolving ideas in radio interviews for the Australian Broadcasting Corporation's Radio National network *Books and Arts* program several times in the early years of the research—a terrific experience which prompted gratifying engagement by the broader public with the project's ideas.

I thank my research assistant, Dr. Kevin Patrick, for coming on board in the project's early years and intelligently sourcing a mountain of primary and secondary literature that I literally worked through for years. My colleagues at Monash University's School of Languages, Literatures, Cultures and Linguistics and the Centre for the Book helpfully read and commented upon my research at various stages, from draft grant applications to book proposals, and convincingly feigned interest throughout: Robin Gerster, Melinda Harvey, Anna Poletti, and Patrick Spedding. Further afield, University of Melbourne colleagues Beth Driscoll and Clara Tuite engineered invitations to present my research, gave thoughtful feedback at conferences and seminars, and were in all ways congenial intellectual fellow travelers. The annual SHARP conference has long been my favorite academic forum for its by now well-established openness to contemporary publishing developments, broad interdisciplinarity, and general conviviality. I thank fellow SHARPists for their intellectual companionship and good humor over many years: Sarah Brouillette, David Carter, Beth Driscoll, Simon Frost, Danielle Fuller, Per Henningsgaard, Cora Krömer, Stevie Marsden, Marianne Martens, Melanie Ramdarshan Bold, DeNel Rehberg Sedo, Simon Rowberry, Claire Squires, Ann Steiner, Shafquat Towheed, and Alexis Weedon.

Two anonymous referees for Johns Hopkins University Press read the draft manuscript in its entirety. Their scrupulous attention to the text and astute sense of disciplinary siting tightened the project's analysis and refined its expression. I am immensely grateful for their intellectual generosity, time, and expertise. David Goehring put the entire manuscript through a copyedit both assiduous and tactful.

By convention, the personal thanks come last, though those closest to the coalface of a project invest the most and typically reap the least intellectual reward. It hardly seems fair. I hope this can be partial recompense. On the home front I thank Kieran Hagan, Helen Murray-Gould, Rod Gould, Geoffrey and Heather Hagan, the Posse members (both financial and honorary), Rebekah Bull, and Rebecca Emmert. This book is dedicated to Elliot Hagan who, in a positive sign for the future, sees no contradiction between books and computers.

The Digital Literary Sphere

Charting the Digital Literary Sphere

What is the relationship between digital communication technologies and contemporary literary culture? In some ways, it is a question rarely posed at present, largely because it has been posed so often before and the often grandiose predictions formulated in response have so lamentably failed to materialize. Since the late 1980s, proponents of literary hypertext and later network-inspired variants such as remix fiction and Twitterature have challenged literature's traditionally linear-narrative and single-author characteristics (Bolter, 1990; Coover, 1992, 1993; Landow, 1992, 1994; Delaney and Landow, 1994; Douglas, 2000; Page and Thomas, 2011). Roughly simultaneously, since the early 1990s, constant academic speculation over the imminent "death of the book" cast doubt upon literature's traditional print-culture format (Spender, 1995; Nunberg, 1996). Yet e-books have demonstrably failed to eliminate codex book sales to date, and even the most critically acclaimed hypertext fictions remain mere curiosities in the literary canon, their dissemination beset by problems of software and hardware obsolescence (Montfort and Wardrip-Fruin, 2004; Ensslin, 2006; Moulthrop and Grigar, 2017). These facts have rendered the question of digital technologies' impact on contemporary literary culture a passé, almost embarrassingly naïve, inquiry in the eyes of mainstream literary studies. There is a weary sense that, as a discipline, we have been around this block before.

Yet the manifest failure of futurists' more eschatological predictions to come to pass is not reason to abandon the question of the digital's significance for literary culture. Rather, it should serve as a spur to provide better answers—newer, alert to the risks of rhetorical overreaching, and attentive to the varied and sometimes contradictory permutations of contemporary digital culture. For the Internet offers an abundance of what in earlier print- and broadcast-dominated eras was collectively termed "book talk": book review websites, self-cataloging library networks, author home pages, publishers' portals, online book retailers, archived writers' festival panel sessions, and recorded celebrity author readings. Indeed, the challenge for contemporary bibliophiles is not to *locate* literary content of interest online but, rather, to sift the perspicacious and illuminating wheat from the chaff of vapid adulation and naked self-promotion (Sullivan, 2013a, 2013b). For literary studies to ignore this rich seam of online biblio-enthusiasm simply because the question of the digital literary interface has been posed before and the answers found wanting risks looking like smug self-satisfaction on the part of print culture's erstwhile defenders in the face of earlier waves of digital boosterism. More pervasively, for a discipline fearful of the impact of neoliberal political agendas on research funding allocations, student enrollments, and graduate employment prospects, it is needlessly self-limiting to dismiss such ample evidence of continued public enthusiasm for matters literary (English, 2012; Collins, 2013).

This is not to suggest that academe has, since the turn of the millennium, remained silent on the relationship of digital media to literary culture—conceived of broadly as the study of not only textual characteristics, authorial styles, and genre categorizations but the entire institutional apparatus governing the producing, disseminating, and consuming of literary culture. Insightful and productive work on the significance of electronic publishing and self-publishing, the game-changing role of online book retailers, and the impact of digital media on reading practices exists (Miller, 2006; Siemens and Schreibman, 2007; Darnton, 2009; Striphas, 2009; Collins, 2010; Lang, 2012). But most striking is how often it is found, piecemeal, at the fringes of better-established disciplines such as book history (whose very choice of name signals its unease with contemporary developments), nationalist literary studies (despite the Internet's structural undermining of national boundaries), cultural sociology (though traditionally restive with specifically literary judgments), and cultural studies (long more attuned to screen media than the codex). Lacking is a unifying term that could give focus and coherence to a currently scattered body of work. This book therefore deploys the umbrella term "the digital literary sphere." The phrase's Habermasian echoes are deliberate. The German sociologist's influential study of how print communication fostered the growth of national bourgeois public spheres in various western European nations from the early eighteenth century provides a handy model of a multi-actor system that can account for the complex interplay of intellectual, political, and economic forces. But since the translation of his key work, *The Structural Transformation of the Public Sphere* (1962), appeared in English in 1989, Habermas has been a thinker adopted principally in sociology, philosophy, political science, and media studies, not by and large in literary studies.[1] This is despite Habermas's contention that the literary public sphere was the precursor of the genuinely political public sphere (30–33, 55–56). Equally, the periodicals, coffee houses, and salons on which he bases his theorizations ranged freely between what we now demarcate as fiction and nonfiction categories: "the two forms of public sphere blended with each other" (55). Granted, historians of nationalist literatures have occasionally deployed Habermasian models, albeit heavily inflected by the work of Benedict Anderson (1983), to demonstrate how national print publications nurtured a developing sense of "imagined community." But for most literary scholars engaged with *contemporary* literature, Habermas remains emphatically marginal—other disciplines' go-to theorist for analyzing social, institutional, and material contexts typically regarded as other disciplines' bailiwick.[2]

It is clear that e-book formats are undeniably encroaching upon the codex as literature's dominant platform, and that pockets of specialist interest in niche digital literary experiments such as the Electronic Literature Organization (ELO) remain; nonetheless, the vast majority of online literary discussion concerns traditionally linear, single-author narratives published either in print form or in e-book versions that mimic the codex experience. What is required academically to do justice to these developments is a sociocultural conceptualization of the digital-literature interface that is both *contextual* in focus (rather than belletristic or technocentric) and *contemporary* in outlook, so we may gain greater insight into digital media's role in fashioning twenty-first-century authorial careers, publisher prospects, public understandings of literature, critical judgments, and reader behaviors. By the second decade of the twenty-first century, digital environments have clearly ceased to be severable appendages to a properly print-focused literary universe. But it is equally true—perhaps contrary to some of the more imperializing claims of media studies—that literary discourse and its characteristic dispositions continue to shape the nature and norms of online book talk, rendering it distinct from online discussion of other cultural forms. It is this complex interface of literary-digital mutual interpenetration that demands detailed analysis so that literary studies may document and better comprehend an epochal moment of literary culture's adaptation to and colonization of a newer communications format—an era of veritable digital incunabula.

Research in Cognate Fields

The current project's charting of the digital literary sphere operates at the confluence of three dynamic academic fields: book history / print culture studies, media studies, and electronic/digital literary studies. While each discipline is expanding, they have thus far too often failed to engage with one another directly.

Book History / Print Culture Studies

While "the author" is a foundational concept in literary studies, its theorization was not prevalent in the Anglophone scholarly world until translations of Roland Barthes's and Michel Foucault's interventions of the late 1960s drew attention to the way in which academic veneration of the "author figure" functioned to shut down the innate polysemy of texts ([1968] 1986; [1969] 2006). During roughly the same period, but starting from a diametrically opposed empiricist position, the bibliographically inspired discipline of book history has sought to reconstruct the historical, institutional, and material characteristics of authorship's development. These crystallized in the early twentieth-century appearance of the professional (typically male) author—able to live by his pen, vigilant in protecting his international copyrights through the medium of a literary agent, and staging strategic interventions into the public sphere (Hepburn, 1968; West, 1988; McDonald, 1997; Delany, 2002; Gillies, 2007). Situated methodologically between these two approaches has been a third strand of culturally inflected legal scholarship that traces the emergence of the author as a foundational concept in the growth of intellectual property (Rose, 1993; Woodmansee and Jaszi, 1993; Biriotti and Miller, 1993). The most recent wave of book history–inspired authorship studies has emerged over the last decade and a half. It focuses upon the intriguing phenomenon of celebrity literary authorship. Such studies comprise in part a subset of the exponentially growing field of celebrity studies within media and cultural studies generally. But they can be distinguished from this larger field in key regards. First, their focus is the avowedly minority interest of self-described "literature" (as opposed to popular mass culture). Second, they display an uncharacteristic attention to a *print* medium (as opposed to most celebrity studies' preoccupation with screen media) (Gardiner, 2000a; 2000b; Moran, 2000; Glass, 2004; York, 2007; Squires, 2007; Brouillette, 2007; Ommundsen, 2009; Rooney, 2009).

The contextual preconditions for the late twentieth-century celebrity author include structural realignments such as the concentration of publishing houses within multimedia conglomerates, the related shift to sales- and marketing-driven frontlist publishing (those books published in the current season), and the proliferation of creative writing courses in universities (including outside their traditional heartland of North America). In such a context, the author does not (as post-structuralists might have it) disappear from the text so much as continuously offer pronouncements on how readers should interpret it. These can be proffered via public readings and meet-the-author events, profile pieces in broadsheet newspapers, or personality-centered arts (and even news) television programming. The fact that many scholars of celebrity authorship are trained in literary studies predisposes the majority of their work toward sequential textual analysis of case studies—scrutinizing the works of star authors for signs of their invocation, evasion, or subversion of the celebrity author trope (Moran, 2000;

Glass, 2004; Brouillette, 2007; York, 2007). This disciplinary tic has often had the unfortunate effect of confining the contextual and sociological conditions for the rise and maintenance of celebrity authorship to the introductory chapters of such full-length studies. But, still more problematically for a discipline striving to interpret contemporary cultural formations, celebrity author studies are overwhelmingly biased toward print and broadcast media. As a result they offer only the most glancing analysis of how the characteristic affordances of the *digital* literary sphere may be redrawing the contours of contemporary celebrity authorship.

Media Studies

The rapid expansion and uptake of the Internet during the 1990s made "new media studies" initially a burgeoning subfield of media and cultural studies. But now, given all communications formats' conversion to binary-based systems, the entire discipline of media studies is by definition digital in nature. As with the emergence of any new medium, attention was initially on how the Internet differed from extant communication formats, particularly the formerly dominant medium of broadcast television. To this end, the decentralized, networked structure, interactive capability, global reach, and lower barriers to entry characterizing digital media have been thoroughly analyzed in social theory and media studies since the mid-1990s. In spite of these fields' predominant attention to television and film, the implications of networked logics also began to make themselves felt during roughly the same period in the discipline of print culture studies. Indeed, "the future of the book" became almost a 1990s cliché of scholarly book chapters, special journal issues, and academic conferences. Many of the more dire predictions of the "death of the book" may appear risible in retrospect. But digital networks' tendency to "disintermediate" the formerly linearly conceived "publishing chain" by cutting out various middlemen, the fragmenting of the once singular book into a bundle of adaptable and repurposable rights, and the potential usurpation of the publisher role by other communication-circuit agents are all revolutionizing trends (Kotha, 1998; Epstein, 2001; Erickson, 2003; Wirtén, 2004; Thompson, 2005, 2010; Murray, 2006, 2007; Ray Murray and Squires, 2013; Dietz, 2015).[3] The technophoria of the mid-1990s has, however, left an unfortunate legacy: digital media and print culture studies' avid attention to changing e-book formats and digital rights skirmishes has distracted both fields from considering the surprising resilience of *literary* discussion on the Internet itself. Such literary habits persist, as mentioned above, in the form of digital-sphere cultural magazines, heavily trafficked book blogs, and book cataloging and recommendation sites.

Electronic/Digital Literary Studies

The forum in which we might reasonably expect the digital literary sphere to be most fully analyzed is the currently burgeoning discipline of electronic (or, more recently, digital) literary studies, itself a subset of liberal arts faculties' current Great White Hope, the "digital humanities" (also known by the acronym DH). Electronic/digital literary studies, though still very much an outlier to mainstream literary studies, has nevertheless cohered around several established nodes. The first of these, *qualitative* studies, typically use digital databases and archives to undertake philological, bibliographical, and textual scholarship of past works and often primarily self-classify according to a particular author or historical period (for example, digitized medieval manuscripts, Early English Books Online, even early versions of Jerome McGann's The Rossetti Archive) (McGann, 2001). This alignment with a broadly chronological literary taxonomy is revealing; such studies tend to conceive of digital resources principally as aids (or impediments) to standard paper-based critical methodologies, rarely as objects of scholarship in their own right (McGann, 2001: 17; 2004: 411). As Matthew Kirschenbaum, a leading digital literary studies scholar, states, "textual critics have tended to treat the computer mainly as a platform-independent venue for studying the artifacts of *other* media" (2008: 16).[4] A related qualitative digital literary methodology derives from the long-standing subfield of literary computing. Such work, which Thomas Rommel clusters under the useful term of "stylo-statistical studies" (2004), involves computer-assisted analysis of the literary or linguistic characteristics of large corpora through text mining (for example, digital concordances, pattern matching, and author attribution studies) (Jockers and Witten, 2010; Wilkens, 2012, 2015; Jockers, 2013).

A third qualitative research stream theorizes or, more recently, performs textual analysis of born-digital literary works such as hypertext fictions (Hayles, 2002, 2005, 2008, 2012; Kirschenbaum, 2008; Bell, 2010; Bell, Ensslin, and Rustad, 2014; Hayles and Pressman, 2013). This is the field which ought, by rights, to provide the richest fodder for analyses of the contemporary digital literary sphere. Such research, often carried out by scholars under the aegis of the ELO, has been pathbreaking in foregrounding questions of medium that traditional literary studies had tended to overlook, erroneously assuming "literature" was coterminous with the codex format. Once texts are digital-born, literary studies' relatively settled, long-cozy triad of author-text-reader is thrown into the air. Electronic literary studies has, since its emergence in the late 1980s, reveled in the profoundly destabilizing implications and exciting potentialities of screen-based literary works:

multilinear narrative paths; increased reader agency; incorporation of graphic, audio, animated, and kinetic features; textual mutability; distributed authorship; and real-time creation, dissemination, and consumption. As digital media have evolved from CD-ROMs, through the emergence of the Internet, to Web 2.0 and social media, electronic literary studies has continued to explore the interface of literature and technology in ways that pose far-reaching, frequently highly theoretical questions for literary studies as a whole.

And yet, while many in the literary studies mainstream may consider these various strands of digital literary studies radically confronting, they are in some ways standard literary-critical hermeneutic operations simply carried out by means of a new tool. This is because each of these diverse approaches remains obdurately text-, author-, or medium-centric, rather than adopting a cultural-sociological approach focusing upon the *context* or material and institutional cultural systems influencing the emergence and circulation of specific literary texts.[5] For all of digital literary studies' self-conscious avant-gardism, it has evinced a noticeable conservatism in methodology, hewing close to cognate humanities and creative arts disciplines such as philosophy and visual cultures but fighting shy of more social-sciences-style approaches derived from cultural sociology or political economy.[6]

Complementing digital literary studies' various text-based, close-reading approaches is another digital literary studies stream of *quantitative* studies that use digital technology to engage in "distant reading"—compiling statistical data derived from mass literary corpora (for example, St Clair, 2004; Moretti, 2005, 2013; Bode and Dixon, 2009; Goldstone and Underwood, 2014). This approach, unlike the others, moves beyond the aesthetic or cultural-political considerations of the individual text/s to incorporate a more systematizing dimension. Its benefit is the ability to demonstrate patterns in literary development at mass scale, highlighting specific texts that may then lend themselves to close reading in recursive fashion (Piper, 2015). However, the gaze of such researchers is typically retrospective with a preference for earlier literary-historical periods being strongly marked, and as a result their research throws little light on contemporary literary developments. Copyright laws are a strong contributor to this situation, with most twentieth-century works remaining in copyright. For example, Andrew Piper, director of McGill University's .txtLAB, is helming the large-scale, multi-institutional grant NovelTM: Text Mining the Novel. While .txtLAB describes itself as interested in "approaches to understand literature and culture in both the past and present," project outputs to date deal predominantly with earlier eras.[7] The sample corpus of books used in Piper's study of "conversional" reading spans three languages and a "century-and-a-half," from "the late eighteenth century to the early twentieth," strongly suggesting that only out-of-copyright (in US legal terms, pre-1923) works have been consulted (2015: 85, 67).[8] This leaves Piper's model unable to be tested on the last approximately one hundred years of literary output, let alone that of the twenty-first century, as a consequence profoundly limiting its utility to elucidate the contemporary literary moment. The situation may, however, be showing signs of gradual improvement, with a recent round of grants from the HathiTrust focusing specifically on projects analyzing in-copyright works, and thus encompassing topics such as the US novel in the second half of the twentieth century, or the history and personnel involved in the Iowa Writers' Workshop (1936–present).[9] The outcomes of such research projects promise to throw light if not on the contemporary literary scene (defined as the twenty-first century), then at least on its late twentieth-century seedbed.

A third and final digital literary studies research node is *institutional* studies, which features a diverse array of work on digital libraries and archives, especially relating to budgets, informational access, and preservation; electronic scholarly publishing, open access, and peer review (and the implications of these for hiring and tenure decisions); the changing patterns of academic careers; and pedagogical uses for digital resources (Thompson, 2005, 2010; Darnton, 2009; Fish, 2011b). While the outward-looking, materially engaged, and strongly contemporary orientation of such research recommends itself, literary studies per se—or even the humanities more broadly—is rarely the focus of attention.

Hence, digital literary studies as it currently stands largely divides into using computers either to study texts that manifestly predate the arrival of digital media, or to study texts that can *only* be understood through digital platforms because they presuppose reading in digital environments. Recreating this scholarly lacuna on the more macro, *inter*disciplinary level, scholarly dialogue that might have been expected to take place between and among book history / print culture studies, media studies, and digital literary studies has to date largely failed to occur. Too often divided by departmental structures and attendance at different academic conference circuits, and, in some cases, hamstrung by divergent entrenched research methodologies, each of these disciplines has so far gestured at rather than explored the contemporary digital literary sphere. Omitted by all parties as a result is the vast range of contemporary literary discussion that takes place at the liminal zone between print and digital, such as online discussion of predominantly print texts, or examination of the way digital technologies publicize, market, and sell fiction—which is then read (perhaps) in print, only for readers to then reconnect online through book clubs, fan sites, personal library cataloging sites, book reviewing blogs, and so on. Put briefly, what is currently missing and is urgently needed is a digital literary studies that is both contemporary *and* contextual. This hinterland zone of contemporary print-digital literary overlap is the focus of the present volume. My motivation in writing this book is partly to better comprehend the key transitional period through which we are living, but also, more self-reflexively, to examine the effects of this print-digital coexistence for our broader conceptualization of the literary studies discipline. In short, the project asks: What is the significance of digital media for contemporary Anglophone literary culture?

Components of the Digital Literary Sphere

To begin mapping the vast scope of the digital literary sphere, I propose a matrix diagram (table below)—a model that incorporates various traditional literary "processes" along the horizontal axis: performing authorship, "selling" literature, curating the public life of literature, consecrating the literary, and entering literary discussion. The vertical axis, by contrast, is constituted by various subcategories of websites broadly based on sectoral origin. The dots represent points of intersection between items on the two axes—namely, websites engaged in particular literary processes. The benefit of such dual process / category axes is that they both acknowledge institutional processes created during the period of print culture's dominance (and their continuing power) while also granting due attention to digital culture's transformation—the collapsing and "disintermediation" of the traditional print-centric communications circuit (Darnton [1982] 1990; Thompson, 2005: 310). The matrix aims to do justice diagrammatically to English-language literary culture at a key period of transition, where the influence of the old ways perceptibly remains but the logics of the new digital environment have wrought such changes that the digital can no longer be regarded as a mere supplement to inherited print culture structures.[10]

It is impossible in this introduction to more than gesture toward the range of bibliocentric content falling into each of the seven website categories, but I summarize here some of the major players to indicate the ways in which they are instituting change in each of the five highlighted processes, before considering the analytical issues these changes raise for literary studies as a discipline. The book's five core chapters examine in turn each of the various literary processes situated on the horizontal axis, fleshing out and adding nuance to the discussion of website categories below.

Matrix Model of the Digital Literary Sphere

Website categories	Processes				
	Performing authorship	"Selling" literature	Curating the public life of literature	Consecrating the literary	Entering literary discussion
Print-originated media	•	•	•	•	•
Born-digital media	•	•		•	•
Author	•	•	•	•	•
Publisher	•	•	•	•	•
Retailer	•	•		•	•
"Reader"	•	•		•	•
Cultural policy entities	•		•	•	•

Print-Originated Media

(For example: *New York Times Book Review* (*NYTBR*), *Times Literary Supplement* (*TLS*), *New York Review of Books* (*NYRB*), *London Review of Books* (*LRB*), *Guardian* Books section)

It is clear that print-originated literary supplements have, since at least the mid-1990s, consciously parlayed their laboriously built status as offline literary arbiters into the digital environment. In so doing, they have increasingly adopted the technical affordances of digital media to engage their "readerships" in a variety of ways that wed consumers more closely to the masthead's brand. These methods include blogs; podcasts; PowerPoint slideshows; discussion forums; competitions; reader reviews; online reading groups; Twitter feeds; archives; personalized booklists; and audiovisual recordings of author readings, panel sessions, and public lectures. While long engaged with consecrating varieties of literary achievement by publishing influential book reviews, and thus to some extent also with undertaking a quasi-cultural-policy role in shepherding public conceptions of literature, such mastheads' digital incarnations are increasingly also engaging in author-making and (e-)book retailing through self-publishing ventures. They clearly aim to be dominant players at all stages of book creation, circulation, and consumption. By additionally hosting interactive forums such as online book clubs, showcasing rotating rosters of literary bloggers, and archiving audiovisual book-event content, these print-originated brands aspire to convert offline reader familiarity into online loyalty by becoming the discerning reader's digital first port of call.

Born-Digital Media

(For example: *Salon, Slate, The Elegant Variation, Bookslut, The Complete Review,* SlowTV)

Born-digital media incarnations tend to foreground communicative modes not available to traditional print culture—immediate interactivity, multimedia content, hyperlinking—though it is noticeable how frequently their print-originated rival websites have now cannibalized many of these formerly unique selling points. The rise of a new breed of book bloggers unaffiliated with traditional print-media outlets provides an exciting case study of the assertion and accumulation of literary capital by those previously outside the network of established consecrators. Such literary bloggers trumpet their freedom to provide frank and fearless book reviews because they are uncompromised by the commercial conflicts of interest and indebted backscratching allegedly characterizing their print-media rivals. Yet amateur bloggers have nevertheless become increasingly enmeshed in commercial book-world realities through inter-blogger status rivalries and the potential to sell onsite advertising arising from high levels of Internet traffic.[11] Around twenty book bloggers in 2005 banded together as the Litblog Co-op to increase participants' online visibility (the group has since disbanded), while others, still blogging, promise publishers review coverage of submitted titles during an agreed period in exchange for free copies of books.[12] Such generation of online "book buzz" places "amateur" bloggers in direct competition with avowedly commercial entities such as NetGalley, a business distributing prepublication digital galley proofs to key opinion influencers.[13] The existence of book bloggers further problematizes book reviewers' already liminal status between the amateur and professional domains. It moreover illustrates the digital literary sphere's dissolving of the traditional distinction between an autonomous, after-the-event "reader" and previously publisher-coordinated marketing and publicity functions.

Author

For literary authors, particularly in the "star" echelon, elaborate websites provide direct communication to readerships untrammeled by the potentially pesky agendas of publisher publicity departments, profile-compiling journalists, or literary festival organizers. Frequently such official websites are fairly standoffish, one-way, setting-the-record-straight affairs, often outsourced to a web-design professional. Exceptions to this category include Joyce Carol Oates, whose characteristic prolificness now extends to sending multiple daily Twitter messages to her approximately 178,000 followers,[14] or Margaret Atwood, dubbed "doyenne of digital-savvy authors" for her avid tweeting, experimentation with Kindle Serials publishing, and enthusiastic backing of the start-up fan-writer interactive portal Fanado (Baddeley, 2013).[15] More typically, younger and digital-native authors, especially those targeting young adult readerships, have enthusiastically embraced an interactive—even distributed—model of managing their online presence, such as John Green's *vlogbrothers* YouTube channel and even a competition for his fans to design the paperback cover of his novel *An Abundance of Katherines* (2006).[16] In the digital sphere, the author's role extends far beyond providing the content, followed by production and marketing self-effacement, schematized in Robert Darnton's influential "communications circuit" ([1982] 1990). Now the author is engaged in one-to-many or even one-to-one real-time relationships with readers, providing updates on the progress of writing projects, plugging future in-store or media appearances, intervening in current political or cultural debates, passing judgment on the work of other writers (whether established or novice), and selectively endorsing, correcting, or otherwise mediating reader discussions of their work. Instead of the broadcast era's authorial phasing in and out of public consciousness according to the publicity cycle for a new book, the digital-era author now aims for consistency and "stickiness" (in web parlance) of reader-writer relationships. As Anne Groell, fantasy author George R. R. Martin's editor at Random House, recently summarized the contemporary author's role, "outreach and building community with readers is the single most important thing you can do for your book these days. You need to make them feel invested in your career" (Miller, 2011).

Publisher

While book publishers' websites have, since their mid-1990s inception, been primarily geared toward publicizing and retailing house titles, contemporary websites of both multinational firms and independents have more recently expanded their ambit. They are now moreover involved in activities that might be described as consecrating the literary in a manner previously left to literary critics or cultural-policy bodies, as well as to facilitating readers' entry into literary discussion. This expanded range of activities is manifested in phenomena such as publisher-awarded prizes (especially for unpublished manuscripts), audiovisual recordings of literary events, social media feeds, and online book clubs. Digitally savvy publishers have even established dedicated YouTube channels hosting book trailers for house titles[17] as well as Pinterest "pin boards" filled with bibliophilic images for digital sharing to encourage further reader-publisher identification.[18] As digital media threatens to render redundant publishers' traditional intermediary role between author and reader, publishers have responded in part by insisting on their colophon as a guarantee of quality control in readers' minds. But, ambitiously, publishers have moreover attempted to inveigle themselves into every phase of the author-reader encounter: acting as points of information on author backgrounds and new releases, retailer-independent sources of both print and e-book sales, arbiters of literary value, and curators of book lovers' online home.

Retailer

(For example: Amazon, Book Depository, Barnes & Noble, Waterstones)

Book retailers, whether traditional brick-and-mortar or solely online, have not taken lying down publishers' attempts to bypass them by excluding retailer markup and selling direct to the consumer. Rather, they have retaliated by invoking a similar tactic and attempting to exclude publishers themselves from the publishing chain. In perhaps the digital literary sphere's most dramatic imperializing gesture, book retailer websites, principally industry behemoth Amazon, have attempted to dominate all phases of books' lives, across all media. Book retailing websites have expanded from mere sales outlets to become diverse and highly active literary communities through features like reader reviews (frequently ranked to stoke inter-reviewer competition); algorithmically generated "personal" book recommendations; book-browsing functionality; online-, self-, and serial-publishing; author home pages; blogs; email newsletters; and book groups. Avowedly commercial in intent, such book retailer websites nevertheless frequently invoke the language of cultural connoisseurship and curatorship formerly the province of academic literary studies. Indeed, despite their online location and typically international customer base, some bookselling websites, particularly those affiliated with local independent stores, may invoke the ethical consumerist rhetoric of supporting local businesses as a mark of enlightened cultural consumption.[19]

"Reader"

(For example: Goodreads, LibraryThing, BookCrossing)

One of the digital literary sphere's most intriguing phenomena is the emergence of what present as user-generated forums allowing avid readers to catalog and annotate their book collections, connect with those of similar tastes, receive and make recommendations, and rate and discuss particular titles. Omnipresent in the self-descriptions by such sites is the rhetoric of selfhood and individuality, with membership of an online bibliophilic community promoted as providing opportunities for cultural self-fashioning and literary display to a global audience of presumably like-minded types. However, despite their air of community co-creation, these sites are typically corporate undertakings and have in many cases been partially or wholly acquired by Amazon as it attempts to concentrate all varieties of online bibliophilia under its own umbrella (Newman, 2008; Nakamura, 2013).[20] Public criticism of such sites has tended to focus on various self-reviewing scandals facilitated by reviewer pseudonyms and site owners' responses to these abuses in tightening their reviewer guidelines. Such a focus has occluded deeper investigation of how such sites extensively infiltrate ostensibly cultural evaluations with a commercial agenda, such as listing "sponsored links" (that is to say, advertising) next to search results for specific titles or authors. In a telling instance of what new media theorist Jodi Dean terms "communicative capitalism," the core content of such "reader" websites—the reviews themselves—is created entirely by volunteer labor. The sites' "Terms of Use" policies reserve all intellectual property in reviews for the corporation, including the power to sell reviewer-created content to third parties, but those same policies hold reviewers themselves solely liable for any damage their reviews may generate (2003: 102).[21] Conspicuous cultural consumption here morphs into unwaged content provision in a manner characteristic of Web 2.0 environments but new to the realm of literary connoisseurship.

Cultural Policy Entities

(For example: national and state-based or provincial-based arts councils, writers' festivals, UNESCO-anointed Cities of Literature)

Because cultural policy has traditionally been formulated and enacted by national or state governments, its geographic specificity made it a natural partner for promoting nationalist (and especially postcolonial) literary paradigms during the second half of the twentieth century. But cultural policy, for the same reason, represents a less natural bedfellow for the jurisdiction-defying Internet. Curiously, during the same mid-1990s period when national and state boundaries were losing their robustness in cultural policy spheres, the role of the city as a key site for cultural innovation began to expand with the mainstreaming of creative industries discourse in both politics and academe (Landry, 1996; Leadbeater, 1999; Florida, 2002; Hartley, 2005; Hesmondhalgh, 2007; Cunningham, 2008). Such works' proposal of a loose international network of significant creative cities has been foregrounded in literary terms by UNESCO's dubbing of specific metropoles "Cities of Literature": first Edinburgh (2004), then Melbourne (2008) and Iowa City (2008), and later Dublin (2010), Reykjavik (2011), Norwich (UK) (2012), Krakow (2013) and Dunedin (2014), among a growing list (Brouillette, 2014; Driscoll, 2014; Hamilton and Seale, 2014). The concept of a network of cosmopolitan sites concentrating literary activity echoes (and in some cases has piggybacked upon) an existing circuit of prominent international Anglophone literary festivals and writers' workshops, such as the Edinburgh International Book Festival, the Melbourne Writers Festival, the Sydney Writers' Festival, the Iowa Writers' Workshop, the Hay Festival (UK), Adelaide Writers' Week, and Toronto's International Festival of Authors (Murray, 2012). The digital literary sphere has found a natural complementarity with such a denationalized and disseminated pattern of literary festival-going. Rather than being rendered obsolete by the Internet's year-round, 24/7, global literary discussion, literary festivals have seized upon digital technology's potential to extend the life and audience for face-to-face events through audiovisual recordings, podcasts, guest blogs, Twitter feeds, real-time web chats, and inter-festival live linkups. Indeed, several online-only writers' festivals have emerged in recent years that positively celebrate their ability to flout geographic limitations.[22] Even the online incarnations of embodied literary festivals thus not only preserve ex post facto festival events; they increasingly comprise the *content* of the festival itself, with online competitions prior to the event's start, live-tweeting throughout the proceedings, and guest bloggers providing commentary on events that are frequently still underway. Such a digital efflorescence of the writers' festival permits organizers to make compelling arguments to government sponsors about expanding audiences and extending the life of events at a time of shrinking cultural policy budgets. This tactic, in symbiotic fashion, permits successful festivals in turn to lend their weight to local government pitches for UNESCO recognition of the host city.

Key Concepts and Theoretical Framework

The characterizing of authorship as a *performance* in the table above signals this book's concern with the increasing importance of authorial personae for literary texts. This contention may, at first glance, appear counterintuitive. After all, compared with exclusively oral cultures, the defining characteristic of written communication is its *detachment* of the message from its originating author (McLuhan, 1962; Ong, 1982; Olson, 1994). By contrast, scholars of celebrity media culture have elaborated since the 1950s upon radio, film, and television's creation of a "para-social" dynamic, whereby audiences feel a quasi-kinship with the *persona* of the communicator (be it program host, charismatic star, or special guest) (Horton and Wohl, 1956; Turner, 2004; Marshall, 2006). Celebrity studies recognizes these consciously constructed and deployed communicative personae as having no necessary relationship to the biological being with which they are customarily associated. So long as the literary author's physical image and personal biography remained largely tangential to book culture (confined, perhaps, to paratextual matter such as back-flap author photographs and brief biographical notes), the writerly persona could be considered largely a matter of textual effects and implied author roles (Iser, 1974; Genette, 1997). But the late twentieth-century flourishing of author tours, writers' festivals, television and radio book-talk programs, live broadcasts of book-prize ceremonies, real-time linkups between writers' week events occurring on different continents, and the archiving of all of these online via massively popular audiovisual content-aggregator sites such as YouTube has meant that authorial embodiment and performativity have come to be key—and controversial—criteria in the marketing, reception, and evaluation of literary fiction (McPhee, 2001; Lurie, 2004; Donadio, 2005; Starke, 2006; Squires, 2007; Ommundsen, 2004, 2009). Routine advice columns in professional publications such as the Authors Guild's *Bulletin* or the UK Society of Authors' *The Author* on how to perform at writers' festivals, create a podcast, or engage readers through social media testify to the fact that theatrical norms of performance and conscious self-fashioning increasingly infiltrate the literary sphere. Despite their everyday familiarity to humanities academics, these manifestations of what David Carter and Kay Ferres (2001) broadly term "the public life of literature" have to date been barely acknowledged in literary studies proper. Their specifically *digital-realm* manifestations remain, as outlined above, even more lamentably underexplored. This omission is particularly glaring on the issue of how disintermediation and real-time interactivity fundamentally alter the nature of writer-reader encounters—even to the extent of collapsing that traditional print culture dyad.

The present project's focus on specifically *literary* creative writing also requires some explanation, as it may seem to fly in the face of cultural studies' now decades-old project to dismantle cultural hierarchies. Owing perhaps to the discipline-changing impact of British cultural studies' anti-Arnoldian critiques of literary canon-formation, the majority of academic research about creative writing on the Internet focuses upon popular fiction, the exponentially growing category of fan fiction, and mass-authored wikinovels (Tushnet, 1996; 2007; Pugh, 2005; Jenkins, 2006; Mason and Thomas, 2008; Page and Thomas, 2011; Guthrie, 2013).

Such genres and forms represent easier fits with the democratically oriented, anti-aestheticist rubrics of cultural studies' original intellectual project. Yet, over the course of the last decade and a half, there is strong evidence emerging from within cultural studies itself of dissatisfaction with such populist and relativist orthodoxies. Selected critics have noted public thirst for a surprisingly resilient brand of cultural self-improvement, investigating contemporary audiences' willingness to seek out and act upon markers of cultural prestige such as book prizes, film awards, and blockbuster traveling art exhibitions (Buckridge, Murray, and Macleod, 1995; Collins, 2002, 2010; Bérubé, 2005). In play here are formerly settled assumptions about high/pop cultural hierarchies, the relative determinism of cultural institutions, and the relationship between objectivist and subjectivist understandings of the category of "literature."

The chief aim of the present book is to straddle these shifting tectonic plates of literary studies and cultural sociology at a critical juncture in both disciplines' development. My discussion is situated squarely at their point of overlap: the subfield of *the sociology of literature* (English, 2010). This recently reenergized research area attempts to account for literature's resilience as a book-world category outside of academic environments, as witnessed by phenomena such as the flourishing of book clubs in both face-to-face and audiovisual environments, city-based mass reading events, and the proliferation of "great books" applications for e-book devices such as Amazon's Kindle and Apple's iPhone and iPad. Leading theorists in the most recent wave of literary sociology tackle this seeming discrepancy head-on. Tony Bennett, Michael Emmison, and John Frow undertake a Bourdieu-inspired statistically based analysis of contemporary Australian cultural life in *Accounting for Tastes* (1999), arguing compellingly that high culture now constitutes a distinct subsector of mass culture. Also invoking Bourdieu's idea of the "field" (*champ*), James F. English's groundbreaking *The Economy of Prestige* (2005) posits a stock-exchange metaphor for the social evaluation of cultural commodities. Here the cultural prize serves as the mechanism of exchange between distinct forms of cultural and economic capital. Neither work, however—nor joint research into celebrity literary authorship undertaken by English and Frow (2006)—specifically addresses the flourishing *online* dimensions of contemporary literary culture.

This book also adopts as its underpinning theoretical framework Bourdieu's characteristically sociological, contextually minded, and anti-aestheticist perspective. But it does so to stage a critical encounter with Bourdieusian theory, interrogating its applicability to the twenty-first-century literary sphere. Bourdieu's academically fertile field theory provides a capacious device to conceptualize the digital literary sphere in its totality. In fact, Bourdieu's field theory appears especially applicable to the online environment, given the Internet's rapidly fluctuating constellation of agents and institutions, and its demarcation as a "universe of belief" by all participants' self-identification as "literary" adherents (a distinction literary and cultural theory has in recent decades held to be largely unsupportable on any objectivist grounds) (Bourdieu, 1993: 82). Nevertheless, the advent of the Internet throws many of Bourdieu's pronouncements into sharp relief, casting doubt upon the alleged universality of his structuralist-inflected "rules" of cultural functioning by highlighting their French (and, especially, Parisian) specificity. They are thus doubtfully applicable to the de-territorialized (and, in the case of the current project, Anglophone) digital domain. Bourdieu's *The Field of Cultural Production* (1993) and *The Rules of Art* (1996) trace a literary field whose agents are overwhelmingly elite actors collectively possessing a virtual monopoly on the award of symbolic capital in the form of access to publication, literary prizes, and critical endorsements. By contrast, it is precisely the contemporary digital literary sphere's mass democratic accessibility, its vocal celebration of amateur self-expression, and the preponderance of born-digital start-ups that generate its cultural energy and dynamism. Unlike Bourdieu's cultural kingmakers, operating in the largely veiled contexts of literary coteries and exclusive salons, the digital literary sphere renders the actual functioning of cultural brokerage more transparent and more readily documentable than ever before. Further, how can Bourdieu's cast of human and institutional actors account for the preeminent importance of search engine optimization (SEO) and algorithmically determined "discoverability" in online book marketing? Technologies such as Amazon's proprietary Amabot recommendation software present themselves innocuously as simple aggregators of mass popular taste. However, the self-perpetuating logic of the popular becoming more popular that such technologies facilitate, and the commercially oriented ways in which consumer data is stored, combed, and displayed suggest that Bourdieu's critical take on capitalist cultural systems remains indispensable in the digital era.[23] In short, Bourdieu's conceptual vocabulary provides a productive model for challenging the textually exclusivist critical paradigms still constituting literary studies orthodoxy. But his models require sensitive reformulation and reframing to engage meaningfully with twenty-first-century digital cultural phenomena. Thus, over and above this book's core objectives of charting and analyzing the contemporary digital literary sphere, it aims to pose far-reaching *theoretical* questions for the broader sociology of literature, and for literary studies at large.

Conclusion: Contributions and Challenges

The benefits of understanding the digital literary sphere are multiple. Charting the breadth, diversity, and major nodes of digital literary networks gives us a fix on how literatures are being made in the twenty-first century. This insight in turn illuminates the complementary role of print and digital formats and moves discussion on from dated and tired "death of the book" and binary print-versus-digital formulations. As I hope this introduction's quick survey of the digital literary sphere has illustrated, it allows us to analyze changes in the roles and types of literary stakeholders, both the blurring of production, distribution, and consumption contexts as well as the impact of nontraditional industry entrants (for example, Amazon, Google, and Apple). At its broadest level, the project calls into question literary studies' still marginal engagement with sociological perspectives and interrogates the boundaries between text-centric humanities approaches and contextual, social science-inflected research methodologies. And while textual analysis is far from the main focus of the current project, more detailed analysis of institutional, economic, and cultural context nevertheless promises to illuminate the genres and styles of literary writing now being produced and achieving popular and/or academic acclaim.

But let me also be frank about the challenges of such a research undertaking. How to get a fix on a phenomenon so vast and constantly mutating? How to discern the bigger picture from amid the cacophony of individual tweets, blog posts, online reviews, and authorial podcasts, each with its own mix of commercial and community-building motivations? How to rank the importance and influence of specific sites outside of the usual print-culture protocols for assessing significance (such as publisher revenues, retailer sales volume, newspaper circulation and syndication figures, or academic credentials of critics)? Clearly, quantitative rankings generated by the Internet industry itself are indispensable here (for example, site-hit calculators, Google search-result rankings, and Amazon reviewer hierarchies). Yet researcher reliance on such data must be tempered by awareness of the investment of the compiler in specific result outcomes. In the digital literary sphere—as in Heisenberg's uncertainty principle—there is no way to stand outside of the phenomenon in order to analyze it; the researcher is always already enmeshed in that which she researches.

With these practical research caveats openly declared, let me conclude by touching upon some of the more abstract disciplinary issues that charting the digital literary sphere promises to reframe. These potentially thorny topics go to the heart of especially productive, self-reflexive disciplinary debates.

The digital literary sphere puts ever-greater pressure on the specialized niche of "literature" within the broader category of print-based narratives. The distinction has been under sustained attack since at least the cultural-relativist incursions of cultural studies in the 1960s and 1970s, but the digital literary sphere further erodes many of the traditional gatekeeper roles that had kept a vestigial literature / popular fiction distinction viable (for example, "publisher," "editor," and "critic"). The digital literary sphere radically undercuts the cultural arbiter status of professional literary critics within an online context of mass amateur criticism and reflex popular evaluation. Similarly, received understandings of a "real" writer as one who has been published are destabilized, if not rendered meaningless, in an era of self-publishing, online fan fiction, beta readers, and their resultant reader-writer blurring. Hence the digital literary sphere presents an unparalleled, real-time laboratory for examining "literature" not as a preexistent, aesthetically determined category, but as a denomination of cultural value in the act of being brokered by a fluid assemblage of highly disputatious and sometimes fiercely contentious cultural agents. "Literature" thus represents not the simple acknowledgment of a work's always present (if at times misperceived) aesthetic superiority, but rather the veteran's medal of having successfully navigated a hazardous terrain of valorizing and consecrating authorities. In a manner perhaps highly discomforting to traditional literary studies self-conceptions, "literature" to a large extent becomes what the digital literary sphere *deems* to be literature.

The Internet's demonstrably global infrastructure also puts severe pressure on nationalist conceptions of the literary canon by which departmental structures, research funding bodies, and the academic conference circuit have long taxonomically classified the discipline. Nation-state cultural-policy bodies and professional authors' associations have already had to wrestle with such issues, while literary careers defy neat national jurisdictions through the mechanisms of multinational publishing houses, transnational literary agencies, and foreign rights sales. While replacing nationally prescribed geographic territories with a mid-level category such as language-spheres as the key apparatus for classifying our object of study might appear a way out of the problem, a monolingual approach itself imposes paradigmatic distortions, bracketing off cross-cultural translation flows as the key determinant of the implicitly cosmopolitan "world republic of letters" (Casanova, 2004). While literary translation requires significant capital investment in individually unique cultural products, it clearly does not represent an insuperable barrier to the geographic expansion of authorial reputation (even if translation flows between the Anglosphere and elsewhere remain markedly asymmetrical). But if literary studies is to comprise the study of *all* creative writing in *all* languages (and potentially also cognate fields such as drama, film, television, opera, musicals, and computer gaming), there is a real risk of it becoming analytically unwieldy by being submerged into a general study of "culture." Cultural studies veterans of academic skirmishes over the last few decades may remain placidly unruffled by such an eventuality but, intriguingly, the classification misrepresents the sense of the "literary" as inherently *different* which pervades digital literary participants' rhetoric—thus risking misrepresentation of the phenomenon itself.

The subfield of digital literary studies has, since the early 1990s, considered at length what new teaching practices, assessment protocols, and rethinking of the student-teacher hierarchy might be required to teach nonlinear, time-based, and manifestly unstable digital genres such as hypertext fiction, wikinovels, and Twitterature (Landow, 2006; Pressman, 2007; Bell, Ensslin, and Rustad, 2014). Yet literary studies more broadly has been slow to grapple with how to make the wealth of contemporary online materials that our students routinely access in the course of their studies not just a slightly disreputable addendum to "proper" print-based literary resources, but revealing artifacts of contemporary literary culture in their own right. Internet-era literary phenomena such as book trailers, authorial blog-tours, online writers' festivals, and social media–hosted book clubs constitute digital paratexts that crucially mediate the author-reader encounter, and hence deserve the same scrutiny as "thresholds of interpretation" that Gérard Genette brought to the study of cover design, dedications, and prefaces (1997). Book history coalesced as a discipline by taking issue with mainstream literary studies' insistent dematerializing of the literary object as "text." It should nevertheless not be beyond it to acknowledge that *virtual* literary phenomena come similarly charged with sociocultural and economic interpretive significance. In short, literary academe of all stripes has much to gain in shifting from a posture of sniffy dismissal of a manifestly flourishing digital literary sphere to instead embracing digital environments as vital components of contemporary literary culture.

CHAPTER ONE

Performing Authorship in the
Digital Literary Sphere

The popular novelist, dependent upon a public for his living, frequently making it by regular contributions to the magazines . . . is now in the closest touch with his readers, both directly by "fan mail" and by way of such middlemen [journalists and literary agents] as have been considered in the previous chapter, in a fashion and to a degree that would have surprised Emily Brontë, amused Jane Austen, and outraged Henry James.

Q. D. Leavis ([1932] 1979: 47)

These natural laws of digital authorship are yet only in the beginning stage of development. We can expect that someday they will constitute the formative conditions for a new regime of authorship with its own definition of author's [sic] rights; its own practices of distribution, editing, and production; and its own legal, political, and economic configuration.

Mark Poster (2001: 93)

Paul Ewen's satirical novel *Francis Plug: How to Be a Public Author* (2014) presents itself as a field guide to contemporary literary authorship.[1] Noting that the authorial job description has expanded significantly beyond solitary creation to encompass author talks, literary festivals, and public readings, eponymous antihero Francis Plug takes it upon himself to compile a how-to guide for would-be authors intent on entering the public spotlight. Chaotic, alcoholic, and utterly lacking in self-awareness, Plug undertakes "fieldwork" across the UK: from charity events in secondhand bookshops to the Hay Festival, from concert halls to writers' workshops, to the Man Booker Prize ceremony itself, Plug the amateur literary anthropologist launches himself onto the literary scene. His typical modus operandi is to drink himself into inebriation, gate-crash a tony literary talkfest, humiliate himself in myriad ways, and waylay typically bemused real-life Booker Prize–winners with requests that they sign his pilfered first editions. To a large extent Ewen's humorous riffs on the game of public authorship could have been penned at any time since the literary festival boom of the 1980s: appropriate book-signing etiquette; how to appear pensive yet alluring in author photos; and the finer points

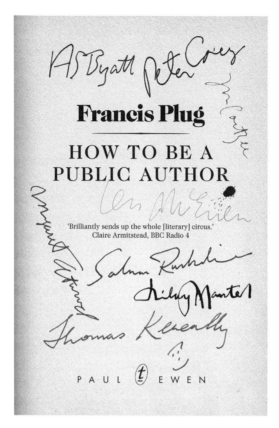

W. H. Chong's cover design for Paul Ewen's *Francis Plug: How to Be a Public Author* (Text Publishing, 2014): multiply-signed title page as front cover. © W. H. Chong

of authorial fashion, grooming, and microphone technique. Yet when Plug notes the ways that digital media increasingly infiltrate literary events—the recording of Salman Rushdie's talk for a podcast (9), pressure on authors to join Twitter and Facebook (84)—it becomes clear that twenty-first-century authorship has mutated in distinctive ways: "On top of their events, authors are also expected to be more interactive with their readers online. They're now encouraged to 'connect' with their audience and 'make friends' on social networking websites and the like. Maybe some authors are comfortable making 'cyber friends.' But I'd rather spend my spare time writing a book than writing about what I had for lunch. Writers don't make friends, they lose them. Especially drunk writers" (21).

In a rare moment of lucidity, Plug here taps into the way digital media have changed the nature of contemporary authorship: not only who gains access to the traditionally sanctified author role, but also the location and mode of author-reader interactions, their frequency, and even blurring of the traditional creative author / passive reader distinction. The Internet, a medium which is typically discussed as having profoundly democratized literary culture, has simultaneously amplified traditional Romantic concepts of authorial genius—to the point where the Internet in general, and Web 2.0 social media technologies in particular, have had the counterintuitive effect of reinforcing extant offline literary celebrity.

If Francis Plug is right in his guiding belief that public authorship is a role that anyone with the requisite advice and training can learn, it is worth asking: What are the implications of considering authorship as an ongoing performance—something cultivated though conscious choices even when authorial control can never be absolute? This holds true even—or especially—when authorial desire for fame is disavowed. There is no little irony in the verb choice "perform," given, as Canadian literary scholar Lorraine York notes, it would be harder to think of a less visually compelling, more sedentary mode of activity than an author sitting down writing (York, 2007: 12–13). In a similar vein, Kerry Myler notes TV book clubs' inherent difficulty with "the extremely camera-unfriendly medium of writing" (2011: 93). Yet there is precedent for considering authorship in a performative light. The collaborative project Research on Authorship as Performance (RAP), which ran between 2009 and 2014 at Ghent University in Belgium, investigated "to what extent the concept of performativity can be made fruitful for historical research on literary authorship in English studies" (Berensmeyer, Buelens, and Demoor, 2012: 7).[2] While the expansive historical remit of the project allowed the research team to empirically document fluctuation between various "weak" and "strong" author concepts across five centuries and various geographic areas, it is disappointing (from the perspective of the current investigation) that their research did not extend far into the twentieth century and the contemporary era.[3] For just as authors have, since the last decades of the nineteenth century, organized themselves into professional lobby groups and engaged literary agents, so too authorial identity has come increasingly to be conceived by the literary industry and by authors themselves as something to be professionally managed. The mainstreaming of digital communications, and especially Web 2.0–enabled social media after the turn of the millennium, has given authors unprecedented opportunities to directly shape and constantly micromanage their public image. It is a facility of which authors, from wannabes to acknowledged stars, have availed themselves with alacrity, with far-reaching repercussions for contemporary literary culture. As Jacob Silverman lamented in an opinion piece for web-based periodical *Slate* about the decline of critical literary culture: "Twitter and Tumblr form the superstructure of today's literary world. The salons and independent book-stores are disappearing, so this is where we congregate, allowing us to collapse geography at the expense of solitary thinking. This is where links are passed around, recommendations exchanged, news spread, contacts and friendships made. It is also where everyone is selling himself and where debate and dissent are easily snuffed" (2012).

But what Silverman reads as critics' and readers' loss is, conversely, potentially authors' gain. Digital media permit mass admission to the category of Author, lively interactivity with readerships, and the chance to cultivate a highly nuanced authorial identity across multiple communication channels and with a frequency impossible by means of codex publication alone. The impact of the digital literary sphere requires not techno-futurist boosterism nor print-loyalist denunciation so much as clear-eyed and nonpartisan description, at least as an investigative starting point. How does this constellation of new communications technologies change the object, parameters, and nature of contemporary literary discussion—what Ed Finn terms "the public game of literary culture" to which the Internet is increasingly central (2012: 178)?

Celebrity Author Studies

During the 1990s a vital and energetic area of research emerged that rethought the "author" figure not as literary studies' traditional Romantic embodiment of creative genius, but as a legal, economic and—above all—*institutional* category, a brand to differentiate products in a crowded literary market, and a label that writers in their works and professional practice either relished, or chafed at, or both simultaneously (Biriotti and Miller, 1993; Rose, 1993; Woodmansee and Jaszi, 1993; Woodmansee, 1994; Coombe, 1998, [1998] 2006). The whole trajectory of authorship studies since Barthes's famously liberatory declaration "The Death of the Author" (1968) and Foucault's more circumspect riposte "What Is an Author?" (1969) had been to denaturalize the category of author in literary studies (Burke, 1998). Principally this change has involved substituting inherited author-centric modes of hermeneutic control with graded levels of interpretative power that fluctuate between author-, text-, and reader-centrism. Yet, particularly since around the turn of the millennium, scholars in literary studies, cultural studies, and increasingly also media studies have probed the lives of contemporary authors *beyond* the book, examining the seemingly oxymoronic phenomenon of literary celebrity.[4] Key foci have included authors' embodied performances at writers' festivals, their political engagements, and their continuing hermeneutic agency in popular culture (Ommundsen, 1999, 2004, 2007, 2009; York, 2000, 2007, 2013a,

2013b; Glass, 2004; Brouillette, 2007, 2014; Stewart, 2010a; Murray, 2012; Fuller and Rehberg Sedo, 2013; Driscoll, 2014; Weber, 2015). It has even become something of a cliché in authorship studies to note that, Barthes's assertion notwithstanding, in the late twentieth and early twenty-first century authors are far from dead and have been, if anything, positively revivified (Sage, 1998: 265, 276; Gardiner, 2000a: 257; K. Douglas, 2001: 806, 812, 820–21; Ommundsen, 2007: 247; 2009: 32; Hartling, 2007: 291, 295; Murray, 2012: 34; Busse, 2013: 49, 54). Indeed, Nicholas Rombes has argued, "The recent surge in personal websites and blogs—rather than diluting the author concept—has helped to create a tyrannical authorship presence . . . [which] has only compounded the cult of the author" (2005). We appear to have come full circle here, with Rombes deploying exactly the same adjective—"tyrannical"—as had Barthes decades earlier to describe the stranglehold over literary interpretation exerted by the proper name of the author. Except that the cult of the author within (French) academic criticism against which Barthes railed seems now to have been extended to whole reading populations.

Despite this frequently remarked-upon expansion of the authorial remit, and despite the fact that authorial personae are increasingly projected via digital media, there has been a paucity of authorship studies analyzing the specific changes in authorial performance made possible by digital media technologies. For example, Joe Moran's *Star Authors* (2000), the earliest book-length study of contemporary celebrity authorship, adopts Bourdieusian terminology of the field to situate the phenomenon of literary celebrity in America: "The author represents both cultural capital and marketable commodity," with the intersection between the two value systems complex and inherently unstable (2000: 6). Moran's work is important for its subtle placing of celebrity at "the intersection between the textual and contextual aspects of American writing" (10). Yet his book (despite its publication date) is overwhelmingly preoccupied with print and broadcast media (especially television) (10). His analysis of the role of the "mediagenic" author focuses on TV talk show appearances, personality-focused broadsheet newspaper profiles, headline-grabbing book advances, multi-city book tours, and the like (35). The Internet is confined in the index to a mere two mentions, despite Moran's noting that the multinational conglomerates that overwhelmingly dominate book publishing frequently also have holdings in "CD-Roms [*sic*] and on-line services" (39). The peripheral role Moran accords the digital realm in constructing contemporary authorship perhaps reflects his book's origins as a PhD thesis, presumably written during the mid- to late-1990s, when the Internet was moving toward, but did not yet fully occupy, the center of contemporary cultural life.

Similarly, James F. English and John Frow, writing six years later, also adopt an explicitly Bourdieusian framework of intertwined cultural and commercial capital, where the contestability of celebrity author figures stems from their sitting "at the intersection of competing regimes of value" (2006: 48). The construction of literary celebrity they analyze "takes place in the press and on television," specifically via newspapers, magazines, and literary journals in the former media category and TV (and to a lesser extent radio) in the latter (51). For Sarah Brouillette, well-trafficked book-centric websites such as the *Guardian*'s and *Salon* are noteworthy as vehicles for marketing "literary fiction for a cultured audience," but she does not explicitly factor in the digital literary sphere to the *construction* of celebrity authorship, which her study *Postcolonial Writers in the Global Literary Marketplace* analyzes principally through the literary works of prominent postcolonial authors (2007: 55; see also York, 2007). Kerry Myler examines the importance of the (frequently female) performing authorial body to the television book club, in particular its ability to collapse author/narrator/character distinctions for the TV audience, but does not fully explore the quite different dynamics characterizing the online dimensions of such book clubs (2011: 89; 92–3). Equally, Andres Ohlsson, Torbjörn Forslid, and Ann Steiner note in passing the importance of "social media, apps etc." to contemporary book promotion, but their larger analysis of "the commodification and mediatisation of the author" draws exclusively on broadcast media and makes no distinction between analog and digital media modes and affordances in the conduct of literary celebrity (2014: 33, 41).

There thus appears to be an analytical lag between the proliferation of literary discussion in online spaces that almost all literary academics encounter on a daily basis, and in which they may well participate, and the take-up of these developments at the level of cultural theory. The author as a cultural figure is, as book historians have abundantly chronicled, indivisibly intertwined with the emergence of Gutenbergian print culture and its concomitant regimes of textual fixity, copyright, and academic literary studies (Eisenstein, 1979). The disruptive changes in communication experienced since the mainstreaming of the Internet in the early- to mid-1990s have had a similarly profound impact on admission to the previously semi-sacrosanct category of author, as well as on the practice of authorial identity for those admitted.

Yet during the same period the idea of the author has been far from absent in discussions of electronic literature. Since the early 1990s researchers have investigated how digital media recasts traditional conceptions of the author, especially as regards electronic media's alleged downgrading of authorial control over a text and the concomitant elevation of the reader's role, who was now recast as hybrid reader/writer, or even coauthor (Bolter, 1990, 2001; Landow, 1992, 1997, 2006;

Coover, 1992; Hartling, 2007; Skains, 2010; cf. Burke, 1998). But it is notable that such work tends to be exclusively text- and medium-centric, concerned principally with the relative power of authors and readers to order narratives and to determine textual meaning. Early electronic literature theorists were therefore very much reinforcing the textual exclusivity of New Critical, Leavisite, and Structuralist literary studies methodological protocols (however much they presented themselves, and were certainly viewed, as iconoclasts). As outlined in this book's introduction, the field of electronic literary studies has so far granted almost no attention to modes of authorial digital media use *outside* of the text (for example to cultivate and project a public image, to publicize and market a work, and to interact with actual—as opposed to idealized—readers).

Some related work has appeared regarding academic nonfiction authorship and the both exciting and somewhat disconcerting experience for humanities academics of collaborative and interactive authorship facilitated by digital media (Fitzpatrick, 2011a, 2011b; Berensmeyer, Buelens, and Demoor, 2012).[5] In the more media studies–inflected end of literary studies there has also emerged work regarding nonfiction bloggers and identity-construction via interaction on social media (Whitlock, 2007; Smith and Watson, 2014). Yet, such works hew closer to life-writing modes of analysis than fiction-based models.

The most radical undermining of literary studies' traditional writer-reader distinction takes place in the world of fan fiction, where amateur writers not only freely appropriate the characters, plots, and settings of professionally produced texts, but act as simultaneous reader, writer, and critic by posting beta-reader feedback on other fanfic authors' works (Thomas, 2011a, 2011b; Busse, 2013). Written texts raided by fanfic authors run the full gamut from highly canonical classics through popular fiction down to unapologetic genre fiction (with the bulk of fanfics occupying the middle to lower end of traditional cultural-prestige hierarchies). But even Jane Austen fanfic is unlikely to be recognized by any but the most dyed-in-the-wool cultural relativist as "literature." Fan fiction therefore remains beyond the ambit of the current book. As I argue in my introduction, taking inspiration from Stanley Fish's enduringly fecund idea of "interpretive communities," definitions of "literature" are not determined by any innate textual qualities, but are rather brokered through ongoing social, economic, and institutional consensus. Given this fact, the absence of consensus around fanfic's literary status necessarily marks it as beyond the scope of the present study.

This brief survey of extant work in authorship studies thus returns us to this chapter's key question: What is the impact of digital media on the performance of contemporary literary authorship? Very little theoretical work on the question currently exists, despite evidence of authorial performance occurring daily online, and its implications for writers' working lives being frequently debated on anec- dotal or empirical levels in literary-sphere publications such as the *Guardian*'s Books section, *TLS, NYTBR*, and the periodicals of national author societies (cf. Burdick et al., 2012: 11). Once even fictional literary anthropologists have begun to itemize digital media's impact on the literary landscape, it is clearly time that the academy sat up and began to take note of the changes underway and to devise a theoretical schema for comprehending them.

How Digital Media Restructure Authorial Identity-Performance

Clearly, restricting analysis of celebrity authorship to analog media obscures the particular ways in which the characteristic affordances of digital media fundamen- tally alter existing conceptions and practices of celebrity authorship, namely:

- Disintermediation: This denotes the ability of (would-be) authors to pub- lish, publicize, and sell their work without the gatekeeper approval of main- stream media arbiters (agents, publishers, marketers, publicists, and retail- ers). It amounts to a do-it-yourself (DIY) revolution in authorial construction and ongoing control over an author's public persona. The trend represents in part a resurrection (or at least further complication) of the Romantic myth of the genuine literary author as divorced from the grubby commer- cialism of the marketplace, as online self-publishing and direct mainte- nance of reader-author interactions bypass many offline book industry intermediaries. However, such a descendent of early-1990s-style Internet utopianism must remain willfully blind to the thoroughly capitalist ethos of information and communication technology (ICT) hardware and soft- ware producers upon whom the digital literary sphere is dependent, not to mention the role of digital literary sphere corporate behemoths Amazon, Google, and Facebook (the "Big Three"). Besides these three, we also need to consider the commercial self-interest of smaller-scale online self-publishing enterprises, themselves often subsidiaries of the digital literary sphere's Big Three.
- Interactivity: The digital domain offers authors the possibility of rapid or even real-time interaction with readers irrespective of their geographic lo- cation, and publicly accessible archiving of such interactions. This includes use of both "push" (websites, blogs, vlogs) and "pull" (RSS feeds, Facebook updates, Twitter followings) digital media technologies to maintain quasi- intimate connection with readers (potentially themselves also writers). Reader

impact upon an author, previously only belated and indirect (hence represented tentatively as a dotted line in Robert Darnton's famous communications circuit model) is here made manifest, as feedback may come not only months or years following publication through reviews, fan letters, and the like, but during the course of literary composition ([1982] 1990). Rare authors even solicit reader-fan participation through commentary on blog posts or book drafts (for example, Wark, 2004, 2007; Anderson, 2006; Fitzpatrick, 2011a).

· Para-sociality: The digital literary sphere massively amplifies literature's traditional illusion of the authorial voice that speaks seemingly unmediated to the reader in one-to-one communion (although readers have traditionally rarely spoken back). Consequently, digital mediums foster substantial upswing in author-reader para-social pseudo-intimacy, on top of the actual interaction they facilitate (Horton and Wohl, 1956). However, they do so within strict, and often author-enforced, constraints.

As English and Frow remark on a "paradox" of analog celebrity literary culture, "the readerly desire for authorial authenticity continues to inflect the branded, quality-controlled seriality of industrialized literary production" (2006: 52, 51). A Romantic notion of communion with the "superior" artistic mind of the author is, however illogically, harnessed to the intellectual property regimes and economic heft of the contemporary cultural industries. However, the contradiction might appear less jarring in the context of the digital literary sphere, where far lower barriers to entry and a higher degree of direct authorial control over content make the illusion of authorial communion less industrially confected. A *newer* contradiction presented by the digital literary sphere, however, is one of scale: unlike the reader-fan asking a question in a public forum such as a literary festival or requesting that an author sign their book copy, in the digital literary sphere the nature of the intimate authorial revelation is always profoundly asymmetrical, with an individual author communicating to any number of typically unknown and unseen online followers, who are themselves typically unknown to and unseen by each other (Gruzd and Rehberg Sedo, 2012). In cases of particularly dedicated and energetic fan communities it is possible selected fans may be known to each other through their active and highly visible roles in an authorial fan subgroup. But here too power imbalances predominate with the always fragile communitarian rhetoric of fan solidarity undercut by deeply ingrained hierarchical impulses among fans. Serving as webmaster of a leading author-tribute site, having a message retweeted by a literary celebrity, or being seen by lower-ranking fans to be having one-to-one communications with a celebrity author create spaces not only for the performance of authorial identities, but also—importantly—for the enacting of fannish identities in relation to that author.

Disintermediation/Reintermediation

It has become a truism that the Internet's greatest impact on the book industry is that anyone can now become an author through one of the ever-mushrooming digital self-publishing enterprises, of which Lulu, XLibris, Smashwords, Scribd, and CreateSpace are among the better known. Such services typically allow would-be authors to upload their manuscript, apply a variety of layout templates and cover designs, and set a price. The site then coordinates print-on-demand publication, taking a cut of any sales revenue. These sites' constant reiteration of the generous royalty percentages on offer to self-published authors is disingenuous: with sales of a self-published book typically below 150 copies, they can afford to be generous (Lynch, 2001; Donadio, 2008; Fowler and Trachtenberg, 2010; Bradley et al., 2011; Adsett, 2012). In the words of *New York Review of Books* journalist Steve Coll, "The trouble is 70 percent of nothing is nothing" (2014).

Interestingly, this is far from the vision of literature's digital future prognosticated by electronic literature enthusiasts of the early 1990s. Theorist-practitioners such as Robert Coover foresaw digital technologies doing away not only with the printed codex as an output form, but with the author figure to boot. Coover's infamous 1992 article for the *NYTBR*, "The End of Books," forecast the literary future as a democratic sphere of collaboratively written, "essentially anonymous text fragments" floating in the digital ether.[6] These texts would demonstrate a thoroughly postmodern smash-and-grab attitude to creative property, with text rearranged, sampled, and rewritten in an implicit rejection of the author-worshipping individualism of the Romantic literary tradition. In fact, the opposite has come to pass, with amateur writers eager to seize the prestigious mantle of Published Author and to have a hard-copy book as tangible evidence of their admission to this formerly elite stratum. Still, the very fact of mass admission to the category of author should in itself effectively have atomized the concept of a literary elite. As lead researchers from the Research on Authorship as Performance project have noted about the publication boom of the eighteenth century, artistic coteries cannot long withstand a stampede for membership: "When authorship becomes a mass phenomenon, it is no longer special and noteworthy" (Berensmeyer, Buelens, and Demoor, 2012: 17).[7]

But, again, executing the death of the author not by critical fiat but by throwing open the doors to all and sundry seems not to have worked in practice. Another digital permutation of the publishing landscape unforeseen by early-1990s electronic literature enthusiasts, working as they then were on the technological model of the freestanding computer and CD-ROM, has been the rise of crowdfunded book publications. A revival of the practice of subscription publishing prevalent in the eighteenth and nineteenth centuries, under this model the writing and production of a book are funded by the pledges of would-be readers (Finkelstein and McCleery, 2013: 63, 76). Crowdfunded literary publication projects are not only housed on general crowdfunding websites such as Kickstarter and Pozible but even have their own dedicated portal in UK website Unbound (Booth, 2015).[8] Would-be authors pitch projects to Unbound's membership, set a financial target and a deadline for pledges, and, if their threshold is met, interact digitally with their future readership through author question-and-answer sessions, updates on progress, and advance marketing. Pledging readers receive their copy of the printed book at the end of the process, significantly changing the traditional author-publisher-reader dynamic whereby the author and publisher seek to recover their sunk costs in terms of time and money by luring a capricious and unindebted readership. The crowdfunded model of digital publishing ought also to have dethroned the Romantic author figure from the eminence of creative genius dispensing his insights to the masses below, to more of a journeyman figure producing works for hire and beholden to a pre-identified reader-market. In fact, it is this more prosaic model of writer-as-artisan that predominated prior to the invention of the cultural category of the author in the late eighteenth century, buoyed by Romanticism's philosophical proclamation of the author-as-original-genius and protected by the embryonic legal regime of copyright (Woodmansee, 1984). Over two hundred years later, the author figure may have been killed off in academic circles but still exerts a charismatic pull from beyond the grave in the minds of the digitally enabled general public.

What have become increasingly evident since the first flush of enthusiasm for self-publishing are the practical impediments confronting authors of self-published titles: newspapers refuse to review them; brick-and-mortar retailers decline to stock them; and, without a background in marketing and publicity, most self-published authors struggle to attract mainstream media attention (Clark and Phillips, 2008: 91; Donadio, 2008; Fowler and Trachtenberg, 2010; Bradley et al., 2011; Jameson, 2012: 9; Wilcockson, 2012: 125; Williams, 2012: 128). While self-published authors may have their work published in the culturally esteemed format of the printed codex and gain legal admission to the category of author in terms of intellectual property ownership, their continuing exclusion from the circuits of literary estimation and consecration still denies them the halo of creative superiority that has proven authorship's most lingering allure. As Antoine Compagnon has noted, "On the Internet, contradictory courses tend toward both the disappearance but also the strengthening of the figure of the author" (2005: 230–31). We have, in response, witnessed a de facto resuscitation of the author as an elite category and a revalorization of the gatekeeping intermediaries that traditionally stamped printed publications with their imprimatur as a guarantee of merit and quality control.

Publishing's back-to-the-future impulse takes the form of a perhaps counterintuitive phenomenon—reintermediation: self-publishing has come to replace the publisher's and (later) literary agent's slush-pile of unsolicited manuscripts as the unofficial research and development (R&D) arm of print publishing (Murray, 2012: 55). Perhaps more surprisingly, for Internet visionaries who foresaw the wholesale replacement of print publication by digital distribution, self-publishers have increasingly come to define *themselves* in this role of handmaid to their erstwhile print publishing rivals. For example, the UK Arts Council–sponsored website YouWriteOn allows registered writers to post sample chapters or short stories for peer review and comment, with the ten most popular being reviewed monthly by multinational publishers Random House and Orion.[9] Interestingly, the website prominently and proudly displays former "YouWriteOn Book of the Year Award Winners" who went on to achieve "real" (namely, print) publication through the mainstream publisher attention given to their writing via the site. Here, the editorial scrutiny and quality assurance represented by print publishing's gatekeepers is celebrated by digital self-publishing outfits, and online publication is explicitly positioned as a potential entry point to valorized *print* publication.

Nor is this rhetorical self-positioning unusual: Amazon's Encore program plucks from the deluge of self-published titles a promising few, then edits and distributes them online and through print retailers (Fowler and Trachtenberg, 2010).[10] Self-publishing circles abound with discussion of DIY novelists who went on to achieve mainstream publishing success, such as Australian thriller writer Matthew Reilly or, most (in)famously, *Fifty Shades of Grey* (2012) author E. L. James. Equally, the blogosphere bristles with authors keen to garner a quantifiable audience to demonstrate to print publishers an existing readership for their work, in the hope that this will translate into a paying market (Nelson, 2006: 6). Blog analyst Aimée Morrison notes the plethora of blogs by "aspiring writers seeking both audiences and book contracts with provocative and literate projects" (2007: 378; see also Baverstock, 2008: 166; Pedersen, 2008; Thompson, 2010: 159). Again, self-publishing enterprises are complicit in this process: leading self-publishing website Lulu.com's sponsorship of the jokily named "Blooker Prize" for the best blog self-published as a book positively solicits mainstream media attention, and the Hollywood adaptation of former winner Julie Powell's *Julie and Julia* (2005) has provided Lulu.com with a potent exemplar for self-published writers as to what can be achieved. When online publishing businesses themselves posit digital publishing as a second-best option to the ultimate goal of legitimate *print* publication, clearly something more complex than simple disintermediation is in play.

Commentators have remarked that the boom in online self-publishing tends to be either idealized as innately democratic and evidence of information's desire to be free, or castigated and bemoaned in jeremiads about the end of literary quality in the twenty-first century (van der Weel, 2015). Yet the effect of the digital literary sphere, taken as a whole, is neither one of simple mass democratization nor further reification of print-based celebrity. Rather, we are witnessing polarization between, on one hand, a near-limitless influx of self-published amateur writers seeking sales and audiences and, on the other, celebrity authors importing their offline profile into the digital sphere and enhancing it. It is the middle ground of both this debate and the digital literary sphere that proves most interesting, meriting more detailed examination of the liminal zone where print and digital publishing converge. Publishing's two modes appear to have brokered a fragile means for coexisting; just as mass democratization of publishing erupts, new filtering mechanisms emerge simultaneously to weigh and evaluate the mass of newly published material. The best of this material is, predominantly, siphoned off by the traditional book publishing industry for the cultural anointment of "proper" print publication, thus bestowing the mantle of "genuine" authorship upon its creators. Hence, e-publishing has, far from having replaced print publishing, rather cast itself as an R&D arm for the industry—often doing so explicitly in its advertising to would-be authors. Here digital media exists in a handmaid relationship to print culture, in a significant disruption of simplistic views of print and digital media based on a model of serial eclipse and replacement.

The challenge for an analyst of the digital literary sphere is, then, to analyze the *interrelationships* between these two fields, and to identify the new filters and mediators that restrict or permit flow between these two poles. Book history has long recognized the crucial significance of mediators (publishers, printers, shippers, booksellers, binders, and others) between literary studies' traditionally preferred categories of author and reader. The challenge is to bring this literary-sociological mindset to bear upon the new set of circumstances, institutions, and practices sponsored by the digital literary sphere. To do so facilitates explanation of how digital media can be simultaneously democratizing and sacralizing literary authorship.

Interactivity

In the twenty-first century the author's traditional mode of communication with readerships via printed codex has expanded not only to encompass delivery of print content through digital forms (such as e-books) but, much more radically, also across a large variety of Internet platforms. To this extent, the author's creative offering has been reconceptualized as only the kernel, around which is wrapped a panoply of other, less formally couched but vitally relationship-sustaining author-reader communications. A personal website has become the standard minimal accoutrement of contemporary authorship, to the extent that the Authors Guild (US) offers members website-building templates through its Sitebuilder software, plus minimal monthly hosting fees and domain name registration.[11] But, as even fictional authorial wannabe Francis Plug understands, much more is expected of today's professional author. The Australian Society of Authors' guidebook *The Adaptable Author: Coping with Change in the Digital Age* summarizes its advice for authors as "Re-design your 'brand' with all the digital bells and whistles" (Masson, 2014: 259). These digital accoutrements typically include a blog, a Facebook page, and a Twitter account, but can also span more arcane (at least for traditionally late-adopting literary authors) digital technologies such as podcasting, video-blogging (vlogging), Instagram, Pinterest, webfora, and Skype. In a crucial shift in tone from the 1990s heyday of Web 1.0, take-up of digital technologies is now presented less as an avant-garde opportunity for boundary-pushing authors than a bare professional necessity. Publicist Ruth Killick, writing in the UK Society of Authors' journal, sets its membership straight: "*Embrace new media.* There really is no choice. Your website is your shop window and we're happy to advise on filling and dressing it. Likewise, get set up on Twitter and Facebook; research blogs; suggest guest blogs—we'll retweet your links and do everything we can to spread the word electronically" (2013: 64). Authors cannot rely on an overtaxed publicist to hustle on their behalf; in the era of one-stroke dissemination of one's thoughts to global audiences, conscientious engagement in DIY modes of publicity is mandatory. Publicity professionals will commit themselves only to amplifying authors' own efforts. Constantly reiterated in such professional-advice columns is the need not only to be present on such social media platforms, but to engage with them frequently and with appropriate savvy. Authors are reminded of the imperative to keep their website content and blog posts current, since frequency of updating optimizes a site's ranking with search engines such as Google (Katz, 2010: 48; Thompson, 2010: 254–55; Miller, P., 2013; Thompson, R., 2013; Wilkins, 2014: 7). As online book marketer Rachel Thompson spells out the equation for any foot-dragging, recalcitrant authors: "More visitors = more comments = more interaction = potential sales / readers" (2013).

Internalizing appropriate netiquette is essential if traditionally one-way communicators such as literary authors are to use an interactive platform like Twitter successfully, that is to "genuinely use it as a diary and conversational tool rather than just for publicity" (Harrad, 2012). Inept social media use can be more damaging to an author than refusal to engage at all. As publicist Gabrielle Gantz warns, "It's a place to share interesting thoughts and ideas with each other, not just self-promote" (quoted in Radford, 2012). Simply using Twitter for one-way self-promotion is known within the Twitterverse by the disparaging, and appropriately media-generationalist, tag of "broadcasting" (Cannold, 2011: 14).[12] When self-promotion seems necessary (and when, under the new literary dispensation, does it not?), authors are advised coyly to do it via third-party endorsement: "To wit, retweeting congratulatory or praiseworthy tweets by others about you" (Cannold, 2011: 15).

Motivations for Social Media Adoption

This is not to deny the large number of authors who have eagerly embraced social media of their own accord and have found it a liberating, energizing, and, above all, tremendously fun experience. It is impossible to overestimate the hard slog of social isolation in which most literary creativity takes place and, conversely, the creative and social fillip provided by interacting multiple times daily with peers and readerships via social media. The tenuous sense of belonging to an imagined literary community that many writers discuss in interviews is here strengthened through the digital literary sphere's ability to make that community manifest, and to bring the peer interactions, information-sharing, and gossip formerly confined to physical bookish settings such as writers' festivals, book launches, and publisher parties into the author's place of creation via the intimate technologies of the tablet computer and mobile phone. In addition, writers value social media's bypassing of publisher and media gatekeepers in providing a direct channel of communication with their readerships, at a time and rate determined by themselves. Canadian-Australian crime writer and former model Tara Moss, who has long been the target of much sniping about the eclipse of talent by marketability in the book industries, describes blogging as professionally liberating: "At last my words and ideas were out there, unmediated and unedited, and people could read what I had to say and decide for themselves if they were interested in read-ing more" (2013: 25).

However, while social media's permeation of the literary industries has served to enhance many authors' sense of personal agency and readerly community building, there is no denying that structural transformations in the book industry have also played their part. Large-scale changes in book industry roles are fre-quently retrofitted with a discourse of authorial empowerment to smooth the way for authors to shoulder more of the financial and time burden for publicizing and marketing their own work. The underlying causes for this shift have been evident since the waves of conglomeration that engulfed book publishing during the 1980s. Publishers experiencing pressure on their marketing and publicity budgets have put more money behind "big books," thus squeezing out publicity and market-ing of midlist titles (Moran, 2000: 38–39; Spender, 2004: 245; Squires, 2007: 36–39; Thompson, J., 2010: 243–51; Masson, 2014: 26, 31). Claire Squires memora-bly terms the upshot of this process "a hierarchy of marketability" (2007: 36–37). Midlist or first-time authors have the option of either picking up the marketing and publicity crumbs of their publisher's budget (if there are any) or ramping up their self-publicizing efforts: "The rest have to make do with publicity that can be gained for free, or that the author him- or herself can generate" (Squires, 2007: 38). Agents and publishers are increasingly interested in potential authors who have a DIY approach to marketing and publicizing their work—ideally even be-fore publication—by having a promotable "platform" or "hook" for media interest (Marshall, 2006: 794; Katz, 2010: 47; Thompson, J., 2010: 86; Wilkins, 2014: 6). Preferably authors will also have low-cost but widely disseminated online pres-ences to target potential book purchasers (for example, a heavily trafficked web-site, widely read and commented-upon blog, much-"liked" Facebook page, and/or widely subscribed Twitter feed) (Clark and Phillips, 2008: 88; Thompson, J., 2010: 257; York, 2013a: 128–29; Delaney, 2014: 12; Dietz, 2015: 200). Such evidence of quantifiable public interest in the author and/or their work helps to reduce the financial risk inherent in the decision to publish. Much in the way that, pre-Internet, an author's visual appeal and skill at public performance could be cru-cial in swinging marketing executives at acquisition board meetings, "in the in-ternet age," writes John B. Thompson, "these new forms of online marketing are becoming more and more decisive in shaping the visibility of books and their fate" (2010: 257). The ease with which a rhetoric of author empowerment can fit hand in glove with industrial cost shifting should give enthusiasts of digital media's uptake in the book world pause. The synchronicity of these phenomena seems to verify a point made by writer Elmo Keep in a charged, profoundly disillusioned blog post for the *Australian Author* website which she titled "Nobody Cares about Your Personal Brand." Recounting her experiences as both a practicing author and educator of would-be writers, Keep asserts that, from the advent of blogging around 1999 to the 2008 heyday of Twitter, "being on the Internet had turned from an expression of egocentric naïveté into one of perfectly calibrated, narcissistic professional identity."

Varieties of Authorial Digital Performance

Young adult (YA) novelist John Green is one of the most accomplished authorial users of social media to engage his vast international, and largely millennial-generation, readership. His social media profile is multifaceted and ubiquitous: the *vlogbrothers* YouTube channel (established in 2007 to communicate with his brother Hank and now with over three million subscribers);[13] his online Nerd-fighters community championing bookish, outsider teenagers by cultivating collective nerd-pride; and the reader cover-design competition engineered for the US paperback edition of his novel *An Abundance of Katherines* (2006) (Alter, 2014; Brockes, 2014; Wind, 2014; Talbot, 2014). Green is a near-daily communicator with his readership, whether through his YouTube channel, Twitter or Tumblr accounts, or the newer project of Crash Course educational videos aimed at high schoolers (Carpenter, 2012; Hawker, 2014). Posts in his better-established digital media channels range from chronicling his daily routine, whether at home or on the road, proffering advice on surviving "middle-school misery" and mental health problems, and even videoblogging his acceptance of the MTV Movie Awards Best Movie statuette for the adaptation of his fourth, and best known, novel, *The Fault in Our Stars* (book, 2012; movie, 2014).[14] It would be difficult, at this point in Green's career, for a reader to encounter his fiction without some familiarity with the author's extra-textual persona, so pervasive is his online authorial presence. Crucially, Green's audience interactions are not quarantined to the key marketing window around a new novel's release (which might be regarded as calculatingly exploitative "broadcasting"), but are instead ongoing: he has communicated about failing to write, he has read early drafts of subsequently abandoned projects, and he has documented the entire adaptation process for *Fault* from casting to film premiere. He claims that maintaining the tone of genuine and (to the extent possible given his subscriber numbers) reciprocal reader engagement is of paramount importance. Itemizing so exhaustively the industrial processes around a book's publication, marketing, publicity, and subsequent adaptation risks potentially inhibiting reader immersion in the book's fictional world. But for Green's networked fan base the author's behind-the-scenes information sharing appears

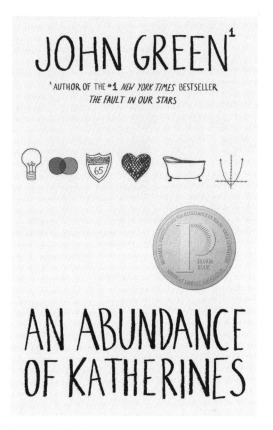

Cover of the 2008 US paperback edition of John Green's *An Abundance of Katherines* (2006), designed by then seventeen-year-old competition winner Sarah Turbin. Reproduced by permission of Penguin Random House

to work in the opposite direction: demystifying the book- and film-world star-making machinery through his everyman, aw-shucks, goofily affable persona invites audience identification and accords readers a vicarious stake in Green's career success.

The astonishing frequency of Green's authorial interactions could only be maintained in the social media era. Writing back in 1977, "in a culture where so much communication is mediated by newspapers, radio and television," John G. Cawelti observed—accurately for the time—that a writer could have "contact with individual members of his public and with the small coteries of his acquaintance," but that "there is no way for him to have a complex relationship with the large and diverse public which constitutes, at least potentially, his audience" (164–65).

YA author John Green (*far left*) accepting the MTV Movie Awards Best Movie statuette for *The Fault in Our Stars* (2014), accompanied by the cast of the film, as chronicled on his *vlogbrothers* YouTube channel (2015).

Green, by contrast, cultivates a thoroughly distributed and digitally interactive authorial persona motivated by his very Web 2.0 belief that "people are more likely to read books if they feel a personal connection to the person who created it, and to the process" (quoted in Morrison, K., 2014). As Margaret Talbot aptly summarizes this new model of the book as an entree to an ongoing social media relationship: "For many young people today . . . reading is not an act of private communication with an author whom they imagine vaguely, if at all, but a prelude to a social experience—following the author on Twitter, meeting other readers, collaborating with them on projects, writing fan fiction. In our connected age, even books have become interactive phenomena" (2014).

While social media performance may be most evident among YA authors writing for digital natives, its uptake spans writers of all genres and age groups. The UK newspaper *The Observer* in 2013 lauded Canadian literary luminary Margaret Atwood as "doyenne of digital-savvy authors" (Baddeley, 2013), especially given her age, for her avid uptake and championing of a series of digital technologies. This digital acumen dates back to 2006 with Atwood's joint invention and public demonstrations of "The LongPen" device: a computer with a mechanical arm able to be controlled remotely that allows authors to sign copies of books virtually ("Author," 2006; Burkeman, 2006; Atwood, 2006; York, 2013a: 137, 152–58). More recently, Atwood has been an enthusiastic experimenter with Twitter (over 1.65 million followers), online serial publication via Amazon's Kindle Serials platform,

Margaret Atwood demonstrates her jointly designed remote book-signing device, The Long-Pen (2006). Photo by David Cooper / Getty Images

a participant in the #TwitterFiction Festival, and patron of community-writing site Wattpad (Dobby, 2012; Baddeley, 2013; Keating, 2013; York, 2013a: 145–52).[15] In 2012, moreover, Atwood co-founded Fanado, a start-up specializing in managing digital creator-fan relationships that dubs itself "the promotional tour online": "Fanado is where artists meet audiences. Reach beyond the press tour—whenever, wherever you want, without travel or entourage. Fanado is Anytime, AnyPlace: meet, greet and sign. Save money and earn revenue. Reward your fans and discover new ones. Fanado is live and intimate, with that 'Kodak Moment' stickiness that will make it the most effective and lasting tool in your social media mix."[16]

While Atwood is an enthused, curious, even evangelistic user of Twitter, praising it as "a combination of your own little radio show and a party," some authors have been forced onto Twitter as a defensive move to preempt false Twitter accounts springing up under their name and gaining quasi-authorized status ("Can Writers," 2014). Atwood herself recounts attempting to set up a Twitter account in the lead-up to a new novel's release and, disconcertingly, finding one already using her name and image. She continues in wry, Browning-esque mode: "This grew; I gave commands; then all other Margaret Atwoods stopped together" (Atwood, 2010). In similar vein, fantasy author George R. R. Martin conceded to belatedly join Twitter in 2014 as "a defensive measure against the various fake Twitter accounts that have sprung up." Lest his stance be mistaken as an old-school print-culture disdain for digital networks, he adds, "Essentially my minions will be using it to echo news and comments from my Not A Blog" (Steger, 2014). Thus the prime purpose of the Twitter account is to demarcate Martin's blog as the authoritative and "genuine" digital-sector source of news from the *Game of Thrones* author. Interesting here is the frank and seemingly untroubled acknowledgment that Martin himself will not be authoring the tweets distributed under his name. How is this to be squared with Twitter's much espoused creation of intimacy with literary celebrities? Is the person whose up-close-and-personal Twitter messages the reader-fan thrills to actually the same person who writes the books? Authorship has always been a slippery construct, with an "authentic" one-to-one match between a particular human being and an authorial persona complicated by the shifting frames of anonymity, pseudonymity, ghostwriting, and collaborative writing. Authorial use of social media promises to transcend but in fact compounds this much older dilemma of how to attribute a particular set of words to some physical being who can be variously enshrined or prosecuted as a message's legitimate source.

Writing back in 1999, before the advent of social media early in the new millennium, publishing commentator Hugh Look observed, "Few authors, agents or publishers have any clear idea of how they are going to handle a much more interactive relationship with fans" (Look, 1999: 22). Given the time of writing, Look's focus was predominantly on author-tribute websites owned and managed by fans, with all the problems of content management, quality control, and intellectual property disputes attendant upon media industry–fan interactions (Look, 1999: 22; Murray, 2004b). Seeming to bear out Look's late twentieth-century prognostications is the number of shadow sites devoted to bemoaning the time Martin is taking to write the next installment in his A Song of Ice and Fire multi-book series (Miller, L., 2011). A subset of fans appeared enraged that production of the television adaptations might catch up to the already published books, or even that Martin may (selfishly) die before concluding the sequence.[17] The level of vituperation directed at an author whose novels the site's creators claim to love is extraordinary. Martin's belated adoption of social media technologies such as blogging, and even more belated and confessedly vicarious adoption of Twitter, need to be understood in this context as forms of public image management. Interactivity with readerships appears to be less desired for its own sake than necessary to prevent the discontent of a subset of specifically book-focused fans infecting his broader (predominantly television-sustained) fan base. The double-edged sword of author-reader interactivity is revealed starkly here, making it easy to sympathize with Martin when he reflects on the Sisyphean labor of authorial fan service: "The more readers you have, the harder it is to keep up, and then you can't get any writing done" (Miller, L., 2011).

Lyle Skains (2010) is one of few scholars to have investigated authors' interactive relationships with readers via digital technology, focusing on highly active web communities surrounding cult UK-born authors Neil Gaiman and Jasper Fforde. She draws a connection between the fact that, like Martin, both write in the broad science fiction fantasy (SFF) genre and appeal to core YA readerships, among whom take-up of digital technologies, and specifically Web 2.0 social media, is highest (97, 100–102). Fforde offers online communities the chance to prolong and deepen engagement in the world of his playfully metafictional Thursday Next series of novels via fan fiction, contests, games, and puzzles. Defying the demarcation between author and reader inscribed in the regime of copyright, Fforde has even thanked named members of his site's webforum for fan fiction contributions which he subsequently incorporated into a print novel (104). For his part Gaiman, long an experimenter with digital media via a long-running blog, online videos of book readings, and a collaboratively written Twitter novel, has used his website to engage extensively with fans, answering their questions, soliciting reader feedback, and responding to fan-recommended books, films, TV shows, and games.[18] Skains concludes that such experiments constitute the vanguard in print-authors' use of digital media and foreshadow an interactive storytelling future as soon as readers learn to overcome their print-inculcated passivity and resistance: "Online communities, in particular those which expand the author-reader relationship, provide one model of such an intermediate stage, drawing print readers into a digital world" (102).

While Skains's pioneering research into online modes of authorial performance is commendable, events since her article's 2010 appearance cast her rather digital-determinist conclusions in a different, more problematic, light. In 2014 Gaiman, then the world's most prolific and highly followed authorial tweeter, announced to his approximately 2.3 million Twitter followers that he was taking a four-month holiday from the technology ("Neil," n.d.; Power, 2015: 14). Its demands for constant interactivity were unreasonably colonizing the quiet, contemplative space he needed to gestate writing; the incessant demand to feed and curate reader discussion of his work had grown to the point of actually inhibiting production of new work. Creative fecundity required a certain period of authorial fallowness and insularity, Gaiman insisted. His surprising Twitter moratorium foregrounds strikingly the real authorial costs in terms of time and energy involved in maintaining an online persona (Dietz, 2015: 201). As with Martin, Gaiman's experience with social media suggests that, to the detriment of the actual writing, the publicity tail appears to have begun wagging the authorial dog.

If any author might be considered well equipped to handle social media's unending pressure to provide new content it would be Joyce Carol Oates, who, on par with her prolific literary output, was by December 2013 tweeting up to twenty-two times daily.[19] Like her almost exact contemporary and critical peer, Margaret Atwood, Oates relishes the creative affordances of social media, confessing to surprise at the "high, poetic quality of Twitter—it lends itself to a surreal sort of self-expression" (Muzaffar, 2013). Like Atwood, Oates also praises the sense of social embedding and community maintenance Twitter interactivity offers: "Advantage of Twitter: access to a galaxy of others' (fleeting) thoughts and insights. Disadvantage of Twitter: repeat above" (Muzaffar, 2013). Oates knows this cost personally, having been the target of an online campaign criticizing some of her tweets for alleged racism and Islamophobia. In May 2014 *Gawker* blogger Michelle Dean released an open letter decrying Oates's oversharing of "disconnected, abbreviated, context-free thoughts" (this may seem rich coming from a blogger) and advising Oates to delete her Twitter account: "Your continued presence there does nothing but undermine your own authority and annoy other people" (Dean, 2014). *Flavorwire* blogger Jason Diamond weighed in to the Internet-shaming free-for-all suggesting that the habit of considered, polished thought for which published authors are praised is innately incompatible with the impromptu Twitter format: "These authors [Oates and Stephen King][20] run the risk of tarnishing their reputations the more they share their unprocessed opinions and observations with the world" (2014). An unrepentant Oates continues, however, to tweet prolifically, with her posts, in line with the general trajectory of Twitter usage, increasingly incorporating photographic and video content (Rettberg, 2014: 15–16). This Twitter-verse turn to increased visuality raises new issues. If finely honed literary expression is the hallmark of literary authorship, does this skillset maintain purchase in an environment now presumably better geared toward visual artists? On the other hand, if globally disseminating random thoughts is landing prominent authors in hot water, perhaps a shift to the kind of scenic landscapes and wildlife images Oates favors in her more recent Twitter images may constitute a tactical retreat to less controversial ground.

US novelist Jonathan Franzen has been the most high-profile critic of social media publicity's opportunity cost for authors in terms of time for literary creation and paid freelance work. Franzen's droll 2013 article for the *Guardian*, titled "What's Wrong with the Modern World," was an extract from his book *The Kraus*

Project (2013) and lamented contemporary America's techno-fetishism and mania for media distraction. This article triggered a Twitter controversy on the basis of a passing observation from Franzen: "I confess to feeling some version of his [Kraus's] disappointment when a novelist who I believe ought to have known better, Salman Rushdie, succumbs to Twitter." Franzen also used the piece to deride the "phony kind of individuality" of Facebook pages and gullible hero worship of alleged techno-visionaries. While well written, this critique is of a piece with Franzen's long-cultivated stance decrying the deleterious effects of contemporary pop culture and his anachronistically high-Romantic conception of the novelist's role in supporting "serious" "high" culture (for instance, his 1996 *Harper's* essay "Perchance to Dream: In the Age of Images, A Reason to Write Novels," his confession to the *New York Times* that he often wrote with both earmuffs and a blindfold to block out the world around him, and his infamous disquiet with *The Corrections* [2001] being selected for Oprah's Book Club) (Eakin, 2001; Franzen, 2001; Farr, 2005; Farr and Harker, 2008).[21] Social media enthusiast Rushdie, who has said in praise of such technologies "I like reaching a new audience. The dialogue is invigorating," was quick to retaliate via Twitter (Holson, 2012: L1): "Dear #Franzen: @MargaretAtwood @JoyceCarolOates @nycnovel @NathanEnglander @Shteyngart and I are fine with Twitter. Enjoy your ivory tower."[22] Chick-lit novelist Jennifer Weiner, namechecked by Franzen in the same article as representing the nadir of vapid social media self-promotion, then jumped into the pile-on with a riposte for the *New Republic* entitled "What Jonathan Franzen Misunderstands about Me" (2013). Franzen, refusing to be cowed by the Twitter backlash his *Guardian* piece instigated, the following month continued his *j'accuse* campaign against the literary world's uncritical embrace of digital media with the following comment in a BBC Radio 4 interview: "What I find particularly alarming from the point of view of American fiction is that [social media] is a coercive development, agents will now tell young writers: 'I won't even look at your manuscript if you don't have 250 followers on Twitter.'. . . I see people who ought to be spending their time developing their craft, and people who used to be able to make a living as freelance writers, I see them making nothing and coerced into this constant self-promotion" ("Jonathan," 2013).[23]

Here Franzen echoes a decades-old critique that the writers' festival circuit unduly favors good *performers* over good writers (Murray and Weber, 2017). Others have lamented this extension of the imperative of marketability from analog media into new media domains; Jacob Silverman similarly notes that blogs and Twitter are "having a chilling effect on literary culture, creating an environment where writers are vaunted for their personal biographies or their online followings rather than for their work on the page" (2012). However, if writers' festival and TV appearances tended to promote the physically attractive ("authors with great hair," as Mark Crispin Miller witheringly termed them), blogs and tweets do at least have the advantage of being *written* communication, thus playing to authors' traditionally strongest suit (14).

All parties to the Franzen-Rushdie dispute were presumably engaged in it with one eye on their public profile—indisputably Weiner and Rushdie, but equally Franzen, for whom borderline-Luddite techno truth-telling has become a core part of his public persona. Hence, his refusal to participate in online authorial performance comprises not a rejection of authorial performativity per se but a dispute, fundamentally, about the appropriate media forums for such self-fashioning: analog or digital. To that extent, Franzen's stance is disingenuous: his aversion to Twitter self-publicity is *itself* a constituent part of his authorial image. Much as literary celebrities J. D. Salinger, Thomas Pynchon, J. M. Coetzee, David Foster Wallace, and Elena Ferrante have, to varying degrees, made rejection of publicity a kind of literary anti-brand, Franzen becomes enmeshed in that which he seeks to repudiate (Sage, 1998: 267). Franzen ultimately enacted perhaps his most effective revenge on those who derided him as a hopelessly out of touch Luddite

The character of psychoanalyst "Dr. Franzen" tweets distractedly mid-consultation in the book trailer for Gary Shteyngart's memoir, *Little Failure* (2013).

not by rejecting but, counterintuitively, by embracing digital media in the form of the book trailer. His cameo appearance in the unlikely guise of a New York psychoanalyst who taps away distractedly on his mobile phone mid-consultation in Gary Shteyngart's celebrity-studded book trailer for *Little Failure* (2013) is surely designed as one in the eye for his recent detractors.[24]

"Twitter is a time vampire."[25]

Franzen's attempt to position himself rhetorically in a place outside of literary celebrity may be untenable, but his attack on the normalizing of social media performance for novelists and his drawing attention to the real of costs of such work in terms of time and paid labor forgone warrant attention. Unable to be dismissed out of hand as the complaints of some digital refusenik, Franzen's gripes closely echo reservations expressed by high-profile social media communicators Neil Gaiman and George R. R. Martin. If such authorial stars, with paid "minions" deputized to communicate on the author's behalf, find feeding the insatiable maw of social media unduly onerous, how much more so must it be for midlist or aspirant writers who must typically combine writing with other employment and life roles?

It is indisputable that author-reader relationships have been fundamentally reconfigured in the digital literary sphere. Professional advisers caution that a one-way, Web 1.0 mentality premised upon a predominantly passive conception of the audience as recipient of the author's intended communications is unengaging and unsustainable: "We are past the days of a come-and-see website. . . . It's come and chat" (Wind, 2014: 33). But how authors will manage to balance this obligation of virtual sociability with their core creative work is still being brokered among the various parties that, collectively, comprise the digital literary sphere. In this regard, Franzen is right to note that social media engagement has shifted from being a voluntary add-on to the authorial job description to becoming a mandatory minimum requirement for even being considered for admission. Like Elmo Keep in her dispirited and jaundiced blog post, authors articulate various reservations about engaging with social media ranging from an (implicit) belief that self-marketing is meretricious and a stain on the cult of the commercially disinterested, purely aesthetic Romantic author, through a dislike of "performing" in public and airing personal material, to a confessed lack of skill in self-promotion, whether technical or social. But preeminently, authors return to the problem of having insufficient time to write at all, let alone to write "peripheral," unremunerated content: "Social media management has become a never-satisfied beast that I just can't keep feeding, if I want to write a novel a year" (Thompson, R., 2013).

The situation is exacerbated by the justified suspicion that talk of authorial empowerment through fostering direct relationships with readers in fact serves as a convenient fig leaf for cash-strapped publishers to outsource formerly in-house tasks onto authors themselves. Examining the contours of contemporary authorial performance in the digital literary sphere raises the question of whether online-presence management is part of the main game of contemporary authorship, or ultimately a distraction from it. If the former, has authorial performance, while never exactly detachable from the authorial role, now grown so vast, multifaceted, and time-consuming as to become coterminous with the act of authorship itself? How, authors plaintively ask, is a writer trapped in an endless cycle of performing "writerliness" ever to get any actual writing done?

Para-Sociality: Intimacy Achieved or Perpetually Postponed?

One of literary criticism's abiding preoccupations has been with the nature of the author-reader textual encounter, specifically with how the "personality" of the author infuses their work and communicates to the reader. This generalized "reader" had, under the reign of Leavisite and New Critical approaches, various textual interpretations attributed to him. With the importation of audience research methodologies into Anglophone literary studies from the 1970s via reader-response theory and cultural studies, concern with a text's "implied author" and "implied reader" was supplemented by ethnographic research into actual readers, whether historical or present day (Iser, 1974; 1978; Radway, 1984, 1997; Rose, J., 1992, 2001; Lyons and Taksa, 1992; Altick, 1998; Long, 2003).[26] These readers, it was documented, may variously accept, reject, or complexly negotiate with intended authorial messages. Yet even this empirical turn still prioritized the printed codex as the sole platform for the author-reader encounter. The last decades of the twentieth century saw venues for author-reader exchanges proliferate well beyond the book, especially with the growth of authorial writers' festival appearances, book signings, and star author performances on broadcast media (Franzen, 1996: 50; Turner, 2004: 18). As stated in the introduction to this chapter, recognition that these extra-textual dimensions of authorial identity-performance themselves warrant analysis has been relatively recent: Ohlsson, Forslid, and Steiner rightly insist in this regard that "the public *persona* of an author is undoubtedly an important part of his or her authorship" (2014: 42). If authorship has expanded well beyond the book, so too have the forums for readerly encounters with authorial personae.

US sociologists Donald Horton and R. Richard Wohl in 1956 analyzed the cultivation of pseudo-intimacy by mass-media talent such as TV chat-show pre-senters and radio hosts in an article which has become fundamental to the stream of celebrity studies research emanating from media and cultural studies. Their emphasis was on the media host's "persona": a media-sustained construct that may bear little relationship to the biography of the person commonly associated with it, but that allows audiences to feel they enjoy a quasi-social form of famil-iarity and even interpersonal intimacy with the performer (216). Given that Hor-ton and Wohl were writing during the mid-twentieth-century heyday of broadcast media, they had necessarily to conceive of audience interactions as para-social because the then architecture of radio and television supported barely any audi-ence interactivity beyond the proxy function of studio audiences and talk-back radio callers. As their article's subtitle maintained, any performer-audience inti-macy thus achieved had, necessarily, to be "at a distance."

Today, audience members may remain geographically distant from media ce-lebrities, but their role has expanded to encompass not only para-social inter-action but genuine, albeit digitally mediated, interactivity. If Web 1.0 offered the limited and typically asynchronous interactivity of email, Web 2.0 offers greatly enhanced opportunities for an author to directly engage readers in close to real time in the form of blog posts, Facebook updates, and Twitter messages. Cru-cially, readers can now also reply directly. Web 2.0 social media technologies thus foster an "up-close-and-personal" sense of relationship to an esteemed author, with social media updates providing "backstage" insight into the author's routines, thoughts, and enthusiasms rather like a real-time mass-accessible diary (Mar-wick and boyd, 2011: 140; Totanes, 2011: 189; Gruzd and Rehberg Sedo, 2012).[27] The fact that social media are now typically engaged with via the portable, highly personalized platforms of the mobile phone and tablet computer cultivates a sense of readers being always-available for authorial updating. Moreover, blog-ging, Twitter, and Instagram permit readers, at least in theory, the possibility of bringing themselves to the attention of the favored author—the ultimate fannish goal. Having an author respond to a blog comment, retweet a Twitter message, or otherwise acknowledge an individual reader's existence is, however momen-tarily and conditionally, to be granted access to what media sociologist Nick Coul-dry terms "the mediated centre"—the zone of public visibility that constitutes the epicenter of power in a society like ours ruled by the attention economy (2003: 2). Still more spectacle-like, fan-celebrity virtual interactions via social media allow the fan to perform to the same audience their own version of nano-celebrity; bask-ing in the reflected glow of "real" celebrity, they nevertheless demonstrate their superior status relative to other (fully anonymous) fans (Marwick and boyd, 2011: 145, 150). Performed intimacy thus constitutes the currency of social media encounters for celebrities and fans alike.

However, regardless of the democratizing potential of social media technologies, their actual deployment tends to reinforce rather than dissolve boundaries between the known and unknowns. In part, authorial celebrities have compelling practical reasons for rationing the access to the mediated center they vicariously permit to others: after all, constant status updates as to an author's location and activities are irresistible temptations for would-be stalkers (Groskop, 2010a). But, more theoretically, too much redirecting of the readerly gaze back to members of the readership may frustrate reader-fans (it is, after all, the author they seek) as well as threatening the exclusivity inherent in the nature of celebrity itself. Actual author use of social media can perversely *enhance* the lopsidedness of the author-reader encounter by providing the illusion of a direct means of communicating with the authorial persona but one which the author takes up only at their own discretion, if at all. For example, actor, author, and erstwhile new media enthusiast Stephen Fry's Twitter profile informed his six million-plus "followers" (note the term) that he "NEVER reads Direct Messages" (that is, private, one-on-one Twitter conversations).[28] Similarly, Leslie Cannold, writing in 2011, informs us that "Margaret Atwood has more than 166,500 people signed up to get her tweets, but chooses to receive tweets from just 157" (14).[29] Here, authors appear to be engaged in a profoundly lopsided transaction: availing themselves of the interactive capabilities of social media to communicate "unmediated" with their followers but withholding the possibility of a direct two-way exchange on more equal terms.

The most dramatic undercutting of the implicitly interactive and mass-democratic potential of social media use as it relates to literature occurs when the platform degenerates into a quasi-broadcast architecture whereby the majority of readers are r-duced to the role of spectators looking in at a mediated center in which famous authors interact predominantly with each other. This is the ultimate significance of the Franzen-Rushdie Twitter spat: not so much the persuasiveness or otherwise of Franzen's passing lament at the banality of Twitter (made, of course, in newsprint and codex) but the voyeuristic thrill Rushdie's Twitter riposte provided us in observing famed authors having the kind of celebrity dustup previously only reported on secondhand in literary gossip columns or rehashed years after the event in literary biographies (Groskop, 2010b; Khanna, 2013).

To note the confected nature of authorial social media performance is not to assume, however, that readers are ignorant of the medium's potential for role-playing and dissembling. After all, one of the questions most frequently posed to authors on social media is along the lines of "Do you write the messages yourself or have a PR flak compose them for you?" (Marwick and boyd, 2011: 142, 149). In an era in which reality TV star-making formats minutely itemized the construction of celebrity, only for audiences to embrace the star-making machinery's products all the more enthusiastically, it smacks of Frankfurt School–style false consciousness to argue that merely exposing the workings of the fame machinery to the public gaze will necessarily lead to mass disillusionment. There is, after all, a certain pleasure in watching the mechanics of the celebrity industry in motion—in relation to literature as much as any other cultural sector. This complex mixture of promised equalizing *and* voyeuristic spectatorship, of desire for authorial authenticity *and* self-ironic appreciation of the performativity of social media identity-construction, is encapsulated in UK journalist Kate Harrad's comments about the bittersweet pleasures of following literary authors on Twitter: "It's like being friends with [famous authors], except they have no idea who you are, but it doesn't matter because this is still closer than you'd ever normally get. *The illusion of intimacy* is fun, providing you remain aware that it's an illusion" (2012; italics added).

Conclusion: Literary Culture's Haunting by Oral Communication

Since the last decade of the twentieth century, literary culture has witnessed successive waves of technological utopianism giving way repeatedly to disenchantment: the medium—whether email, websites, blogging, Facebook, Twitter, or Instagram—that promises to collapse distance and provide unmediated access to the intimate thoughts of an author in real time is revealed to be incrementally commercialized and colonized by corporate interests. Each new platform's vaunted transparency is rendered suddenly disconcertingly visible and economically confected. Viewed in this light, social media channels are not therefore radically "disruptive" breaks in the history of literary media but are, rather, notable for their perpetuation of a long-evident pattern—the thwarted promise they seem to offer to transcend mediation and attain the holy grail of literary culture: intimate mind-to-mind communion between author and reader.

Our formerly book-dominated and now digital media–saturated culture finds itself haunted by oral communication's dynamic of co-presence, hankering after the real-time, multisensory, and interactive communication that is the hallmark of embodied conversation. Yet, a culture for some five hundred years transformed by the printed codex's ability to sustain narratives of unprecedented length, complexity, and relative fixity could never reconcile itself with purely oral communication's necessary brevity, instability, and transience. Therefore, it is not the uniqueness of social media that is notable in the history of authorship, but its forcible returning us to a fundamental, irresolvable problem inherent in the nature of literary communication itself. Mediation both makes literary communication possible and, by exempting the author from the same time and place as the reader, inserts a note of inauthenticity into the very encounter. Socrates's well-rehearsed suspicion of writing, as related (ironically) *in* writing by Plato in the dialogue *Phaedrus*, is often the starting point for chronologically structured undergraduate courses on the history of written and print communication (2005).[30] These surveys now typically conclude with some discussion of how digital media and specifically e-books have changed the format and nature of the literary encounter. But such pedagogically handy Gutenberg-to-Google trajectories disguise how much digital media's multimodality, interactivity, democratic accessibility, and real-time affordances return us to the same, long-standing quandary: it is the absence of the author that makes literature possible, yet powerful literature typically provokes a desire in readers to get closer to the author. This search for the author behind the work may be conducted by means of biographies, published correspondence and house museums in the case of deceased authors or via embodied and social media encounters in the case of living writers. Authors may variously deny, evade, or positively revel in this paradoxical fact through formalist play or textual role-taking, but there is ultimately no way out of the conundrum of the author's simultaneous presence and absence for literary culture at large.

CHAPTER TWO

"Selling" Literature

Cultivating Community in the Digital Literary Sphere

News that market-leading online retailer Amazon.com was to open a brick-and-mortar bookstore in its hometown of Seattle, Washington, spread like media wildfire in November 2015 (Denham, 2015; Halzack, 2015; Streitfeld, 2015; Ruddick, 2015).[1] The announcement—irresistible in its seeming perversity—appeared to demonstrate that book retailing had come full circle. It verified that there are aspects of the in-store retailing experience that e-commerce, for all its vast inventory, "Search Inside the Book" functions, and recommendation algorithms, simply could not emulate, let alone surpass.[2] Was it perhaps a response to the indisputable plateauing of e-book sales globally? To others more cynical, the store's opening appeared an adroit publicity stunt on Amazon's part—reinforcing its brand name in the public mind and underlining how much the firm had revolutionized the world's shopping behavior in only twenty years. Viewed in such a light, the opening of the first Amazon Books physical bookstore is the exception that proves the rule—an apparently quirky folly aimed strategically at highlighting how the firm itself had rendered independent local booksellers almost a historical curiosity. Was it perhaps designed to function as a Trojan horse: ostensibly conceding the resilient appeal of brick-and-mortar book retailing but in fact designed as a shopfront for Amazon's Kindle e-reader devices?

In announcing the Seattle opening, Amazon executives were at pains to emphasize the new bookstore's fusion of online and offline affordances: the comparatively limited physical stock holdings would be selected on the basis of Amazon's top-selling titles online; printed customer reviews would be displayed in front of relevant books; and the firm's various hardware devices would be available for customers to try out. For Amazon Books Vice President Jennifer Cast, this balance represented the ultimate synthesis of old-school community bookselling and digital-era tech savvy: it was, she averred, "data with a heart" (Tokars, 2015).

This latest twist in ongoing debates over the nature of bookish community and its uneasy relationship with commerce provides an appropriate entry point to this chapter's consideration of how the Internet has changed the marketing, publicizing, and retailing of literature over the past twenty-five years. With the rise of first-generation Internet retailers such as Amazon, and specifically since the advent of Web 2.0 early in the new millennium, the manner in which readers discover, purchase, and communicate about books has been transformed by the digital literary sphere. Bookish dispositions and activities born in the analog era are not simply carried over en masse into digital platforms but are reconstituted in the process, in terms of who both the gatekeepers and the participants are in online literary culture. Equally, new practices of instigating literary sociability and hosting discussion around books have been incubated in online environments and may be conceivable only in digitally distributed spaces. In such a transitional environment, long-standing concerns about the political economy of the book world do not disappear, but their contours are radically altered and their ortho-doxies upended, meriting fresh examination of the myriad ways in which litera-ture is "sold" in the contemporary era.

In using the verb "selling" in referring to literature, I am deliberating playing on the double meaning of the word. I mean both the fundamental fact of the commercial transaction that is the bedrock of the book trade, as well as the more diffuse, colloquial sense of "selling," meaning to advertise or promote. In the Amazon world, whether or not we actively purchase any given title, we are being constantly sold the flattering image of ourselves as bibliophiles—literary con-noisseurs belonging to an almost secret society of book lovers, replete with its own lingo, rituals, and enthusiasms. Other academic commentators have noted this crucial aspect of Amazon's corporate design, one evident, as this chapter pro-ceeds to explore, from the website's earliest incarnations. Cultural studies scholar Ted Striphas terms this particular brand of digital community atmospherics Am-azon's "ethos of bookishness" (2009: 101), while literary historian and scholar of the post–World War II institutionalization of literature, Mark McGurl, writes of Amazon's "existential commitment to the idea of literature, to getting inside lit-erature, to *being literary*" (2016: 449; italics in the original). Both of these scholars' investigations into Amazon are valuable because they contribute to the tiny body of critical analysis that offsets a vast and mostly celebratory genre of business journalism and corporate hagiography (for example, Spector, 2000). Nevethe-less, conspicuous by its absence from the work of both scholars is any reference to research drawn from the discipline of book history. Despite the retrospective orientation implied by the discipline's name, the history of the book has, in re-cent years, proven a fertile field for analyzing the *contemporary* book trade, includ-ing its digital permutations.[3] This chapter invokes book historian Claire Squires's expansive definition of book "marketing" as the instigation of desire in consum-ers to possess a particular work: "Marketing in publishing is . . . a vital, dynamic act, the creator of the literary marketplace" (2007: 51)—and also, we might add in Amazon's case, the creator of a particular kind of digital literary sensibility.

Digital media's data-generating and -archiving capabilities enable researchers to document and analyze the publishing industry's mysterious "word of mouth" factor either in real time or retrospectively—from advance publicity for a title, through waves of critical and customer reviews, plus the long afterlife of social media discussion and tagging. In this sense analyzing *digital* book marketing has distinct advantages over analyzing its analog predecessors. Traditionally publishers have evinced a certain wariness of book marketing and publicity on the grounds that they could rarely calibrate the precise relationship between a particular campaign, advertisement, or author appearance and a book's sales. Whereas in the digital realm, authorial and publisher-led marketing activities can be tracked in real time and, particularly in an integrated IT system such as Amazon's, "eyeballs" that morph into "click-throughs" and then become "customers" can be logged with heretofore undreamed of metrical precision (Wright, 2012: 112). Spearheading these digital changes and often acting as an advanced social research laboratory is the young adult (YA) book sector which, given that its target audience comprises digital natives, has invested heavily in web portals that avidly solicit teen engagement through quizzes, games, and even content co-creation (Martens, 2016). For book historian and former children's book publisher Marianne Martens, this constitutes the evidentiary high-water mark that digital technologies have irreversibly blurred the formerly distinct roles of "author," "marketer," "reviewer," and "consumer" (3, 6).

My method in this chapter is not to examine this new frontier of online book marketing from a how-to perspective (about which there exist books already)[4] but from a *critical* one—to explore the implications of the digital literary sphere for a materialist understanding of literature and its conditions of existence in the twenty-first century. How in particular do the marketing, publicizing, and retailing of literature in digital environments capitalize on and transform contemporary conceptions and practices of literary "community"?

Algorithmic Culture's Challenge to the Bourdieusian Field

In online forums, established literary credentials matter less than search engine optimization (SEO) and discoverability, as prominence and user recommendations increasingly drive authorial profile and book sales (Compagnon, 2005: 229; Schnittman, 2008: 139–40; Clifton, 2010: 108; Kaiser, 2012: 32; Parsons, 2013: 20; Delaney, 2014: 12; Friedman, 2016: 278–79). Hence algorithms have partially eclipsed the decades- or centuries-old human literary gatekeepers that have long regulated access to "legitimate" print culture. Reputation becomes less a question of accrued symbolic or social capital than of mathematics. The academic subfield of critical code studies (CCS) has emerged to examine such cultural, social, political, and economic effects of software programs, particularly as they affect relations between individuals and corporate and/or state entities and between and among users themselves.[5] It thus brings cultural and media studies, humanities, and social science perspectives to bear on information and communication technologies: "Software studies and its kin are the collision of computer science and cultural studies" (Kirschenbaum, 2009). While CCS scholars such as Mark Marino (2006), Matthew Kirschenbaum (2009), and Lev Manovich (2013) write extensively about the significance of "cultural software," they rarely make explicit connection with the book industries (Manovich, 2013: 20). Yet CCS possesses great significance for book studies because selection filters that operate between authors and readers are increasingly automated. Immensely influential algorithms such as Amazon's Amabot tool and Google's PageRank software, or the recommendation systems of YouTube, Facebook, Twitter, and Netflix, tend to be "black boxes" (systems whose internal workings are opaque because of proprietary and commercial-in-confidence restrictions and whose workings may only be inferred from observing inputs and outputs). More recently, Ted Striphas has usefully christened this rapidly expanding digital regime of cultural decision making with the term "algorithmic culture" (2010b, 2012, 2015; Hallinan and Striphas, 2016: 119).[6]

Theoretically, a shift from a sociological, Bourdieusian field of book-world individuals collectively brokering cultural capital to a model based on the workings of opaque mathematical formulas has momentous significance for the study of the contemporary literary sphere. In terms of disciplinary location, it nudges the study of print culture further from its humanities and social-science origins toward the burgeoning digital humanities fold. Whether or not humanities-trained scholars understand the mathematical complexities involved in typically closely guarded proprietary algorithms, it is incumbent upon us to analyze their *effects* and not simply to surrender the field to the technological imperatives of computer scientists or the bland assurances of media economists.

Two specific challenges to print culture scholars' now habitual recourse to Bourdieusian field theory present themselves in an era of CCS. Bourdieu's key innovation was to stage a leftist critique of the social investments of high culture by highlighting the class-interested nature of cultural gatekeepers' seemingly "disinterested" pronouncements on aesthetic worth (specifically, in the literary realm, those emanating from reviewers, prize committees, and academics) (1993, 1996). Given Bourdieu's sociological mindset, the agents operative upon the literary field were conceived of less as specific individuals than as representatives of various institutions, whereby a small number of individuals allied to the same organization (for example, a literary masthead, a publishing house, or a prize committee) mask their individual investments behind a smokescreen of collective, institutional value judgments (1993: 121–22). But once cultural gatekeeping functions shift to computer programs, sociological critiques of individual or small-group agency become far harder to sustain. It is not that algorithms function without social or political investments (far from it) but rather that their mathematical nature lends them a powerful air of scientific objectivity, thus rendering their encoded social and cultural priorities harder to identify and interrogate. Cultural arbitration is thus removed from the sphere of public debate via an incremental process of "privatization" (Striphas, 2015: 406). Such outsourcing of cultural evaluation from public figures to corporate-owned computer programs is all the more powerful and stealthy as such programs' aggregation and mining of vast datasets appear to represent transparently the very concept of the "public."

Bourdieu's consecrators of symbolic capital saw themselves as functioning in advance of high cultural trends—initiating trends through their avant-garde tastes—whereas algorithmic culture, on the other hand, functions retrospectively or in real time: ranking and thus reinforcing that which is *currently* popular and encouraging wider consumption of already bestselling items.[7] Clearly this has a self-reinforcing effect: that which is already popular becomes more popular through mass validation, polarizing the book market into what J. B. Thompson terms "big books" at one end and Chris Anderson's oft-cited "long tail" of also-rans at the other (2010: 187; 2006). Cultural journalists Malcolm Knox (2005) and Gideon Haigh (2006) have previously explored the similarly self-perpetuating logic within the cultural sphere of two other quantitative tools: respectively, the bookselling point-of-sale subscription database BookScan, and Google's search engine. The air of reportage algorithmic culture enjoys—ostensibly merely aggregating that which users already consume without implicit value judgments—makes Bourdieu-style critiques harder to mount. For what previously read as an attack on a self-appointed minority avant-garde now presents as an attack on majority taste (Striphas, 2010b). If anything, critiquing the effect of algorithmic culture on perpetuating mass-cultural trends paints the Bourdieusian critic him/ herself as self-appointed cultural arbiter—a stance wildly at odds with the cultural-studies relativism which most adopters of Bourdieu's theories have strongly internalized. In mounting a critique of algorithmic culture we thus sail dangerously close to rearticulating the elite cultural pessimism of the Frankfurt School theorists. Nevertheless, refusing to be scared off by the default, catchall putdown "elitist" is essential if we are to understand the transformative effects of algorithmic culture on the "selling" of contemporary literature.

Amazon and the Commodification of "Community"

As a pioneer in online bookselling, Amazon faced the significant challenge that its lack of physical locations for customer interactions necessitated that all retailer-consumer rapport be generated through the website alone, both discursively via landing-page content and as well as through backstage technological tools. Hence it was words (rather than images, given the primitive state of Internet browsers at Amazon's 1995 inception) that had to sustain the kind of ambiance that brick-and-mortar retailers could evoke through store design, furnishings, lighting, artworks, signage, and staff interactions (Kotha, 1998: 215, 221; Weedon, 2007: 119). The cultivation of bookishness is Amazon's attempt to emulate what, by the 1990s, had become a key attraction for clientele of both independent and chain brick-and-mortar book retailers: a sense of clubbish belonging with likeminded literate people—what Juliet Gardiner terms "customer intimacy" (2002: 165; see also Collins, 2010: 59–62).[8] For Amazon, therefore, the tone of its website was paramount.

Being a rank outsider to literary circles, Jeff Bezos, Amazon's founder, needed to hire in the cultural capital of established literary habitus to cultivate an appropriate tone, which he did with the appointment in 1996 of book reviewer and translator James Marcus as Amazon's first literary editor. Marcus recalls in his wry, self-aware memoir *Amazonia* (2004)—tagged by its publisher with the rather breathless "Five Years at the Epicenter of the Dot.com Juggernaut"—that Bezos wanted the home page's tone to be "eclectic, funny, smart, and discriminating, minus any hint of snobbish superiority" (115).

While visually and technologically more sophisticated today, the Amazon website still echoes this early desire to convince users that they are "getting the same kind of literary feedback they would find in a small independent bookstore" (Spector, 2000: 141). The air of informality and casual news-sharing is, in reality, painstakingly orchestrated. Amazon lists five Editors on its Books subpage, who typically boast long-standing careers in the commercial book trade. Their job is to match current events and consumer trends with topical book titles, post advance reviews of pre-release titles, and curate general literary chat—to consciously replicate on Amazon's website "the trustworthy atmosphere of a quirky independent bookstore with refined literary tastes" (Stone, 2013: 47).

This goal is achieved through giving top billing to a handful of "Best Books of the Month/Year Editor's picks," with awards news, special offers, and *Amazon Book Review*[9] presented in descending order of prime home-page real estate. Interviews with topical authors are prominent; these were initially in text-based Q&A format (Spector, 2000: 87; Marcus, 2004: 32–33), though they are now more commonly video clips. For consumers seeking the reassurance of the mass market, there are multiple bestseller listings provided, ranking top-selling titles on Amazon, or the US industry-defining *New York Times* list, as well as listings by genre subcategories. Specific book-centric markets are actively interpolated on Amazon's home page by links dedicated to best book club picks and books recently adapted for screen, rotated as topicality demands. The remainder of the web page (the less valuable lower sections requiring users to scroll down) displays "personalized" recommendations uniquely customized according to a browser's prior viewing history.

Marcus notes that, during its early years, "It was useful to Amazon, as a business strategy, to convey the feeling of your beloved indie bookstore, full of hip, book-loving people" (quoted in Packer, 2014). His own memoir charts, however, that from 1998 Amazon's books home-page content became increasingly automated and dictated by algorithms and co-operative advertising agreements, rather than curated by humans (2004: 167–69). Featured books, especially those scoring the home page's most coveted top-slot real estate, have long been chosen on the basis of co-op advertising money alone, not necessarily arms-length editorial recommendation (Finn, 2013). In this, Amazon functions like brick-and-mortar book retailers, especially chain stores, who rent out preferential window display-space, prominent front-table positioning, and even the endcaps of bookstore stacks to publishers for set fees (Schiffrin, 2001: 125; Miller, 2006: 101; Thompson, 2010: 327; Packer, 2014; cf. Ray Murray and Squires, 2013: 13).

The gradual nudging out of human literary "habitus" by automation is a recurrent Amazon theme, bearing out what Marcus has dubbed the firm's "mania for quantification, . . . its . . . Culture of Metrics" (3; see also Timberg, 2015). Leveraging Bezos's background in mathematical analysis for a Wall Street investment firm, Amazon strove to secure browsers' community allegiance through technological means. The most innovative of these was Amazon's system of automated personalized recommendations, starting in 1997. These were generated algorithmically by its Amabot software on the basis of each customer's prior purchases, viewing history, and purchases by other customers who bought a viewed item (Kotha, 1998: 218–19; Kumar and Benbasat, 2002: 16; Stone, 2013: 134; Finn, 2013). Bezos's media-friendly descriptions of the program's workings are revealing, not only for their technological explanation but also for the consciously folksy tone in which they are couched. Amazon's personalized recommendation software works "by collaborative filtering. It is a statistical technique that looks at your past purchase stream and finds other people whose past purchase streams are similar. Think of the people it finds as your electronic soul mates. Then we look at that aggregation and see what things your electronic soul mates have bought that you haven't. Those are the books we recommend. And it works" (Sheff, 2000).[10] Hence, by the turn of the millennium, the Amazon web page reconstituted itself—was "rehung" in technical parlance—in uniquely customized form for each individual web user (Marcus, 2004: 198).

Bezos is on record as having modeled the Amabot algorithm on traditional booksellers' hand-selling skills: "I want to transport online bookselling . . . back to the days of the small bookseller, who got to know you very well and would say things like, 'I know you like John Irving, and guess what, here's this new author, I think he's a lot like John Irving'" (quoted in Spector, 2000: 152). As is typical in Bezos's rhetoric, the customer here takes on almost metaphysical proportions— both unappeasable taskmaster and amiable co-explorer of giddy new-economy frontiers.[11] In inverse proportion to this hyperbolic deification of the customer, Amazon as retail behemoth shrinks to mere conduit, pandering to the fickle will of its master, the market. In its founder's most extreme formulation, Amazon recasts itself as a quasi-public service, existing benevolently to enhance customers' satisfaction by uniting them with optimally chosen consumer goods: "Our core business isn't selling things. Our core business is helping people make purchase decisions" (quoted in Sheff, 2000).

But community-creation via collaborative filtering carries with it a reductive, functionalist undertow: by necessity it presents users with an increasingly tightly focused range of choices which imitate both their own earlier choices and those of their likeminded peers. It is driven by a self-reinforcing and confirmatory logic that continually reorients users along consumption paths they have already trod (Robinson, 2010). For the literary-trained Marcus—increasingly by the late 1990s coming to regard himself as an embattled "humanist in the dark wood of the internet boom"—statistical prediction represents a hopelessly blunt tool with which to try to capture the vagaries of literary taste (2004: 157): "Personalization strikes me as a mixed blessing. While it gives the people what they want—or what we think they want—it also engineers spontaneity out of the picture. The happy accident, the freakish discovery, ceases to exist. And that's a problem. From time to time, we want something to arrive out of left field: we want a shocking addition to our statistical universe. A program won't do it. At such moments, only human perversity or sheer error will make us happy" (Marcus, 2004: 200).

At play here are two competing versions of market "choice": one a cornucopia of bookish offerings exceeding the possible stock holdings of a physical bookstore; the other, the economic rationalist fiction of the sovereign consumer perfectly informed and unerringly discriminating in her purchasing choices. Amazon, proudly styling itself "Earth's Biggest Bookstore," has a legitimate claim to offer unparalleled bookish inventory. But the sheer immensity of its virtual holdings induces in consumers a form of analysis paralysis or choice-anxiety. This in turn triggers a search for reassurance and predictability in the form of following previous buying habits, either their own or those of their "electronic soul mates," relying on brand-name authors, genre-confirming cover design, and automated "personalized" recommendations. Publishers, in response, focus their acquisition decisions and promotional efforts on a limited number of (often imitative) bestsellers. The upshot of this seemingly paradoxical coexistence of boundless choice with tractable and docile purchaser behavior is aptly encapsulated in a phrase coined by the late publisher and book industry commentator André Schiffrin: "market censorship" (2001: 103).

Amazon's quantified and commercialized approach to community-building represents an early instance of what, in the Web 2.0 era, we would identify more readily as the surveillance culture of social networking: the harvesting of voluntarily supplied user data to ever more precisely target commercial messages to potential consumers (Striphas, 2010a: 304; Nakamura, 2013: 241–42; Wu, 2013; Davis, 2015: 515; McGurl, 2016: 450). The collapse of the term "community" into "consumer base" is rife across the book industry. As with book blogs maintained by commercial entities, there is a constant reiteration of "community" rather than selling. But in the how-to genre of marketing advice for publishers and retailers, there is an equally insistent refrain of how *not* to sound like you're aggressively shilling a product, while at the same time taking an avid interest in user statistics, sales spikes, best channels for increasing consumer spending, and the like. An example from *Writer's Digest* encapsulates the bait and switch: "People not only noticed, but they felt more valued, and that created authentic connections between them and the author. By the time our marketing message later came down the pipeline, they were much more receptive than they would have been otherwise" (Kaiser, 2012: 33; see also Weinman, 2008: 97; Tian and Martin, 2010: 157–58; Katz, 2010: 49). It is a patently disingenuous stance: sound like you're not selling when of course you are. The net effect is that marketing becomes the practice that dare not speak its name: omnipresent, relentlessly pursued, but rhetorically disavowed through continual recourse to a vocabulary of communal fellow-feeling.

Is this even all that new? Publishers have always unsettled more aesthetically purist doctrines of literature by their close involvement with books as commodities. Additionally, the independent bookstores Amazon's discourse consciously emulated were themselves always indisputably commercial operations, however much they paired that motivation with the mantle of cultural improvement and community service (Miller, Laura J., 2011: 19). Yet differences are discernible. The bookish community ethos operative around such independent bookstores was conceived of as predating the customer's commercial transaction with the bookseller and extending beyond the cash nexus alone. Such instantiations of "community" were never understood as reducible to the floor space of the bookshop itself, let alone that around the cash register. By contrast, the reach and pace of commercialism in digital environments dedicated to books and reading are more pervasive and track "user" purchasing interests more minutely than ever before. Amazon's tactics as an early online bookseller thus represented a difference both in kind and in scale: commerce and community not sitting uneasily side by side and at points pulling in opposite directions (as in Laura J. Miller's oxymoronic denomination of booksellers as "reluctant capitalists") but "community" conceived from its inception as commercial asset. It represented a thoroughgoing subsumption of the social by the commercial facilitated by the disembodied nature of Amazon-customer interactions.

The concept of bookish community has become so saturated with commercialism in online-born literary spheres, and existing real-world book communities have become so co-opted by commercial concerns in their digital incarnations, that it seems timely to rethink the very ontological opposition between community as based on emotional rapport and common interest, and the idea of community as potential market. Is product affiliation the way in which twenty-first-century netizens now *conceive of* community? Such recasting of the relationship between "commerce" and "community" from one of fundamental antipathy and mutual exclusivity has its appeal. However, if we follow this transmutation in the term's meaning through to its logical conclusion, the concept of "community" risks becoming so hollowed out as to be merely interchangeable with "market" or "consumer base." Surely something essential is lost in such a process: social bonds, emotional reciprocity, the possibility of human altruism. Nevertheless, posing the devil's-advocate question of whether "community" can now be equated with "market" usefully alerts us to the intellectual cul-de-sac of continuing to present these two concepts as irreconcilable binaries.[12] Comprehending the deeply intermeshed ways in which older, non-commercial understandings of "community" are increasingly shot through with financial motivations—including within social groupings which self-describe as "communities"—is essential if we are to come to grips with the nature of sociability and group belonging in contemporary digital environments.

Innovations in Online Book Marketing

There is clear industry and academic consensus that twenty-first-century book marketing will increasingly migrate to the digital sphere (Allen, 2009; Clifton, 2010; Thompson, 2010; Steiner, 2010; Crompton, 2013; Taylor, 2013; Kurowski, Miller, and Prufer, 2016). Rather than marketing remaining beholden to an analog-era "campaign" mindset of one-way communication focused upon the narrow six-week window around a book's publication, the interactive affordances of digital media and the Internet's possibilities for sustaining producer-consumer relationships transform marketing into a process of ongoing community cultivation. Marketing and publicity efforts on behalf of a new book will typically accelerate around the date of the new title's publication but, given the Internet's archiving capability, they need never become completely dormant (Voigt, 2013: 682–83). Two of the most intriguing born-digital marketing innovations in the contemporary "selling" of literature are book trailers and blog tours, which merit detailed examination in turn.

Book Trailers

A book trailer is a brief video, typically around two minutes long, which encapsulates the premise and something of the tone of a book, and which is distributed for free, usually via online platforms. The goal is to so entice interested viewers that they are motivated to further promote the trailer by embedding it in their social media posts, retweeting the URL, and increasing its hit rate on video-sharing websites—prior to buying the book itself (Davila, 2010: 33; Paul, 2010: L1; El-Hai, 2014: 25). It is no coincidence that book trailers emerged around 2006, at precisely the point when YouTube exploded into popular consciousness (Dennys, 2006; Deahl, 2007; Rickett, 2007).[13] Since that time, multinational publishers have invested significantly in this new marketing phenomenon, especially in the YA and children's book sectors, with many even setting up dedicated YouTube channels proffering dozens, sometimes hundreds, of videos for house titles.[14] The book trailer's audiovisual medium is seen as a natural fit for the Internet, and more particularly for multifunctional reading devices such as Apple's iPad, which promise to realize the digital marketing holy grail of users viewing a book trailer, purchasing the e-book, and reading the download—all on the same device (Prothero, 2010: 48). Given professional book trailer production budgets of at least $5,000–$10,000, it is typically a publishing house's lead authors who score commissioned book trailers (Allen, 2009; Ronai, 2010; Metz, 2012; Baum, 2012: 17): even the famously reclusive Thomas Pynchon agreed to provide the voiceover for the book trailer accompanying his novel *Inherent Vice* (2009) (signing off rather plaintively, "Or maybe you'll just wanna read the book").[15]

A decade on from the phenomenon's emergence, the time is clearly ripe for literary sociologists to analyze the book trailer—a feature of the book industry landscape that has thus far attracted almost no academic interest.[16] That such scholarly attention is overdue in book studies is made clear by a serendipitous alignment with academic interest developing in a related, though distinct, discipline. In film and television studies, promotional phenomena such as trailers, promos, station identifiers, credit sequences, and other screenic paratexts have recently shifted from the periphery of academic concern—disregarded as so much advertising detritus jeopardizing the claims of cinema studies, and now also television studies, to high art. They have been belatedly admitted to screen cultures' legitimate sphere of analysis because of the way they destabilize simplistic creative/commercial dualisms, as well as for the light they throw on shifting producer-consumer relationships in a period when screen industries are being remade by digital media (Gray, 2010; Gillan, 2015; Grainge and Johnson, 2015).[17] Adopting and reworking print culture theorist Gérard Genette's concept of "paratext" ([1987] 1997), which he used to denote the external wrappings of a codex such as cover designs, prefaces, dedications, and notes, screen scholars have repositioned the film trailer and similar commercial texts as key "filters," which crucially mediate audiences' encounter with a screenic text (Gray, 2010: 3). To invoke the architectural metaphor suggested by the original French title of Genette's work, *Seuils* (thresholds), promotional paratexts act as vestibules to the text proper—spaces, as it were, for audiences to remove their coat and hat, straighten their tie, pause to take a breath, and orient themselves to the key lineaments of the text proper before passing fully from the extradiegetic to the intradiegetic realm. Specifically, screenic paratexts are vital in managing would-be audiences' expectations of a film or television program, establishing genre classification, touting star billing, and habituating audiences to producers' preferred viewing stance by communicating evaluative features such as critical plaudits or box office results. While never determinative in these regards, promotional paratexts nevertheless remain hugely influential. To extend the architectural metaphor, just as would-be house sellers are constantly urged to be mindful of the importance of the first impression their property makes, the expectations established in an audience's first, paratextual encounter with a screen text can be difficult, if not impossible, to dislodge; if misconceived or poorly targeted, the paratextual cues may actually prevent the desired consumption from ever taking place.

Granted, film trailers have been a feature of the screen industries for decades, even if they have only recently attained academic respectability. Their creation typically involves filleting of existing film or television content down to an encapsulation of key dramatic or intriguing moments (Allen, 2009). The book trailer, by contrast, requires generating content ex nihilo, and furthermore involves a transmedial wrench from print to audiovisual communication that may well exceed the author's—and even the publisher's—skillset (Ronai, 2010; Voigt, 2013: 680). Hence, the mainstreaming of book trailers represents a more existentially disruptive trend for the book industries than for screen cultures. The rapidity with which book trailers have multiplied in recent years suggests a kind of desperation on the part of book marketers to find a new promotional form better able to exploit the technical affordances and user behaviors typical of digital environments than the clearly diminishing returns of old-school book promotion techniques such as securing reviews, print media advertising, and direct mailing. As cultural sociologist and book industry analyst John B. Thompson has uncontroversially remarked, "Marketing will increasingly shift to the online environment" (2010: 399, see also 328). But whether the book trailer represents the optimal fit between bookish dispositions and digital architectures remains an open question at this early point in the evolution of the digital literary sphere.

Industry skeptics such as Peter Miller, then Director of Publicity at Bloomsbury Publishing US, cut through the book trailer hype early in remarking, "They're all the rage right now . . . but I would love to see an example of one video that really did generate a lot of sales" (Kachka, 2008; see also Walker, 2012). Insofar as any book trailers have achieved viral popularity and registered on mainstream bookish consciousness to date, US writer Gary Shteyngart leads the field. Shteyngart has cornered the market on celebrity cameos in his book trailers, where A-list literary authors such as Jonathan Franzen, Edmund White, Jeffrey Eugenides, and Jay McInerney—and even Hollywood names James Franco, Paul Giamatti, and Rashida Jones—have appeared.[18] The self-mocking hijinks of these Brahmins of literary culture, and their appearance check by jowl with embodiments of the usually quite distinct domain of film celebrity, positively invite sharing in the form of forwarding, "liking," and retweeting. If ever there were a moment where the authorial celebrity explored in chapter 1 and Hollywood celebrity fused it would

Hollywood star James Franco appears as Gary Shteyngart's husband in the book trailer for Shteyngart's *Little Failure* (2013).

be in actor and occasional fiction writer James Franco's appearance in the book trailer for Shteyngart's memoir *Little Failure* (2013): Franco "stars" as Shteyngart's husband, dropping a consolatory kiss on his disconsolate spouse and engaging in suggestive banter while both sport fluffy pink bathrobes.[19] Shteyngart's book trailers ape gonzo-style amateurism, a pose rather belied by the involvement of his stellar cast and the closing production credits. Other, genuinely lower-budget efforts such as independent publisher Text's wildly successful book trailer for the Australian edition of Adam Mansbach's bestselling spoof children's book *Go the Fuck to Sleep*, may indicate the entry-level potential of the book trailer genre. This trailer, which earned semi-cult status in its national market and has been viewed more than 1.5 million times on YouTube, depicted children's television stalwart and longtime *Play School* presenter Noni Hazelhurst reading the book to the camera in a perfect synthesis of self-mocking presenter and pseudo children's picture book.[20]

James English contends in *The Economy of Prestige* (2005) that the key indicator of any contemporary cultural phenomenon having entered the mainstream is the creation of a prize, either an award for the best or worst of a given genre (2). By this measure, book trailers have manifestly achieved cultural centrality through the establishment of multiple book trailer awards, beginning with the UK *Bookseller*'s inaugural awards in 2007 (Rickett, 2007), reinforced by natural book-trailer enthusiast Amazon's selection of the top five book trailers of the year since

2008 (Paul, 2010), and particularly with US publisher Melville House's 2010 establishment of the semi-serious Moby Awards for book trailers in various best and worst categories (Paul, 2010; "Honoring," 2011; Staskiewicz, 2011: 77).[21] Their inaugural award for Best Performance by an Author went to a well-deserving Dennis Cass for his "Book Launch 2.0," purporting to be one side of a filmed mobile-phone conversation between author and publisher about the perils of on-line book marketing:[22]

> What *am* I doing? Yes, that is the question . . . ah, well . . . oh, book club . . . yeah . . . my neighbour's having a book club! Read the book and . . . yeah, my neighbour. I'm also going to do a big email blast: "that book I wrote a year ago is out, again." Just send that to everybody, select all. . . . No, I never did a website. No, I know, I know, you need to have a website, I know everything has a website, you're right, and I don't. Well, I have my blog. The blog . . . the free one. I've kind of neglected it. I'm guessing that nobody reads it. But I did redesign it recently. Well, I guess I just picked a new template, made it a bit darker, more . . . something. . . . What are those? You mean like those little buttons like "Digg," "Reddit," there's one that looks like the word "delicious" but it's got a bunch of dots in it? . . . oh, it is "Delicious." OK, well it sounds like I need a new website and a new blog. . . . Well I guess technically I'm on MySpace in that I have an account . . . no, I don't have anything for the book on that, it's just me. . . . Well, I'm on Facebook. No, I didn't know you could do that. . . . My *book* can have a Facebook page? I thought you'd need to have someone with a . . . face. . . . So . . . get Second Life, build avatar, meet friends, so I just host a reading. . . . Twitter. What twitters? . . . Anything else while we're jamming this out? YouTube, of course. Coz you know, that's the dream, right? Twenty years ago when I wanted to become a writer, a big part of the dream was to be able to put little videos on the internet. . . . And maybe I'll just stop writing and I'll just do downloads and apps, and widgets and. . . . Hey, you know, I just had an idea: I'm gonna write a hit song and I'm gonna get it on *Guitar Hero 4*. That might help. . . .

Cass's delightfully self-ironic, self-deconstructing take on the book trailer is in fact representative of a veritable subgenre: book trailers frequently display a kind of having-your-cake-and-eating-it-too unease with the whole concept of a book trailer while gleefully engaging in the process.[23] Melville House publisher Dennis Johnson suggests something of the cross-media origins of this disquiet: "In a way the whole concept of making a movie about your book is a denigration of your book" ("Honoring," 2011; see also Arons, 2013; Voigt, 2013). Also of this ambivalent school is the trailer for Lane Smith's picture book *It's a Book* (2010), in which an ape character patiently defends the features of the codex against the digital and interactive obsessions of a presumably younger donkey.[24] Doubtless many of the half-million YouTube users who watched the book trailer thrilled to its stance of bibliophilic one-upmanship over the usually rampaging triumphalism of digital culture. But they nevertheless registered their approval by watching a digitally generated and hosted video and voting for it in an online popularity poll. Australian author Max Barry takes the book trailer to a new level of self-referentiality in his darkly literal webcam reenactment of the plot of his novel *Machine Man* (2011). Recounting to the camera that his publisher has urged him to make a book trailer, to "be creative, maybe re-enact a scene from the book, have fun with it," he proceeds to don protective goggles and rev a circular saw in what we are led to believe will be a dramatization of the moment where Barry's protagonist amputates his own leg to replace it with robotics.[25]

Such authorial high jinks tap into book industry ambivalence about book trailers; the fear is that they epitomize the codex's capitulation to screen culture, shoehorning literary content into an audiovisual medium to which it is ill suited. As award-winning Australian novelist Charlotte Wood has confessed, "I also find the idea kind of depressing—part of the point of a work of literary fiction is that it isn't a film" (Baum, 2012: 17). In such remarks, there is discernible resentment at the book industry's increasing absorption into multimedia conglomerates for whom films, television, and gaming represent far more lucrative sectors and in which books are viewed less as freestanding entities so much as proto-adaptations— "seeds of synergy" in the despairing phrasing of one commentator (Engelhardt, 1997). This echoes preexisting unease over the manner in which optioning of a manuscript for a screenplay can catalyze a book publishing deal for the same content—a phenomenon I have explored elsewhere using the term "twin-track authorship" (Murray, 2012: 42–43).[26] More generally, bookish types frequently express a reservation about book trailers long standard in critiques of adaptations— that they impose a particular visualization of characters and settings on readers' first encounter with a text (Walker, 2012; Metz, 2012; Baum, 2012: 17). But, interestingly, producers of book trailers are keenly aware of the imperative not to stray too close to an outright adaptation of the book's content—though for the quite distinct reason that it might jeopardize the sale of lucrative screen rights; as leading US book trailer producer Jefferson Rabb notes, "Any time I get too specific about the appearance of a character, people start to get very nervous" (Sullivan, J. C., 2009: 23).

None of these fears of literary culture being colonized by a screen industry mindset and marketing practices are exactly allayed by one publisher's analogy of the book trailer as akin to "the bonus material on the DVD" (Paul, 2010: L1).

But—reflexive bibliophilic flinching aside—his remark should prod scholars of the book to take account of the book trailer phenomenon and to question more broadly what it signifies for literary culture's existence in the online environment. Granted, the moment of "peak book trailer" may have now passed (the Mobys were last awarded in 2011) with trailers produced for adult literary titles in decline, although in the lucrative YA and children's markets they continue apace. This is a typical uptake pattern for digital literary sphere innovations: an industry-wide wave, followed by retreat to those market sectors where the tactic has demonstrated consumer traction. That trailers have not remained a key part of the book marketing mix for all titles does not negate their significance, nor does it resolve some of the thorny ontological issues trailers raise for books and reading. As in the screen industries, book trailers constitute key paratexts of contemporary literary works. Has a YouTube viewer who watches the book trailer for *Go the Fuck to Sleep*, which narrates all the words and lingers on each illustrated page, actually "read" the book in a conventional sense?[27] If so, has the actor-persona of a Noni Hazelhurst or Samuel L. Jackson been a semiotically relevant aspect of the viewer's textual encounter, and is the absence of this additional feature for readers who "only" consume the book itself somehow problematic? In such ways book trailers productively complicate neat divisions between the "inside" and "outside" of a text, between what is mere commercial paraphernalia and what constitutes the text proper. They dramatically emblematize the expanding liminal zone in which reader-users morph into co-marketers, publicists, and reviewers.[28]

Blog Tours

Also emerging around 2006, early in the social media era, was the marketing phenomenon of the blog tour (Gomez, 2005: 8–9; Nelson, 2006: 12; Alsever, 2006: 56). A virtual incarnation of the late twentieth-century authorial multi-city book tour, the blog tour promises greater audience reach, without the associated costs and risk of low turnouts inherent in the embodied book tour (Pool, 2007: 120; Parsons, 2013: 20; Baron, 2015: 118; Dietz, 2015: 199). Authors engaged on a blog tour make guest posts, or "stops," on typically twenty to fifty blogs over a concentrated period of days or weeks. Posts may range from op-ed–style pieces, to writer interviews and live webchats, but they can also include more exotic subgenres such as "a character interview, an excerpt or sneak peek, a how-to/behind-the-scenes post, writing tips, research ideas, a review, teaching notes, a book give-away" (Hanke, 2015: 18).[29] The marketing phenomenon's take-up has been greatest in YA, science fiction, and romance genres. This is either because the target readers are digital natives best contacted in the online realm where they already spend their time, or because the genre's fans boast a strong sense of online community which can be precisely targeted and has previously been overlooked by mainstream reviewing outlets (Gomez, 2005: 5; Pool, 2007: 116; Gillieron and Kilgarriff, 2007: 220–23; Delaney, 2014: 12; Hanke, 2015: 18–19). Such defaulting of book publicity to the author rather than the publisher—exploiting the author's sunk-cost investment in the success of a book and reducing the publisher's marketing costs—has not gone unremarked by authors. In a manner strongly reminiscent of the authorial self-marketing quandaries explored in chapter 1, Australian-based fantasy and YA writer Kim Wilkins reflects jadedly on the time sacrifices involved in building a digital "platform":

> A couple of years ago one of my books came out in the United States and I had no market there, I had no audience there, so I had to do a lot of this kind of audience building, this platform building, and what I did was I kept a folder of all the writing that I had to do to build that platform. Things like all the blogs I had to write, the blog tours that I had to go on, long interviews that I had to type the answers into and send off to book web sites and readers' web sites and so on. At the end of the process I added up how much I'd written and it was 12,000 words. That is roughly a month's worth of work as a writer for me. It took a whole month out of my fiction writing just to do this. (2014: 6)

Filling the vacuum left by retreating publisher marketing efforts are websites dedicated solely to coordinating blog tours for authors either inexperienced with, or queasy about, online self-promotion. Some are (currently) free to use, such as BlogTour.org,[30] whereas others, including Virtual Book Tour Café[31] and ATOMR Tours,[32] charge authors or their publishers a fee to compile a tour schedule of willing host bloggers. In this sense, the blog tour can be distinguished in important ways from Amazon's invocation of "community" as analyzed earlier. Amazon's incubation of an online bookish community was designed from its inception as a soft sell for its commercial ambitions: "It was neither a traditional store nor a traditional publication, but a backscratching fusion of the two," in Marcus's terse encapsulation (2004: 106). The blog tour, by contrast, introduces a commercial agenda to online communities first formed to promote discussion among likeminded readers; some degree of authentic, extra-commercial community existed prior to its identification as a target market. Hence commercial motivations have manifested incrementally as the literary blogging medium thrived rather than having been hardwired into its original design.

Nevertheless, creeping product placement should not cast book bloggers themselves in the role of passive bystanders, helplessly witnessing the infiltration of the blogosphere by insidious commercialism. Groups such as the former Litblog Co-op represent self-organized alliances of over a dozen "leading literary weblogs" that agree to discuss a certain book release across all members' blogs during a predetermined period.[33] Litblog Co-op's legacy website is coy as to whether such publicity was paid for, or whether supply of free book copies to over a dozen participating bloggers was sufficient in itself to have a title profiled. The Co-op's only self-justification in its "About" section—that it existed "for the purpose of drawing attention to the best of contemporary fiction, authors and presses that are struggling to be noticed in a flooded marketplace"—seems, at the very least, to have left the door open for commercial arrangements with the book trade. This pattern of coordinated online publicity is replicated in unashamedly commercial entities such as NetGalley, which acts as an online marketing intermediary between the book industry and groups of what it terms "professional readers," such as bloggers, journalists, librarians, educators, and other opinion influencers.[34] Subscribing readers are given the digital equivalent of a title's galley proofs for pre-release publicity generation, with the overall aim being to "ignite buzz and promote sales."

It has been scarcely a decade and a half since the blog's mainstreaming as a new form of public diary-keeping and citizen journalism, one allegedly free of the commercial constraints that bedevil analog media formats such as book publishing, newspapers, magazines, and broadcasting (Lejeune, 2009; Rettberg, J., 2014).[35] It is a pattern of disenchantment we ought to have become inured to before now: the rapidity with which notions of "authentic" community become themselves commodified. Even setting aside the fact that becoming a blogger always involved use of IT hardware, software, and Internet service provision from the corporate sector, bloggers' progressively closer enmeshment in marketplace realities has been undeniable. Whether through publishers' offers of free book copies in exchange for reviewing, the desire to increase their blog's hit rate (with the implications this carries for advertising revenue), or more diffuse motivations such as assuming the mantle of expertise and community esteem, blogging's communitarian and amateur rhetoric has everywhere run up against self-interest and commercialism (Steiner, 2010: 483, 489).[36] Nor are bloggers the only ones ensnared in this simultaneous pursuit and disavowal of commercial intent: author Kim Wilkins blows the whistle on the doublespeak pervading blog tours' ubiquitous talk of bookish "community": "You can't write all the time about your book because that sounds like you are trying to sell people something, and the whole idea is—just quietly, you are trying to sell people something—that you've got to present this kind of persona, this persona that is trying to engage with people on a personal level" (2014: 7).

The common interest and emotional reciprocity that lie at the heart of all concepts of community—whether digital or embodied—are under constant pressure in the digital literary sphere to demonstrate their financial utility. Online literary sociability *must*, it seems, be monetized. In this sense, the blog tour is a quintessentially digital-era book marketing model, one replicable at this cost level or global scale in neither analog nor live environments. But it is also a reminder that traditional political economy concerns with the irresolvable tension between culture and commerce remain absolutely relevant (if too often underexamined) in a digital literary sphere prone to self-idealization.

Pros and Cons of Online Marketing for the Independent Publishing Community

What does book marketing's new digital center of gravity portend for the independent and small press sector in particular? Significantly, the rise of online marketing dramatically levels a playing field long tilted against independent publishers and in favor of multinationals, in a manner often trumpeted by Internet proponents (Kotha, 1998: 213). If independent presses are no longer competing on the basis of advertising spending for access to a limited number of print-culture newspaper and periodical outlets, suddenly there is potential to reach a global market of would-be readers through DIY, quirky, virally circulated content (Schnittman, 2008: 140; Friedman, 2016: 285). For example, Philadelphia-based publishing minnow Quirk Books (established in 2002 and producing only around twenty-five titles per year) achieved enormous sales and imprint recognition for its series of literary classics / pulp fiction mashups, beginning with *Pride and Prejudice and Zombies* (2009), which was itself subsequently adapted for comic book (2010) and film (2016).[37] Especially with the viral success of their parody Austen-adaptation book trailer for *Sense and Sensibility and Sea Monsters* (2009)[38]—awarded top honors in Amazon's 2009 Best Book Video awards—Quirk leapfrogged its multinational competitors to achieve outsized profile on Google and YouTube searches for the term "book trailer." Quirk's especially resonant brand identity in this niche market attracts a demographic of pop culture adherents who may not primarily self-identify as book purchasers, thus pioneering new publishing markets. Such digital publicity tactics build upon the independent press sector's long history of developing strong brand identities and cultivating devoted communities around their content, such as the iconic resonance that UK feminist publisher Virago crafted for their dark-green Modern Classics series during the 1970s–1980s, or the hipster chic with which McSweeney's imbues its format-shifting quarterly and book titles (Murray, 2004a; Hungerford, 2012). The preeminent importance in the Internet era of publisher branding, particularly for independents, is high-lighted by publishing commentator Jane Friedman, in her contention that "the literary publisher needs to be a beacon, to offer a strong signal amidst all the noise, and organize ideas, content, and stories within an identifiable and useful context" (2016: 286).

The shifting and blurring of previously distinct book-industry roles that Mari-anne Martens detects at work in the YA market here register also on the tradi-tionally more conservative literary fiction sector. With the Internet's genuinely interactive capabilities, a literary-identified small press's readership can now be-come a combined focus group, marketing team, and reviewer pool all rolled into one. Indeed, literary periodicals and little magazines, fellow travelers of the small-press community and sometimes financially related undertakings, have had suc-cess in combining new-issue releases with live events, readings, and launch par-ties to reinforce the publication's embedding within a particular kind of local community (Stadler, 2016).[39] This collective identity may, at various times, man-ifest in print-based, virtual, or embodied incarnations without these various guises being seen as in any way mutually exclusive. Even for readerships at considerable geographic remove from the independent publisher's typically inner-metro site of operations, Internet appearances can helpfully supplant reality. Book market-ing practitioner and how-to author Alison Baverstock remarks that "website mar-keting offers smaller publishing houses a huge advantage: you can present the image you want your potential customers to see, even if the reality is that you only have a tiny staff" (2008: 158). If publisher-customer intimacy is successfully gen-erated, readers may even, she writes, "buy directly from you rather than through a [sic] internet retailing superstore" (2008: 158).

But this lowering of the barriers to entry to the publishing marketplace should not blind us to the profound power imbalances that continue to characterize the book market. It is just that the competition lineup has changed. If conglomerates-versus-independent-publisher tensions characterized the 1980s, and superstore-chains-versus-independent-bookseller wars dominated the 1990s, the new mil-lennium presents small publishers with a different big-media lineup, albeit one drawn from outside the traditional book industries. New entrants from IT hard-ware and software manufacturing, first-generation Internet retailing, and online search—preeminently Apple, Amazon, and Google—display inconsistent attitudes toward the independent and small press sector. When starting out, Amazon av-idly solicited the participation of small publishers so it could diversify its inven-tory and add ballast to its claims to be "Earth's Biggest Bookstore," in competition with its brick-and-mortar chain-store rivals (Marcus, 2004: 46; Squires, 2007: 33;

Amazon as cheetah, complete with familiar swoosh logo, in Dan Turk's illustrations for *Inside Digital Book World 2014: News and Highlights*. Reproduced by permission of Dan Turk

Baverstock, 2008: 152; Coll, 2014). James Marcus recalls walking the aisles of trade fair BookExpo America in mid-1997 with colleagues similarly dressed in Amazon livery and being "greeted like heroes" by independent publishers aggrieved by the financial thumbscrews the big-box retailers had been applying to them with increasing force (2004: 91). This warm relationship between small publishers and online retailer was formalized the following year with Amazon's invitation for independent publishers to participate on an equal footing with multinationals in its Publisher's Advantage program (Spector, 2000: 146). Yet, having established its market dominance, Amazon by the turn of the millennium itself proceeded to demand aggressive discounts from small publishers on the basis of such publishers' relatively low-volume sales and the associated administrative costs (Wasserman, 2012; Michell, 2015). Internally, this was infamously dubbed "the Gazelle Project"—after Bezos suggested that "Amazon should approach these small publishers the way a cheetah would pursue a sickly gazelle"—before company lawyers changed the name to the more anodyne "Small Publisher Negotiation Program" (Stone, 2013: 243–44; Packer, 2014; Coll, 2014; Davis, 2015: 525; Timberg, 2015).

Amazon's rapid acquisitions of rival online book destinations Shelfari (2008), Book Depository (2011), and Goodreads (2013) demonstrate its corporate goal to

Independent publishers, depicted as a wounded gazelle with reading glasses, broken horn, and circling flies, attempt to evade Amazon's cheetah. Reproduced by permission of Dan Turk

dominate the market for all things bookish—the imperative that all roads of online book talk lead to Amazon. The online bookseller has also exploited its near-monopoly position by deploying hardball tactics such as its well-publicized battles with the Big Six of corporate publishing over pricing of e-books. This predatory behavior saw Amazon temporarily remove the "buy" buttons from Macmillan titles in 2010 and, again, from Hachette titles in 2014 (Stone and Rich, 2010; Robinson, 2010; Wasserman, 2012; Coll, 2014). Such rancorous disputes, plus related antitrust litigation brought *by Amazon* (remarkably) against Apple for alleged e-book price-fixing in collusion with five multinational publishers, prompted rhetorical slap-downs of Amazon from within the book community for its winner-take-all business practices. The following, from Authors Guild Vice President Richard Russo, is representative: "We believe that [book-world] ecosystem should be as diverse as possible, containing traditional big publishers, smaller publishers, Amazon, Apple, Barnes & Noble and independent bookstores, as well as both e-books and print books. We believe that such an ecosystem cannot exist while entities within it are committed to the eradication of other entities" (2014).

Given bruising market conditions characterized by a de facto monopoly or, at a bare minimum, tight oligopoly, exactly what bargaining power do small presses realistically have vis-à-vis the online behemoth? Book buzz generated through quirky low-budget book trailers and well-targeted blog tours may indeed energize a previously nascent market for particular book titles. But will customer inertia and the mantra of cheaper prices see this new purchaser traffic adroitly redirected to Amazon?

The same contradiction between, on one hand, the near-infinite array of on-line content and, on the other, the routine nature of most web-users' actual brows-ing behavior is also pertinent for small presses' engagement with third-party social media platforms. Publishers, especially small and independent publishers, are everywhere admonished to cultivate online communities on Facebook, Twitter, Instagram, and Pinterest. While concentrating online marketing efforts on these platforms has the advantage of contacting potential readers in familiar territory, it places small publishers' online presence at the mercy of fickle Internet fashions (remember MySpace?) (Byle, 2012: 7; Harvey, 2013: 23). Moreover, like Amazon, such sites' attitudes toward small presses are often inconsistent and reminiscent of "bait-and-switch" tactics. In their early, traffic-maximizing, brand-building phase, social media sites have actively solicited commercial members. But, as seen with Facebook's decision to penalize companies posting unpaid promotional material in their newsfeeds, policy changes are typically unilateral, effective immediately, and could jeopardize the sunk cost in terms of time and wages of laboriously curated small-press online communities (Luckerson, 2014; Loten, Janofsky, and Albergotti, 2014). With book retailers, authors' own websites, and online reading groups all clamoring for readers' attention and offering themselves as one-stop-shops for all of one's book-related needs, publishers building communities in domains they do not themselves control risk ceding yet another tool of market leverage to competitors. Yet, on the other hand, it remains true that swearing off such platforms increases the alternative risks of marketing ineffectualness and industry irrelevance. In the digital domain independent and small press publish-ers are, once again, attempting to further cultural and political causes amid an inimical commercial landscape (Poland, 1999; Murray, 2004a; Freeth, 2007; Davis, 2008).

Conclusion

I close this survey of the significance of the digital sphere for contemporary book marketing, publicity, and retailing with a (perhaps unintentionally) revealing quote from Katie Bond, Fiction Publicity Manager for US publisher Nelson: "We refer to our authors' social media communities as their assets: something they own and will always take with them" (Byle, 2012: 8). Bond's words appear to encapsu-late many of the key trends in the digital transformation of book marketing: entrepreneurial, self-marketing authors growing their online brand through direct author-reader interactions; the paramount importance of one's online presence as precisely calibrated arbiter of one's literary reputation; and an implied sense of the precariousness and ephemerality of professional book-world relationships.

But, specifically, I want to explore Bond's seemingly straightforward and untroubled conflation of "community" with "asset." It is not so much any aberrant quality to Bond's turn of phrase as its very typicality in industry circles that interests me here. For previously there existed some fundamental incommensurability between the implicit commonality signified by the term "community" and the alienated, proprietorial sense of "asset." Community was precisely that which eluded the object-oriented nature of capitalist commodity exchange through its very relationality, its basis in intangible feelings of group-identity and fellow-feeling. Despite some superficial similarities, Bond's viewpoint is a long way from Bourdieu's concept of "social capital," in which prominent and communally well-integrated individuals are able to deploy their networks of friendship and professional association to further their interests.[40] For here it is not a self-maximizing individual jockeying for advantage within a publicly constituted "field" but the entire field *itself* which is reconceived as "asset."

Talk of community has, as this chapter has explored, become ubiquitous in all discussion of twenty-first-century book marketing, which is now by default digital. Scholars working from humanities and/or social science perspectives (rather than marketing practitioners too inside the system to be motivated to question its logic) thus urgently need to analyze this newly charged relationship between the concepts of "community" and "commodity." As outlined earlier, the traditional political-economy, cultural-industries framework which posited these as antithetical values, where any talk of commercialism pollutes and thus invalidates its counterpoising entity, is too broad-brush to be useful—shutting down discussion of precisely the issue we wish to elucidate. And yet, simplistically collapsing "community" into "commodity," as the practitioner Bond appears in her quote to do, risks liquidating at a stroke all those elements of community that previously exceeded the bounds of capitalist exchange, and which thereby testified to alternative ways of viewing human relationships: collective-minded, relational, potentially altruistic. I propose instead a sliding scale to map the complex interrelationship of "community" and "commodity" in the contemporary book industries. Rather like a Venn diagram in which some values belong exclusively to one set while others are shared by both sets, we can distinguish between various conceptions of community at work. At one extreme are book-centered online communities that perceive themselves to lie outside of commercial relations (perhaps amateur book bloggers whose sites trenchantly eschew advertising). Shifting closer toward the center are preexisting online bookish communities whose operations subsequently incorporate commercial agendas (such as the *Bookslut* blog discussed earlier). A third variety of online bookish communities, also situated at the overlap between Venn sets, are devised with combined social and commercial goals in mind (for instance, the corporately owned online reader forum Goodreads, discussed at length in chapter 5).[41] Finally, embodying the most corporatized view of community, are those online forums created specifically as marketing devices (for example, Amazon, whose editorial content, emailed newsletters, and customer reviews were designed from the outset to maximize the website's "stickiness" and thus drive sales). The emphasis here is on the various gradations and interpenetrations of notions of "community" and "commodity," and the diverse ways in which these combinations manifest in the digital literary sphere. Importantly, classification of an online community need not remain static; as the example of the Litblog Co-op shows, an online community created with the goal of "pure" sociability may, through financial pressures or succession problems, subsequently form mutually beneficial alliances with corporate concerns or be sold outright (as in Goodreads' sale to Amazon), significantly affecting its self-conception and modus operandi.

To return to Bond's quote, her remarks flag a second key issue for online book marketing, this time manifest not at the level of subtextual cues about the capture of "community" by commerce but rather evident on the face of her comments. If Bond, as part of a publishing operation, is genuine in viewing authors' social media communities as the *author's* asset, "something they own and will always take with them," what would it mean if authors acted on this assertion? Given that community has become the newly valuable currency of the book world, the key question arises: Who controls it? Historically, publishers were able, through the power of an illustrious colophon and fabled house or imprint list, to present themselves as the natural locus of literary community-building. Authors, on one hand, and readers, on the other, were generally too scattered, too intermediated by the logic of print publication to be able to sustain viable communities, at least until the boom in literary festivals from the 1980s onward normalized embodied author-reader interaction. But with the mainstreaming of Internet use, and particularly social media, by the first decade of the twenty-first century, publishers have faced competition from all sides in their claims to be the epicenter of literary community: celebrity authors use their public profile to brand their own websites and social media forums as the most authentic, unmediated fannish community; book retailers, whether online or off, leverage the practical fact of the commercial

The Right Tool for the Job

Several we spoke to noted that certain social networking platforms were better for specific book genres or authors than others. While these general guidelines have many exceptions, we thought a summary would be helpful:

Book Genre or Type of Content	Recommended Social Platform
All genres and authors	Blogging
Business	Twitter, LinkedIn
Celebrities (e.g., comedians, politicians)	Twitter, Facebook
Fiction in general	Facebook*
Headline-driven content	Twitter
Inspirational	Facebook
Lifestyle	Facebook, LinkedIn
Relevant image content (e.g., food)	Pinterest
Relevant video content (e.g., travel)	YouTube
Self-help	Facebook
Women's issues	Facebook

* Initially, when building one's platform for any book, Twitter is usually the recommended social network. However, after the book deal is signed, a general-interest network such as Facebook is preferred.

Table of optimal social media channels for publicizing books as classified by genre, accompanying John Parsons's article "The Social Publisher" in *Book Business* (2013). Reprinted with permission of *Book Business* magazine, October 2013

transaction into communities that readers may as well serendipitously engage with while making their purchases; readers form their own online communities, invoking a discourse of democratic participation to promote their sites as the most genuinely reader-centric; literary reviewing newspapers and periodicals attempt to counter this shift by deploying the inherited prestige of their mastheads as grantors of quality control, while condescending to the online environment through the addition of interactive affordances such as comments functions.[42] Even self-publishing enterprises, whether crowdfunded or print-on-demand in basis, have attempted to present themselves as natural loci of online community: at the same time as they promise a newly unmediated relationship between author and reader, they attempt to cultivate and prolong this relationship through the medium of the self-publishing enterprise's own website.

Faced with usurpers on all sides, how can publishers retain their precarious and increasingly embattled position as the go-to point for online literary sociability? The challenge of the digital literary sphere is for publishers to become such adept practitioners of online marketing that they ensure their continued centrality to the book-making business, rather than disintermediating themselves out of a job. In this, publishers must be mindful of playing to their strengths. The trump card they hold is their continuing legitimating function—what Bourdieu terms the power to "consecrate" cultural goods—a stamp of expert approval that retains relevance and perhaps is even amplified in the free-for-all environment of digital self-publishing (1993). Publishers can moreover demonstrate a wealth of expertise in online marketing management that few authors can match, advising writers on the optimal mix of social media tools for their particular title.[43] Finally, publishers can act as curators of a title's myriad online identities: providing a point of relative stability in the typically transient online environment by linking all related content under the publisher's brand umbrella. The publishers most successful in retaining and even entrenching their historical position as authorreader intermediaries tend to cultivate pungent brand identities to imbue house titles with a particular cultural/social/political charge that inspires community-building. In this, the typically small and beleaguered independent press sector, perhaps surprisingly, leads the way—identifying potentially global micro-communities who wish to comment upon, communicate about, perhaps contribute to or modify and, yes, purchase a particularly resonant book.

CHAPTER THREE

Curating the Public Life of Literature
Literary Festivals Online

Rae had hoped, this year, to be so well organised that she would be free to wander in and out of events, to stand quietly at the back for long enough to see what worked and what didn't, to scribble notes about the proficiency of chairpersons and the relative success of presentations, especially the digital ones. There was a five-minute loss of connection when George R. R. Martin was beamed in for two thousand impatient Thronies; the marine biologist illustrated his doleful hour with murky clips of giant jellyfish billowing through dead ocean zones. The Norwegian mythic poet entertained a tiny but appreciative audience with blurry animations of Norse gods major and minor cut with music to accompany his verse.

STEPHANIE JOHNSON (2015: 352)

In Stephanie Johnson's novel *The Writers' Festival* (2015), Rae McKay, director of the fictional Oceania Writers' Festival, must contend with digital technology on a daily basis. The novel depicts contemporary literary life as thoroughly interpenetrated by the digital domain—from the rush to get the festival program uploaded to the Internet in time to meet marketing deadlines, through the blizzard of Google alerts and Twitter messages from the global literary world in which the festival organizers operate, to the Skype meet-up of geographically dispersed judges for the festival-hosted Opus Book Award. Johnson was herself co-founder of the Auckland Writers Festival and clearly knows literary festival organizing from the inside, though her slightly coy comment in the book's Acknowledgements that the novel represents an "entirely imaginary literary knees-up" frustrates reading of the text as a roman à clef (372). But whether the various inter-writer rivalries, soured love affairs, pseudonymous hoaxes, and diplomatic standoffs with the Chinese embassy over a dissident writer's invitation are fictional or not, the book *is* accurate in its depiction of digital technology's centrality to writers' festivals by this point in the twenty-first century. It has long been standard for literary festival events to be organized and publicized with the aid of digital technology, and to be subsequently archived online. But a more recent development is digital mediation making possible the festival event itself. The digital now serves not merely as the technological substrate for organizing a literary event but—as the imaginary, though highly plausible, George R. R. Martin live linkup illustrates—as the context in which the festival event itself takes place. More particularly, such digital mediation appears not to cancel out the literary festival's traditional claims to live authenticity and co-presence; counterintuitively, it harnesses virtual incarnations to bolster such claims. Like Paul Ewen's satirical novel *Francis Plug: How to Be a Public Author* (2014), discussed at the beginning of chapter 1, Johnson's *The Writers' Festival* provides a fictional take on the contemporary public life of authors. Through its mostly playful riffs on the game of contemporary literary culture, the novel foregrounds the extent to which the digital literary sphere has colonized real-world literary institutions and how any residual opposition between the two increasingly dissolves.

Cultural festivals' uptake of digital technology this century has been avid; cultural sociologists Yvette Morey, Andrew Bengry-Howell, Christine Griffin, Isabelle Szmigin, and Sarah Riley write of a pervasive "mediation of festivals online" (2014: 255). Literary festivals, with their predilection for the written word, have been especially prominent contributors to this trend, even during the period of Web 1.0's dominance, when the Internet was characterized by mostly unidirectional communication flows. A survey of Australian literary festival audiences conducted by Wenche Ommundsen and others in 2004–2005 found that 31 percent of those surveyed already sourced information about literature from the Internet (Ommundsen, 2009: 27). But it has been since the dawn of Web 2.0 from around 2004, an era characterized by user-generated content-exchange via social media applications, that literary festivals' embrace of digital technologies has massively increased. A search of the global newspaper database Factiva reveals that mentions of social media at literary festivals tended to surge starting in 2012.

Literary festivals' uptake of digital technology over the past twenty-five years reveals a pattern of growing enthusiasm and increasingly multipronged engagement with audiences. Since well before the beginnings of Web 2.0, most festivals had constructed extensive public-facing websites containing programming, ticketing, and logistical information, as well as offering subscribers email newsletters. As the World Wide Web became increasingly capable of hosting larger audiovisual files, literary festivals added audio or video recordings of past events to both their own websites' archives as well as to highly trafficked third-party video-hosting websites such as YouTube and Vimeo. Indeed, dedicated festival YouTube channels are by this point common.[1] The Hay Festival not only podcasts events and has its own iTunes channel but also boasts the "Daily Haycast," hosted by sponsor newspaper the *Guardian*'s website, thus massively increasing its exposure to already book-identified audiences. Currently, the most prominent international writers' festivals make use of a full suite of social media tools: official and guest blogs; Facebook pages; Twitter, Instagram, and Flickr accounts. The live-tweeting of festival events has by now become as standard at literary festivals as it has at academic conferences, with those not physically present able to keep tabs on what unfolds on stage and in the minds of fellow audience tweeters, be they themselves located onsite or at a virtual remove. If, for marketing reasons, festival organizers are prone in their rhetoric to posit literary culture in opposition to the alleged triviality of mass digital culture, in practice they appear to regard the two mediums as thoroughly compatible. So long as digital media drives and expands public engagement with the world of books and reading, festival organizers are all for it.

The Literary Festival: Definitions, Characteristics, Contexts

Whether labeling themselves as "literary festivals," "writers' festivals" (with or without the possessive apostrophe), "book festivals," "readers' festivals," or some combination of these, public celebrations of literature tend to display common characteristics. They take place in a specific, embodied location over a concentrated period of time and are typically annually recurrent. As cultural policy analyst Liana Giorgi observes, literary festivals have traditionally been defined by this "concentration of events in time and space" (2011: 42). As a consequence, festivals' unique selling points have long been the opportunity for readers and writers to see each other live and in the flesh, to share their passion for writing and ideas, and to experience some degree of reader-writer interactivity. There can be no adequate comprehension of how literary culture operates in the twenty-first century without taking into account the transformative impact book-festival culture has had on literature's public face. The global writers' festival circuit reflects the broader stock exchange of literary esteem in all its constant fluctuation. But as well as microcosmically representing the literary field as a whole, literary festivals are themselves actors within the field: providing forums for the accrual or dispersal of cultural capital—and thus influencing one's value in the cultural prestige market—through particularly laudable or egregious authorial performances. Though the fact is still bemoaned in some quarters, festival culture by now to a large extent *is* literary culture.

"The public life of literature" is print culture scholar David Carter's evocative phrase to denote the significance of literary culture beyond the printed page (1999: 140). Its coinage is designed to throw into high relief literary studies' traditional, near-exclusive preoccupation with aesthetic qualities of literariness (Carter and Ferres, 2001). "In what ways," Carter's refreshingly institutionally oriented investigations ask, "does literature circulate in public, commercial and governmental realms?" (2001: 141). In particular, live, community-facing events such as writers' festivals make literary culture concrete in the form of specific individuals, precincts, buildings, and actual audience behaviors. Such events are closely tied to cultural policy regimes at the levels of local, regional, and national governments through funding relationships and claims to contribute to the economy, cultural life, and tourism-branding of host locales (Belfiore and Bennett, 2009).

Compared to the performing arts, literary culture for a long time lacked embodied instances of community because its primarily print-based medium by default placed authors and audiences at some remove from each other. Print culture had instead to make do with proxy abstractions such as Benedict Anderson's "imagined communities" (1983), Jürgen Habermas's "public sphere" ([1962] 1989), or Pascale Casanova's "world republic of letters" (2004).[2] These might involve certain loci of embodied literary conviviality (the coffee house, the salon, the publisher's lunch) but they could not, individually, aspire to encapsulate the public life of literature as a whole (Sapiro, 2016: 7, 10). Literary festivals, by contrast, especially the largest ones, promote themselves as living incarnations of the book world: diverse and lively places where real-life authors interact with flesh-and-blood readers, book-trade deals are done, books are sold by the thousands, and which provide the media and the broader world with definite—albeit evanescent—images of what literary culture actually *looks* like. Hence the media's predilection for talismanic shots of literary culture in "action"—readers sprawled in Penguin Classics–branded deck chairs at the UK's Hay Festival; the celebrity author striking the lectern in declamatory, speaking-truth-to-power fashion at the PEN World Voices Festival in New York City; or any number of black-clad, espresso-drinking, earnestly engaged audience members at any number of inner-urban writers' festivals the world over.

The writers' festival is the most visible of a range of forums in which literary life is curated and choreographed for public consumption, inviting broad(er) participation. Other phenomena, conceptually distinct but in practice often overlapping, include book town festivals, book trade fairs, meet-the-author events in bookstores, libraries, and schools, and book launches. Book towns are largely analogous to literary festivals in that they are convened in a specific locale during a concentrated period of time (commonly over a week or weekend). However, they are distinct in that they typically take place outside metropolitan locations, such as in regional towns or villages with strong heritage associations. Such semi-rural settings make book towns more closely integrated with discourses of regional regeneration and tourism development than writers' festivals based in capital cities (Seaton, 1996, 1999; Brown, 2006: 2; Gibson and Connell, 2011). The book-town model, famously pioneered by the Welsh border town of Hay-on-Wye with its abundance of secondhand bookshops, has inspired global imitators, including the Clunes Booktown Festival in regional Victoria, Australia (Seaton, 1999: 392–96; Murray, 2012: 100–101; Driscoll, 2014: 186–92; 2016).[3] There is even an International Organisation of Book Towns (IOB) to facilitate administrative knowledge-sharing among existing and would-be book towns and to collectively market the global book-town circuit.[4]

Book trade fairs, on the other hand, are significantly less public-facing and define their core constituency as members of the publishing industry itself. The world's largest, the annual Frankfurt Book Fair in Germany, opens its vast halls to the public on the final two days of proceedings, but this opening has the air of an afterthought and civic goodwill gesture rather than delineating the general public as the mighty Buchmesse's prime catchment (Moeran, 2011: 141). Authors, especially Big Names, may attend major book fairs such as Frankfurt, London, or the Children's Book Fair in Bologna, but they tend to do so at their publishers' behest to boost foreign and translation rights sales for big-ticket acquisitions, less so to engage directly with their readerships (Murray, 2012: 82–89). Amazon's James Marcus memorably refers to the US's dominant domestic book-trade fair, the annual BookExpo America, as "a kind of authorial petting zoo," allowing publishing business partners and prospective clients to get up-close-and-personal with celebrity authors (2004: 87).

How can the recipe for writers' festivals, honed since the phenomenon's 1980s boom, take advantage of digital media without diluting the very spatiotemporal immediacy that has made it such a success? Specifically, how do the literary festival's characteristic qualities of location-specificity, authorial authenticity, audience community, and live experience morph under the pressure and potential of digital media? With digital technologies facilitating "extended" festival participation by global audiences, and even online-only writers' festivals beginning to emerge, we may be witnessing the potential redundancy of ideas of liveness and embodiment for the curation of public literary culture (Morey et al., 2014: 251). If so, is anything unique lost when the live author talk becomes recorded, searchable, and infinitely replayable from among the massed archives of online content? Or does the increased virtuality of literary encounters conversely burnish the allure of the writers' festival—signaling to envious outsiders where the *real* epicenters of literary culture are located? Digital media applications both augment and challenge writers' festivals' key role in curating the public life of literature. Understanding how they do so is thus central to grasping the construction and complex functioning of the twenty-first-century digital literary sphere.

Cultural Festival Theory, Growth, and Hierarchy

Particularly since World War II, festivals have become a structural feature of global cultural life. Spanning art forms from cinema to music to contemporary art, and frequently combining multiple arts sectors in the form of the city-branded festival, cultural festivals have secured their centrality to contemporary cultural life through the various overlapping roles that they play (De Valck, 2007; Iordanova and Rhyne, 2009; Larson, 2009; Porton, 2009; Moeran and Pedersen, 2011). At the commercial pole, the festival acts as a means for uniting creators and audiences, frequently through the proxy of industry intermediaries (film distributors, scouts, agents, dealers). The frequency with which festivals award suites of prizes for excellence in a given art form (the Palme d'Or, Golden Bear or Golden Lion, and Audience Choice awards) demonstrates their serviceability in attracting media attention. For members of a particular creative industry, festivals (at least the major ones) constitute a type of professional circuit, at which one may network, do deals, glean gossip, and generally monitor one's standing within the cultural field. For audiences too, festivals serve performative functions: they are a means of demonstrating and reveling in membership of a particular cultural or lifestyle community, initiating or confirming belonging to a like-minded tribe (Gibson and Connell, 2011: 12; Driscoll, 2016). In the abstract sociological vocabulary employed by Andy Bennett and Ian Woodward, the festival "accentuates— and indeed celebrates—a particular form of lifestyle project through using a collectively shared assemblage of images, objects and texts as an occasion for sociality" (2014: 14). This constellation of economic, consecratory, and community-building functions makes successful festivals a potent form of location-branding and cultural tourism, and hence of keen interest to cultural policymakers and local politicians (Bennett, Taylor, and Woodward, 2014).

Literary festivals, as a subset of cultural festivals, may generally lack the glamor and industry heft of Cannes, the self-conscious avant-gardism of the Venice Biennale, the alternative-culture resonance of Burning Man, or the youth-culture iconicity of Glastonbury. But they have come indisputably to punctuate the international book-world calendar. Combining aspects of trade fair, audience outreach exercise, and barometer of authorial reputation, the literary festival serves multiple stakeholders simultaneously, although not without internal tensions (Larson, 2009; Weber, 2016). Stakeholders in literary festivals are numerous: authors,

readers, publishers, literary agents, booksellers, governments of all levels, libraries, educational institutions, and media outlets. Given the disparate and at times
divergent aims of these groups, writers' festivals represent telling instantiations
of Bourdieu's concept of the literary field—constellations of sociological actors
strung between the poles of commercial self-maximization and economic dis-
interestedness. Internal conflicts generally derive from the fundamental incommensurability of the cultural and economic values the festival seeks to span. More
specifically, tension emanates from the festival's own role in brokering economic
exchange value for cultural goods. In selling tickets to hear an esteemed literary
author speak, in awarding prize money to distinguished books, and in accepting
sponsorship from entities who seek to bask vicariously in the kudos of literary
eminence, writers' festivals are irreducibly in the business of transmuting cultural capital into economic forms (English, 2005). They constitute one of the
most important sites of capital exchange in the literary world and, because such
exchanges take place in front of audiences both embodied and mediated, festivals
have come to occupy an outsized place in the public life of literature. Their concentrated nature in terms of time and space means that literary festivals instan-
tiate, in an especially acute manner, ongoing tensions underpinning all creative
industries.

Writers' festivals have proliferated in recent decades, with most major international cities and state capitals now hosting them; in fact, regional towns, local
councils, and even specific suburbs frequently host their own, location-identified
events (Kiley, 1998: 803; Llewellyn, 2005; Stewart, 2010a, 2010b; Giorgi, Sassatelli,
and Delanty, 2011: 2; English, 2011: 64; Masson, 2011: 90; Stewart, 2013; Driscoll,
2014: 152; Bidisha, 2014: 49). The decade of the 1980s appears to have been when
literary festival culture expanded most dramatically (Sapiro, 2016: 12). Flagship
Anglophone literary festivals that date their founding (or splitting-off from more
general, cross-sectoral arts festivals) from this decade include the Edinburgh International Book Festival (1983–), the Melbourne Writers Festival (MWF) (1986–),
and the Hay Festival (1988–), among many other, smaller-scale events. Uptake of
the literary festival formula seems to have been particularly enthusiastic in countries of the British Commonwealth (the UK's Cheltenham Literature Festival,
established in 1949, is generally acknowledged as the world's first stand-alone,
continuously running literary festival) (Bennett, N., 1999). Long-range trends in
the book world that came to a head in the 1980s boosted literary festival culture,
and in turn were reinforced by it: the primacy of marketing and authorial celebrity;
the polarization of the book market into "lead" titles and midlist also-rans; and
the general climate of economic rationalization whereby what had long regarded

itself as a "gentleman's"—almost hobbyist—occupation was forced by an influx of investment capital and market dictates to demonstrate its value in unambiguously bottom-line terms (Schiffrin, 2001; Murray, 2006, 2007; Thompson, J., 2010). For an industry wanting to shake off a stale, residually tweedy, and markedly masculine image, writers' festivals provided an enticing means to broadcast new writing, connect with wider audiences, and promote a highly mediagenic image.

The writers' festival circuit has by now grown so crowded that an exclusive A-list club, the Word Alliance, has emerged, comprising eight of the leading international festivals. This inner sanctum of literary festival prestige describes itself as "a strategic international partnership which supports and showcases the work of writers, facilitates the creation of international literature projects and provides opportunities to enhance each festival's artistic programme."[5] Intriguingly, for the purposes of the present discussion, one of the Alliance's explicit goals is to "further expansion of online content."[6] Founding members of the Alliance are the Edinburgh International Book Festival, the International Festival of Authors (Toronto), the Melbourne Writers Festival (MWF), the Internationales Literaturfestival (Berlin), Étonnants Voyageurs (France, Mali, Haiti), the Jaipur Literature Festival (India), the Bookworm International Literary Festival (Beijing), and PEN World Voices of International Literature (New York). This membership list appears to be a deliberate attempt to reach beyond the Anglophone, developed world, incorporating festivals in large-population Asian countries of growing economic heft, as well as those run predominantly in Continental European languages. The inclusion of the Francophone Étonnants Voyageurs festival is particularly interesting for the light that this peripatetic, multicountry festival throws on postcolonial mutations of the literary festival template. Étonnants Voyageurs runs annually in Saint-Malo, Brittany, with partner festivals running in alternate years in Bamako, Mali, and Port-au-Prince, Haiti. This distributed structure, with its evident postcolonial agenda, thus fundamentally disrupts the centuries-old anchoring of Francophone literary culture in Paris. Still, there is evident tension between, on one hand, the Word Alliance's enthusiasm for what digital technologies offer the literary festival in terms of transnational reach and, on the other, the Alliance's countervailing emphasis on the particular flavor that each host city imparts to a particular festival. The writers' festival is presented as both insistently located but also transcending any specific locale.

Weighing questions of festival hierarchy and exclusivity such as those embodied in the Word Alliance, literary sociologist James F. English encourages us to temper our Habermasian idealism with a little Bourdieusian political economy (2011: 64). Literary festivals exist in a state of fierce competition—for visibility, for

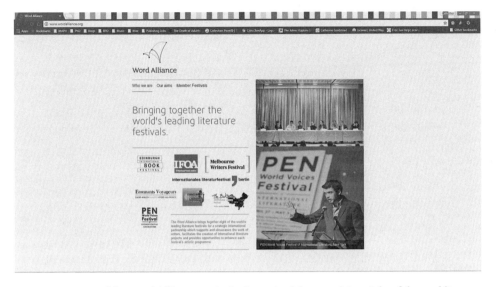

Home page of the Word Alliance, an invitation-only club comprising eight of the world's leading literature festivals.

star-pulling power, and for corporate and public-sector sponsorship: "Festivals . . . play a critical role in shaping [the] geography of the symbolic: determining not just a world public but a world space of hierarchically situated publics, not just a global cultural public sphere but a global field of cultural prestige and power" (2011: 64).

The indisputable reality that literary festivals, for all their talk of the "world republic of letters," are locked in incessant competition with each other has been remarked upon by other literary festival critics such as Cori Stewart, who notes the "hotly contested hierarchy of writers' festivals" (2013: 263). Such competition exists not only between host cities vying to lure the latest Man Booker, Pulitzer, or Nobel laureate to *their* event with alluringly packaged promotional DVDs and YouTube videos, but also between events held simultaneously in the same city.[7] In Stephanie Johnson's *The Writers' Festival*, fierce institutional and deeply personal rivalry exists between the Oceania Writers' Festival and its offshoot Fringe festival, with writers and facilitators miffed at being bumped off the official program and relegated to the lower-profile Fringe. Caro Llewellyn, a former director of the Sydney Writers' Festival and hence a veteran in navigating such ego minefields, makes the same point as James English, albeit expressed more colloquially: "They're [writers' festivals and their organizers] also all competing against one another" (2005).

The status of a given literary festival will determine when it can be scheduled. A-list festivals have their slot on the global literary festival calendar staked out through habit and prime-mover advantage (Jaipur in January, Adelaide in February–March, the *Los Angeles Times* Festival of Books in mid-April, PEN World Voices in late April / early May, Hay and Sydney in late May / early June, Edinburgh and Melbourne in August, Toronto in October). Synchronicity between major festivals taking place on different continents may be tolerated, or even exploited for novelty (as when the Edinburgh and Melbourne festivals in 2008 co-hosted Salman Rushdie in a live linkup, or the new JLF Melbourne—a "pop-up festival" bringing guests of the 2017 Jaipur Literature Festival to Australia in the weeks following the Indian event)[8] (Cassin, 2008). But a new festival seeking entry to the festival circuit must not trespass on an existing festival's chronological slot, or else find that A-list writers, publishers, agents, and media attention are all occupied elsewhere. Moreover, festival organizers must stay alert to the separate circuit of international book fairs that also punctuates the literary calendar, intersecting with but not replicating the literary festival circuit (Moeran and Pedersen, 2011: 5). Like engineers delicately meshing cogs in the literary machine, writers' festival organizers must schedule their festival strategically, and will fiercely defend their place in the book-world calendar if encroached upon by a usurping festival.

Analogous to the Word Alliance, and in several instances overlapping with it, is UNESCO's Creative Cities network, and specifically its subgrouping of UNESCO Cities of Literature.[9] These are not festivals per se (although Cities of Literature often do host important writers' festivals and leverage this fact strategically in their individual UNESCO bids). Rather, a City of Literature is making a claim to year-round literary activity, a strong publishing and book retailing infrastructure, and dynamic and diverse audience involvement in literary life. Notably, UNESCO's Creative Cities program elevates specific metropoles over their host nations as the prime frame for cultural distinction. Cultural geographer Allen J. Scott has emphasized this redundancy of exclusively national frameworks for cultural policy in the globalized era, noting that "creative cites function increasingly within a worldwide system of economic competition and cooperation" (2006: 1). Hence a handful of mostly large, primarily first-world cities have grown to constitute a supranational literary network of their own (13). Yet the scheme is eagerly sought out not by the indisputably global metropoles of the Anglophone literary world (traditionally London and, in more recent decades, equally indisputably New York). Those cities' accumulated commercial heft, institutional critical mass, and long histories of literary self-mythologizing mean UNESCO consecration holds little additional appeal for them. Frankly, why gild the literary lily? It is the second-tier cities, especially those located on the postcolonial periphery of literary empires ruled from these (neo)imperial centers, that most crave UNESCO City of Literature branding: Edinburgh, Melbourne, Dublin, Iowa City, Dunedin . . .

Competition among literary locales in the twenty-first century can also be domestic, with Australia providing an interesting case study in interurban writers' festival rivalries. There is long-running latent and occasionally publicly acrimonious competition between Australia's various capital-city literary festivals: Adelaide Writers' Week (the oldest, and the likeliest draw for Big Names), the Sydney Writers' Festival (the largest in terms of audience numbers and the glossiest), and the Melbourne Writers Festival (the most self-consciously intellectual) for the crown of Australia's leading writers' festival. Smaller state capitals' events such as the Brisbane and Perth Writers Festivals, as well as writers' festivals held in regional centers such as Newcastle, Byron Bay, Wagga Wagga, and Mildura, occupy lower rungs on the ladder of literary prestige (Kiley, 1998: 804; Birmingham, 2010: 13, 15; Stewart, 2010b). The Melbourne Writers Festival's inclusion in the Word Alliance is thus interpreted domestically as a coup for that festival (and that city), and more specifically as an exercise in nose-thumbing at the Sydney Writers' Festival—providing a new literary twist on the long-standing Sydney-Melbourne intercity rivalry.

The proliferation of literary festivals in recent decades has not been matched by a concomitant rise in academic analyses of the phenomenon. There have been some welcome signs of empirical and analytical investigation of literary festival culture over the past twenty years (Ommundsen, 1999, 2007, 2009; Giorgi, 2009, 2011; Stewart, 2010a, 2010b, 2013). But the vast majority of writing about literary festivals is still confined to the cultural supplements of newspapers and book-trade periodicals. The tone of such coverage is either reportage or, if it does attempt analysis, is frequently characterized by denunciation, cultural pessimism, or satire. Theoretical contextualizations of the festival within literary studies, cultural policy, or cultural sociology frameworks are noticeably scant (cf. Weber, 2015, 2016; Sapiro, 2016; Murray and Weber, 2017). Dismissive or pejorative commentary fails to explain authors' increasing participation, demonstrable audience interest, and the use of public money to fund writers' festivals over a now four-decade period, and the raft of (sometimes competing) stakeholder interests that sustains them (Giorgi, 2011: 42). Analyses that take account of digital media's recent impact on the traditional writers' festival formula are even more scant (Driscoll, 2014, 2015).

Elements of Terrestrial Literary Festivals Impacted by Digital Media

It is to address the above research lacuna that the following section of this chapter examines in detail how digital media are radically reconfiguring literary festivals' composition along four key axes: place, authorship, audience, and the live event. It is important to remember, however, that these various elements are complexly interwoven in the digitally mediated festival context where, for example, slippage between author and audience-member status may be precisely the point of a given programming choice.

Place: Civic Branding and Community Identity

The advertising for most literary festivals primarily emphasizes place. Communicated through atmospheric shots on the web page, invoked in marketing rhetoric, and reinforced by the selectively quoted fond recollections of previous guests, the specifics of place imbue a writers' festival with a particular ambience. This sense of place runs from the macro level of the host city itself, with its various tourist and cultural associations, through the festival precinct (whether rural or urban, a parkland, or inner-city setting), down to the proxemic cues of specific event venues (under canvas versus a formal auditorium). Also significantly affecting the experience of place at literary festivals is ticketing policy: festivals such as Adelaide Writers' Week offer predominantly free programming, thereby attracting an often younger, student crowd whereas other main festivals' ticketed events predominantly attract the literary festival's core middle-aged, middle-class demographic, one flush with discretionary income and having time on its hands ("Literary," 2010). A middle choice regarding ticket pricing is one often elected by book towns: charging admission to the festival site and then allowing attendees to choose events within the site at will, a policy that encourages serendipitous grazing rather than the more conservative choosing of headline acts that commonly results from individual-event ticket pricing and seat allocation.

In articulating the literary festival's connection to the broader world beyond the host city, festival organizers are confronted with two alternatives. On one hand there is a cosmopolitan conception of the festival community as defying geographic boundaries and celebrating a Habermasian public based on a shared love of the written word, akin to Casanova's "world republic of letters" (2004; Giorgi, 2011: 35–36, 39; English, 2011: 63; Johanson and Freeman, 2012: 304, 311). The trajectory of such conceptions is centrifugal, outward from the geographic site of the event itself to embrace international writers of diverse stripes and languages, working across an array of genres, and engaging in debates of transcontinental import. Through invocation of such an expansionist rhetoric, a festival lays claim to a spot on the A-list of literary festivals by virtue of the event's demonstrated internationalism. This, reciprocally, consecrates the host city as a significant node on an international cultural festival circuit. It is in this light that we should interpret PEN's choice of the name "World Voices of International Literature" for its New York–based festival, or read the Melbourne Writers Festival's claim that it "connects writers and stories to celebrate a world of literature, explore universal ideas, and inspire *a global community of readers*" (italics added).[10]

The other conception of the literary festival's connection to place is economic: the principal funders of literary festivals internationally are typically the cultural policy divisions of national, state/provincial, and local governments. Given that a sizable proportion of festival funding is derived from taxpayers of a particular locale, those taxpayers have a legitimate desire to see their interests reflected in the resultant event. The dynamic here is centripetal—global interests being brought to bear on a particular locale and illuminating it. There is also a desire, particularly marked in postcolonial settings, to avoid any hint of the usual global literati being flown in to engage in business as usual except in an exotic location. As Bennett and Woodward argue, a cultural festival succeeds only if it weaves the unique characteristics of the host locale into the very fabric of the event: "At the same time as festival discourses point to being open to the swirl of multiple and heterogeneous cultural differences, they also assert the importance of the local and the rooted" (2014: 18). "Flying in" culture is the antithesis of the work the festival seeks to do in terms of showcasing local cultural offerings and cultivating the host city's own literary community. To some extent touting localism may also appeal beyond the local taxpayer base by attracting inbound tourism—fanning the desire of interstate and international visitors to get an evocative, albeit highly choreographed, slice of life in the host city. Of course, building tourist traffic both satisfies the curiosity of travelers while also benefiting the hoteliers, restaurateurs, and taxi drivers of the host city through the so-called festival "multiplier effect"—a beneficial win-win relationship.

Such a delicate balancing of global and local showcasing is, in reality, nearly impossible to pull off, and festival directors who successfully cater to both impulses can expect to see their contracts renewed. Where international community is emphasized over local embedding, festival organizers leave themselves open to criticisms of elitism and resultant funding cuts. Conversely, where localism is overemphasized, festival organizers may weather criticism for the festival's provincialism, a failure to attract "Big Names" that suggests it is not or is no longer an A-list festival, and decline in attendance figures. Somewhat ironically, this scenario also jeopardizes continued public subsidy (Dempster, 2013). Thus, literary festival organizers have for some time experimented with complex strategies to ensure that these two frequently competing senses of community can—however unstably—be mapped onto each other. For example, Toronto's International Festival of Authors (IFOA) has a long-running offshoot "Lit on Tour" program that showcases festival guests in libraries, bookstores, and universities across the province of Ontario.[11] The glamor of visiting literary celebrities is thus maintained, but their stardust is sprinkled more widely, and especially outside the metropolis.

Digital media, with its indiscriminate sense of place, offers further possibilities for extending the geographic reach of a festival. For example, the Sydney Writers' Festival (SWF) in 2015 inaugurated its "Live and Local" program offering livestreaming of selected festival events to libraries and writers' centers across the state of New South Wales (Murray and Weber, 2017). Intriguingly, even in the program's first year, a livestream was offered to the western suburbs of Sydney itself, long regarded as harbor-obsessed Sydney's unloved and unlovely backyard. In reality, the "Live and Local" program strengthened the SWF's claim on public subsidy by undermining geographically entrenched, class-based oppositions in one of the world's most expensive cities.[12] In its first year, "Live and Local" remote participants could ask authors questions via Twitter or text message and receive answers in real time.[13] The following year, building on the program's strategic and popular success, "Live and Local" was rolled out nationally to other capital cities and selected regional centers across Australia, with a now two-way audiovisual channel allowing remote participants to pose their questions to speakers face-to-face.[14] Given the Melbourne-Sydney intercity rivalry alluded to earlier, the "Live and Local" initiative can be interpreted as an imperializing gesture on the part of the SWF, with Sydney seeking to flex its institutional muscles and engage in status display vis-à-vis its southern Word Alliance rival. To be watching a SWF event in UNESCO's apparent Australian City of Literature is to be on the receiving end of a none-too-subtle dig about which is Australia's leading writers' festival.

Viewed less cynically, such programs represent constructive attempts to counter regional taxpayers' common grievances that flagship cultural festivals are unduly concentrated in the metropolis. When the departure of SWF director Jemma Birrell—whose brainchild "Live and Local" had been—was announced in 2016, the program was cited as one of her signature achievements.[15] But in interweaving digital media into the fabric of the literary festival in order to advance laudable aims of increasing access and broadening participation, do festival organizers risk eroding the idea of geographic specificity upon which literary festivals have, since their inception, been premised? Even if this is not the case, and the partic-

Poster for the Sydney Writers' Festival's inaugural 2015 "Live and Local" live streaming program to regional New South Wales locations, including the city of Wollongong in the Illawarra region, about one and a half hours south of Sydney. Reproduced by permission of Sydney Writers' Festival and Merrigong Theatre Company

ular pungency of the host locale remains perceptible in footage livestreamed nationally or online, it risks reinforcing the idea of the particular city as cultural epicenter. Digital audiences may be permitted the equivalent of a cheap seat up in the gods, but the dress circle of literary esteem remains incontestably located in the capital.

Authorial Performativity

A key draw for literary festival audiences is the opportunity to see big-name international and local writers "in the flesh" to see how they measure up against the implied author inferable from their works. This "ritual of authentification" takes literature back to a pre-industrial era when the writer was often a comfortingly familiar, physical presence whose oral performance of a work certified it as their own creation (Meehan, 2005;[16] see also Young, 2015). Another motivation for many attendees is the opportunity for a quasi-papal literary audience by asking a question of the star author in a public forum, or the benediction of the signed book copy. It is hard to escape such sacral language given that literary festivals constitute primary sites for perpetuation of the literary star system (Meehan, 2005; Ommundsen, 2009: 22, 31; Driscoll, 2014: 165–67). Independent publisher and cultural commentator Ivor Indyk some twenty years ago puckishly skewered the atmosphere of religious ritual that pervades the author-reader encounter in festival settings: "The air of adulation is unmistakable: you queue, you sit as a congregation, you listen to oracular utterances by the writers of the day on all the fundamental issues of existence. It is Spring; it is Autumn. They are our gods, and goddesses" (1997: 38).

There has been long-running criticism of writers' festivals in academic debate and, in particular, in cultural-sector commentary on the grounds that they force often introvert authors to become public performers, and encourage evaluation of writers on such theatrical criteria rather than on the allegedly "purer" achievement of their writing (Ommundsen, 1999: 174; 2007: 246–47; 2009: 29–30; Llewellyn, 2005; Starke, 2006: 158–59; Nowra, 2010: 7; Barnes, H., 2010: 11; "Literary," 2010; Johanson and Freeman, 2012: 308; Montenegro, 2013; Driscoll, 2014: 166–67; Lodge, 2015; Young, 2015). This constitutes part of a broader critique that writers' festivals contribute to a debasing and vulgarizing of literary culture (Lurie, 2004; Ommundsen, 2009: 21–22; Giorgi, 2011: 42; Driscoll, 2014: 158). For some commentators, the shoehorning of writing into modes of engagement more typical of the performing arts is at the heart of what is problematic about literary festivals (Sage, 1998: 266–67). Wenche Ommundsen identifies the mismatch thus: "The festival somehow aspires to make the moment of creation and the moment of consumption coincide in time and space, thus changing the fundamental dynamics of the experience" (2009: 21). The asynchronous and disembodied author-reader encounter typical of print culture is allegedly distorted by festival formats such as author readings and panel sessions, introducing notes of awkwardness and falsity. For Liana Giorgi, it is literature's deviation from the norms of "music, film or the visual arts" that renders it "much more difficult to 'stage' as a performance for the general public" (2011: 38). Yet her unproblematic inclusion of film in this list is interesting, as film was obliged by the disembodied nature of its medium to find alternatives to the theatrical rituals of live performance, such as the star's on-stage entrance, the curtain call, and the encore. This led to the invention of the red-carpet ritual, whereby the absence of the film star from the moment of most audiences' consumption of a film is offset by the star's red-carpet walk at the film's premiere. The resultant visual proof of the actor's approbation of the finished film is then circulated through myriad fan magazines, television coverage, and, now, social media posts. Art forms thus demonstrably adopt and adapt modes of performance from other media on an as-needed basis. The fact that Gutenbergian print culture was for many centuries experienced predominantly in the absence of the author does not mean that literary culture need necessarily remain bound to a disembodied dynamic.

The prevailing view of writers' festivals prior to Web 2.0 was "as if the writer [came] out of their locked room"—of typically solitary authors experiencing a brief burst of publicity and sociability prior to returning to self-imposed creative hibernation at home (Llewellyn, 2015). But the online expansion of literary festivals and, in particular, shifts in the nature of authorial performativity via social media as discussed in chapter 1 of the present volume challenge this previously one-shot, binary logic. Now writers may have a long-running program of online-presence management ramp up prior to their main festival appearance, peaking there perhaps, and then provide ongoing commentary about the literary festival through their blog, tweets, Facebook posts, or Instagram images both during and after the event. The governing pattern of authorial performance becomes not so much an on/off, public/private toggle but rather one of gradation, displaying fluctuations in frequency and modes of public communication. What is more, most of the Web 2.0 applications mentioned above refocus attention on the writer as (pithy) *written* communicator, as opposed to the mediagenic talk-show persona prioritized in the era of broadcast media. Even a self-conscious or introvert author not entirely at home with "in conversation"–style festival events can engage in a degree of self-curation vis-à-vis their broader readership through written ex post facto justification, retaliation, or whimsical recaps. Hence, while communicating effectively in the chatty, offhand form of a blog or the haiku-like laconicism demanded by Twitter may be a far cry from literary prose as traditionally conceived, Web 2.0's reinvigoration of the written word may actually counteract many cultural pessimist criticisms of writers' festivals. Rather than broadcast media's relentless focus on authorial voice and appearance, here is an opportunity for savvy authors to turn the literary game back to their own strongest suit.

Just as discernible hierarchies exist between A-list writers' festivals and the rest, hierarchical differences are also abundantly apparent within the program of specific writers' festivals, especially those of the most prominent events. Local authors frequently gripe about being treated as warm-up acts or panel-fillers for star international acts. Comments by Alexis Wright, winner of Australia's most prestigious literary prize, the Miles Franklin Award, encapsulate such chagrin: "It is often the overseas writers people are flocking to see and who the organisers are promoting, to the detriment of local writers" (Heiss, 2003: 126). As an Indigenous woman, Wright sees the hierarchical devaluation allegedly underway at Australian writers' festivals as being doubly detrimental to Aboriginal Australian authors: "It is difficult to encourage Australian audiences to believe that Aboriginal writers had anything worthwhile to say so our sessions are poorly attended" (126). In fairness, Wright's remarks were made in an email to scholar Anita Heiss in 1999, long before her winning the 2007 Miles Franklin Award (among several other prizes) for her novel *Carpentaria* (2006). This career-making prize, and its associated publicity, made Wright a guaranteed invitee to virtually all Australian festivals in the years immediately following, as well as securing her invitations to present at many international writers' festivals, where her indigeneity and her novel's foregrounding of Indigenous issues may well have been programming boons. But it remains true that attendance numbers at festival sessions and the length and fervor of book-signing queues function as brutally shorthand indicators of an author's relative standing in the world republic of letters. Unlike other relentlessly quantitative indicators of literary success, such as manuscript auctions, bestseller lists, and BookScan sales figures, the writers' festival takes place in the physical presence of the author. Writerly mortification thus lurks as an ever-present risk. Given this self-exposure, the online-only writers' festival appears an increasingly attractive option: all the pleasures of direct and real-time communication with actual readers, with threat of embarrassment or humiliation diluted by virtuality. Even if a writer has to endure the terrestrial festival bugbears of thinly-attended sessions, hackneyed or crazed audience questions, or being programmed at the same time as a visiting star in a neighboring venue, at least social media provides tools to retrospectively take ownership of the experience, perhaps turning it into grist for the author's own creative mill.[17]

From "Audience" to "Community"

The concept of the audience for writers' festivals has undergone a sea change since the first Adelaide Writers' Week (note the name) held in 1960. There efforts were made to *exclude* members of the public from what was essentially a writers' workshop, on the grounds that they were mere literary rubberneckers with no good reason to gate-crash proceedings among a rarefied creative elect (Kiley, 1998: 806; Ommundsen, 1999: 175; Starke, 2006: 157; Stewart, 2010: 26; Murray, 2012: 98; Driscoll, 2014: 158). These days, literary festivals have entirely reoriented themselves from the inward-looking workshop model to look decisively outward, recasting audiences as the festival's key constituency and very raison d'être. Expatriate Iranian author Azar Nafisi, writing in *The Republic of Imagination* (2014), records her ebullient response to her adopted hometown of Baltimore's annual Book Festival, but by extension she could be describing any good literary festival. Nafisi celebrates the festival's role in calling forth a Habermasian public sphere of engaged, critical, passionate, joyful readers and writers:

> I can seldom avoid the temptation of a book festival, with its transient sense of festivity and community: all those strangers sharing the same interest, if not exactly the same passions. . . . I love the chaos of book festivals, the way different characters, cultures, stories and times all jumble together to the accompaniment of music, food and art, all the good things in life shared with gusto, but not too seriously. It is as if the abundant variety of human existence contained in the thousands of books under consideration spills over into the sidewalks and streets of the host city. . . . Each city lends something of its character to these events. (291)

As the author of *Reading Lolita in Tehran* (2003), Nafisi is well placed to appreciate the giddy excitement of untrammeled access to ideas and opinions from around the world being shared in a deliberative, and at times hedonistic, manner. But the mode of engagement she describes so ecstatically is chiefly one of cultivated appreciation. Web 2.0–enabled audiences in the era of social media want this sort of engagement, certainly, but are increasingly restive with being confined solely to passive experiential modes. Writing about contemporary music festivals, Morey et al. note that digitally enabled festival-goers now "both consume and produce—or co-create—the festival experience" (2014: 251). Taking the pulse of this community desire for more active modes of engagement, literary festival organizers in turn have reconceptualized audiences as participants: co-publicists, invited commentators and reviewers, and a pool of future programming suggestions (Ommundsen, 2009: 21; Dempster, 2012: 124; Johanson and Freeman, 2012: 305).[18] For example, the widespread uptake of live-tweeting during festival sessions creates a Twitter "back channel" to a standard festival keynote address or panel session, whereby audience members tweet both in response to what is being said on stage, as well as responding to others' tweets (Driscoll, 2014: 185). It gives a newly multilayered density to participation in an event by involving not only those physically present but also conversations occurring in the Twitterverse (among those both physically present and those geographically elsewhere). There is even potential for the virtual to feed back into and influence the "real," such as when a Chair may make reference to audience members' tweeted feedback during the session itself, or put to an author an audience member's question contributed via Twitter. Such two-way, or preferably multi-way, communication between organizers, audiences, and guests gives real substance to long-standing claims that the literary festival functions as a microcosm of an idealized literary world in which no book is complete until it has been responded to by a reader. The fact that readers can now respond to an author face-to-face, as well as (if they prefer to maintain some anonymity) through myriad digital channels, seems decisively to close the loop from author through to reader first tentatively proposed in Robert Darnton's famous communications circuit ([1982] 1990).[19]

Yet there are clear limits to such conceptions of the literary festival as Habermasian public sphere, given the festival's carnivalesque nature as a temporary hiatus in prevailing social norms. Such a sense of belonging as successful terrestrial festivals manage to generate results, as cultural geographers Chris Gibson and John Connell note, in at best "ephemeral communities in place and time" (2011: 5). Equally, the idealized notion of audiences as co-creators overlooks both the residually commercial context of sponsorship, book sales, and ticket pricing in which festivals operate, as well as the persistent markers of hierarchy within the festival program. After all, it would be a rash or foolhardy writers' festival director who allowed an unedited Twitter waterfall to be projected behind a keynote speaker. Ultimately, the literary star system on which festivals thrive is not fully reconcilable with the participatory ideal of community: hierarchical distinctions remain clearly evident between authorial stars and also-rans, between overseas and local writers (as explored above), and between invited guests and ticket holders. Hence much of the more egalitarian, Habermasian discourse around writers' festival community à la Nafisi *is* illusory. Beth Driscoll identifies this conditional and transient dimension of book festival fellow-feeling, dubbing it "temporary community" (2014: 170). To this we might add "policed community." Digital media involvement by audiences in writers' festivals is frequently corralled into manifestations edited and approved by organizers (for example, the SWF's 2015 request for the best photos, tweets, quotes, and blog posts about the festival to be picked up and recirculated through the festival's official channels,[20] or the MWF's 2015 invitation for audience members to share their favorite festival memory in a curated online archive to celebrate the festival's thirtieth anniversary).[21] Audience-generated content is eagerly solicited, certainly, but is incorporated into the festival's official online presence and distributed more widely subject to the organizers' approval. But acknowledging this residual persistence of hierarchy within the festival setting need not lead us to reductive, all-or-nothing conclusions. Arguing that literary festivals fall short of realizing an (always theoretical, probably unattainable) Habermasian ideal is not to deny that the uptake of social media at literary festivals is still a significant advance in rendering festivals' previous us/them structures more porous.

Liveness

Melbourne Writers Festival director Lisa Dempster's observation that the "live connection" is "the point of what a writers' festival is all about" finds emphatic endorsement in myriad surveys of audience members' motivations for attending writers' festivals (2013). Audiences seek, above all, spatiotemporal co-presence with esteemed writers: to be there, to see and hear them, live. Nevertheless, "liveness" as a concept has a complicated intellectual history, especially in relation to literature. The terminology of "liveness" first arose negatively. Prior to the invention of recording technologies, performing arts such as music, theater, opera, and dance were by definition live events. It was only with the late-nineteenth-century invention of the phonograph, radio, film, and—decades later—television, that the term "live" had to be coined in contradistinction to consuming a recorded version of a performed event (Auslander, 2008: 56–57; Conner, 2013: 9–10). With subsequent technological advances in radio and television permitting transmission of epochal events in (close to) real time via "live broadcasts," the concept of liveness underwent a further permutation: liveness and mediation were no longer mutually exclusive (Auslander, 2008: 60, 12–15). Hence the audience for a sporting event, coronation, or moon landing came to understand mediation as extending rather than canceling out the notion of "live."

But this etymology of "liveness" in the performing arts applies only clumsily to book culture. After all, the progressive separation of an author from first their words and later their readership lies at the very heart of written culture. Indeed, it was precisely the inability of the reader to engage the author of a written text in debate that provoked Socrates's famous rejection of writing in Plato's *Phaedrus* (as discussed in chapter 1). Hence, since the invention of writing, and even more so since Gutenbergian print technologies removed the residual trace of the human in the form of the copyist's hand, book culture has been defined by its lack of physical co-presence and simultaneity between author and reader. Literature has long been, by nature of its very format, profoundly mediated. It is the attempt to overcome this inevitable distancing that has given rise to a veritable cult of authorial identity in literary criticism, with pronouncements about an author's signature style, his (typically) ability to create readerly intimacy, and the illusion of direct, mind-to-mind communion. Book culture only became "live" again—in the bardic sense of the creator's recitation to an embodied audience—at the margins:

in Charles Dickens's or Mark Twain's lecture tours of the mid-to-late nineteenth century; in the practices of performance poetry and spoken word; or in the post-1980 boom in writers' festivals. Yet even at these often wildly popular events, audience appreciation and attendance have tended to be driven by prior readerly consumption of, or at least familiarity with, an authorial brand. This brand is primarily a creation of print culture, subsequently parlayed into the theatrical milieu but not born of it.

But, as the above historical parallel with live broadcasting suggests, it would be mistaken to conceive of print culture and liveness as comprising an ontological binary. Most striking, as performance theorist Philip Auslander notes, is "the way mediatization is now explicitly and implicitly embedded within the live experience" (2008: 35). Liveness and mediatization are more accurately conceived as demarcating twin poles of a graded continuum of co-presence: being physically on stage with a writer; asking a question from an audience microphone; registering applause or laughter; being silently present in the same venue; being in another (onsite) venue witnessing a live-feed; viewing a recording made in the same venue; watching a recording online (long) after the event. There is no sense in which liveness and mediation can today be posited as mutually exclusive: in especially large writers' festival events a digital feed of the on-stage author may be projected behind him or her on a giant screen, so that attendees in the most distant seats might enjoy technologically amplified intimacy with the facial expressions and subtle body language cues of the author. Much like a rock concert or action replay in a sporting arena, here technological mediation is provided to *enhance* the sense of live authenticity.

While literary festivals have made commonplace the live potential of literature and now successfully showcase varied gradations of it, they simultaneously risk inscribing new audience hierarchies. Most valued by audiences is physical co-presence with the author, with rungs of decreasing prestige occupied by those who watch a live-feed from another venue, down to those who merely view an archived recording online, perhaps long after the event, and leave some ex post facto comment about it. Archiving video and audio content on a festival's own website or on content-aggregator websites such as YouTube, Vimeo, and SlowTV doubtless expands audiences for a literary festival event, in terms of both geography and chronology. As Morey et al. remark of audience members uploading music festival footage to file-sharing sites, audiences seek to capture for posterity some record of an inevitably transient experience: "an extension of the self beyond the temporal—beyond the duration of the festival event itself *and* beyond the present, into an imagined future" (2014: 265). Yet these altruistic attempts to preserve for a wider audience something of the feeling of experiencing the event firsthand nevertheless carry a self-regarding undertow: "I was there," they proclaim, "I saw it, live." Such cultural bragging rights attach preeminently to the live event, whereas digitally mediated recordings come wreathed in a compensatory discourse—almost making the viewer feel they were there. Equally, festival organizers' laudable audience-maximizing motivations in uploading video or audio recordings of festival events coexist with a desire to reinforce a particular festival's A-list prestige. Such documentary footage effectively broadcasts a celebrity writer's association with *their* event—hence the prominent banners and backdrops inevitably positioned behind the speaker's podium and strategically in the camera shot at writers' festival keynotes. Such practices risk reinscribing the idea of literary coterie, anointing with "insider" status those who can afford to pay for tickets to see big name speakers, who live within range of major literary metropoles, and who have sufficient leisure time. Meanwhile, the remainder of (would-be) audiences are reduced to flapping like moths around the lightbulb of literary fame, making do with whatever digitally mediated glory they can. Canadian literary scholar Lorraine York in her *Margaret Atwood and the Labour of Literary Celebrity* makes a similar point about digital author-reader interactivity not democratically collapsing, but rather reinforcing, hierarchies of access between major metropolitan and regional/rural audiences. Discussing Atwood's LongPen remote book-signing device (as mentioned in chapter 1 of the present volume), York writes, "It vouchsafes access to the body of the celebrity for metropolitan fans while consigning others to a (more) mediated experience" (2013a: 156).[22]

In the twenty-first century, questions of liveness dovetail with newly problematic notions of local specificity, thus complicating writers' festivals' twin claims to the superior experience of spatiotemporal co-presence. Does a member of the newly expanded online audience for a literary event even care where a recorded talk was originally presented? If not, can public money to support such events still be justified in an era of long-standing and ever-tightening cultural policy budget cuts? Why fly star authors (via business class) transcontinentally if the majority of the host nation's book-loving public can view clips of other appearances by the same author online for free? Digital media thus present enticing but potentially self-canceling possibilities for convenors of embodied literary events: the legitimate deployment of digital technologies in expanding the geographic and chronological reach of formerly localized, transient events can easily spill over into a "digital is better" (that is, cheaper) argument on the part of budget-conscious cultural bureaucrats. Conversely, if the sacrosanct nature of the live, embodied authorial encounter is successfully defended by festival organizers, the digitally mediated experience struggles to be presented as other than a "second-best" option, thus undercutting a festival's claims to inclusiveness. In this context of damned-if-you-do, damned-if-you-don't choices, the emergence of solely digital literary festivals, which have no determining tie to any host location, seems inevitable. Yet even within online-only writers' festivals, the situated nature of literary consumption reemerges in often surprising ways.

Online-only Literary Festivals' Challenges to the Terrestrial Paradigm

Online-only literary festivals represent a current limit case for the study of digital technology's role in curating the public life of literature. Rather than the ancillary or complementary role digital media plays in terrestrial writers' festival settings, for online festivals the digital environment constitutes the sine qua non. The digital literary festival is simply inconceivable without digital technology. As a consequence, rather than prompting questions of how digital technologies challenge the standard writers' festival paradigm, such online-only events throw into high relief features of the terrestrial writers' festival previously taken for granted. These include the role of embodiment in the author-reader encounter, the significance of liveness, and the perhaps unexpected resurgence of place as a key concept in defining literary cultures.

Online writers' festivals increasingly engage in digitally hosted programming where "audience" participation in real time is crucial for a festival's success. Lisa Dempster, director of the Melbourne Writers Festival and former director of the Emerging Writers' Festival (EMF), distinguishes among three levels of literary organizations' use of digital technologies:

- using digital media as a supplement to publicise a fairly traditionally-conceived program (for example, keynote addresses; "in conversation with"–style interviews; panel sessions; readings followed by Q&As, etcetera);
- community-building through inviting audience interaction and responses (for example, comments on blogs; official Twitter hashtags; video content); and
- online programming where creativity occurs in the digital sphere and the digital is the assumed (and often only) platform for an event. Audience participation in the event is crucial and typically occurs in real time. (2012: 117–18)

There is currently growing interest among arts administrators in the possibilities of digital technologies for hosting cultural festivals. Underpinning this trend is a perceptible generational shift along the lines Dempster indicates: from conceiving of digital technology as aid and addendum to a terrestrial festival, to putting digital platforms at the center of the festival experience. Arts management scholar Lynne Conner remarks that "Facebook pages and tweets are fine, but often they are employed as mere iterations of the one-to-many communication platforms that characterized most analog-era arts organization's [*sic*] 'outreach' protocols. The vast majority of Facebook pages associated with arts organizations, for instance, aren't much different, structurally and operationally, from printed newsletters and brochures" (2013: 170). As indicated in this chapter's foregoing analysis of audiences at digitally enabled terrestrial writers' festivals, positing digital technology front and center at the festival event shifts the audience role from one of (ideally) appreciative consumption to, increasingly, co-creation. For cultural policy analyst Ben Walmsley, this is the logical consequence of the user empowerment and ease of content-creation offered by social media: "Networked publics in this participatory era seek engagement opportunities that might lead to enrichment, rather than transactional marketing communications that merely seek to attract them" (2016: 76). As such, for the online-only writers' festival, "audiences" are not merely invited to participate (virtually); their involvement is crucial, since without their input the proposed festival events will fall flat.

It is appropriate at this point to consider in detail two examples of online-only writers' festivals to see how they measure up against Dempster's third level of "sophistication" (2012: 117). The #TwitterFiction Festival (#TFF), established in late 2012 and last run in 2015, took place over five consecutive days and billed itself as "about embracing, exploring, and developing the art of storytelling on Twitter" (see also Twyford-Moore, 2012).[23] It boasted heavyweight sponsors in the form of Twitter, Penguin Random House, the Association of American Publishers (AAP), and media partner *USA Today*. The #TFF particularly encouraged literary uses of Twitter beyond just sequential, linear tweets à la Jennifer Egan's "Black Box" (2012). Egan's nine-thousand-word short story, still the best-known example of Twitterature, was related by its Pulitzer Prize–winning author in 140-character installments. These were tweeted from the *New Yorker*'s fiction account over ten nights in 2012 with the magazine subsequently publishing the story in full. By contrast, #TFF organizers invited writers to try their hand at parody accounts, crowdsourced content, tweets incorporating images and video, and those narrated by multiple characters using various Twitter handles. In later iterations of the festival, authors were particularly encouraged to experiment with highly interactive forms of storytelling: soliciting reader feedback on a work in progress; combing reader contributions to choose how to continue a story; or even permitting readers to determine narrative developments through voting. One 2014 #TFF contributor, Tom Mitchell, periodically polled readers on their preference for one of a pair of narrative options, with a reader's choice being indicated through

Twitter's characteristic functions of either "favoriting" or, alternatively, retweeting it (Cain, 2014). Such digital updates on the classic 1980s "Choose-Your-Own-Adventure" formula of codex-based multilinear, interactive fiction represent radical departures from the single-author, sequential-narrative literary norm. They exemplify what Bronwen Thomas, in her work on Twitterature, terms "distributed narrative"—attempts to replicate at the level of story the decentered, highly participatory nature of Web 2.0 environments (2014: 101). Twitterature thereby significantly erodes print culture's foundational author-reader distinction. One dramatic consequence of this newfound interactivity, for authors in particular, is the potential demotion of the god-creator figure in the face of a newly empowered and vocal audience who might aspire to the role of co-creator. In such circumstances, the authorial figure assumes more the role of curator of a narrative's mosaic-like contributing parts, selecting among them, juxtaposing, and arranging them for desired artistic effect. Thus, if terrestrial writers' festivals might be considered curators of the public life of literature—gatekeepers determining via their invitation and programming choices what counts as literature, whose star is in the ascendant, and who has achieved celebrity status—so too might the online-only literary festival. Except that in the latter case authors themselves frequently take on something of the curator's traditionally administrative role, abdicating complete creative control over the literary work in the interests of broader participation.

Yet, upon closer examination, these egalitarian claims are undercut to some extent by the top-down nature of the #TFF as the creation of Twitter itself. Programmed #TFF authors were either "featured" (a diverse group including, for example, Margaret Atwood, Lemony Snicket, Alexander McCall Smith, and Jackie Collins) or among twenty-five contest winners. Meanwhile, members of the public were invited to tweet their contributions to #twitterfiction. The Festival's website also encouraged public engagement via a randomized tweet generator dubbed Instant #TwitterFiction which users could customize to some extent, with results akin to found poetry. Hence a degree of professional/amateur demarcation was hardwired into the festival's design by the organizers, despite frequent invocation of social media's presumed innately democratizing tendencies. The willingness of established literary authors whose status had already been abundantly secured through print publication, however enthusiastic they may be about digital experimentation, was essential for bringing a degree of literary respectability to the initiative. Because it was not at that time typically regarded as a bona fide literary platform, Twitter was at pains to foreground its literary credentials.

A second online-only writers' festival, the Digital Writers' Festival (DWF), first

Logo of the 2014 Digital Writers' Festival, its first year as a stand-alone event. Reproduced by permission of Emerging Writers' Festival

emerged in 2010 as a strand of the Melbourne-coordinated Emerging Writers' Festival, but since 2014 has branched out to become its own event, running annually over twelve days. It describes itself as "an online carnival dedicated to what happens when technology and the written word collide."[24] As befits the brainchild of former EMF director Lisa Dempster, the DWF prides itself on being "playful and participatory, transmedia and transcontinental."[25] For its launch as a stand-alone event in December 2013, then director Connor Tomas O'Brien gave an interview via Twitter (a format he christened with the neologism a "twitterview") (O'Brien, 2013). The DWF comprises an innovative program of hybrid print-digital formats with livestreamed webchats via Google Hangouts predominating. Participation and accessibility (whether geographic, chronological, economic, or social) are the main selling points for the festival, which dubs itself (potentially not without controversy vis-à-vis the #TFF) as the world's first online writers' festival. Openness is a key part of the DWF's pitch; in the words of current DWF director Jane Howard, "If you have a computer, we want you there."[26] The DWF's first iteration in 2014 involved much livestreaming of author panel sessions and discussions, with audience participation mostly confined to tweeting, texting, Facebooking, and other text-based discussion modes. In its later iterations the DWF aimed to expand opportunities for audiences to engage more actively and directly via face-to-face computer-mediated technologies (though technical limitations upon these mean that, in practice, the festival still presupposes a high degree of spectatorship on the part of the majority of its audience).

It is a fair question to ask whether these events, with all their digital bells and whistles, can still be considered writers' festivals, or whether the degree of mediation involved effectively cancels out the traditional festival givens of physical co-presence and spatiotemporal simultaneity. The answer to the first question must be no, in the sense that these online-only festivals manifestly lack the geographic specificity and embodied writer-reader reciprocity still predominantly characterizing the terrestrial writers' festival. But, equally, the answer to the first question might be yes in that both of these online-only festivals perceive the element of liveness to be essential. This is what distinguishes the offerings of such self-described "festivals" from a content-aggregator site or mere archive of an event. For example, #TFF stories are tweeted during preprogrammed periods from authors' Twitter accounts. Andrew Fitzgerald of Twitter emphasizes that liveness was a crucial element of the organizers' strategy: "Our thinking was that: If we bring it all together, all the people experimenting into same chronological space, we can also bring some attention to it" (Popescu, 2014). There are also practical considerations at play: the emphasis on liveness reduces confusion caused by tweets from other accounts in an individual's Twitter feed interrupting a story's narrative flow and thereby inhibiting readerly immersion (Ingleton, 2012). One 2012 #TFF participant, Andrew Shaffer, summed up his contribution to the festival as "real-time storytelling" (Vlieghe, Page, and Rutten, 2016). Of course, this level of liveness surpasses even that of the terrestrial writers' festival. For in such terrestrial settings, authors typically read live from works previously written, redrafted, edited, and proofread, often by the multiple hands of literary agent and editor. Hence the "live" authorial performance in these instances better equates to an actor's live performance of a play script that was written at an earlier period and that achieves whatever spontaneity it offers on the basis of the actor imbuing the words with specific nuances through delivery, or the addition of ad-libbed, off-the-cuff material. But for writers participating in the #TFF, the act of composition *itself* frequently occurs in close to real time, with little time or scope in 140 characters for revision before "publication." It is this sense of the writing act as live creative self-exposure to an audience of unknowable size that caused Josh Gosfield, a participant in the first #TFF, to declare Twitter "the most brilliant tough love editor you will ever have" (Vlieghe, Page, and Rutten, 2016).[27]

It may appear that, of the traditional spatiotemporal dyad characterizing the terrestrial writers' festival, it is the temporal aspect (liveness) that carries over to online-only festivals and that the concept of place has been atomized by the geographic indifference of the Internet. But this is only partially true. In fact, the DWF in particular has, throughout its multiple iterations, evidenced a fascination with the enduring importance of place. For example, the 2015 DWF featured twenty-minute lightning tours of various UNESCO Cites of Literature (including Edinburgh, Melbourne, and Iowa City), all of which were preoccupied with communicating the intangible uniqueness of that place as a locus for literary creativity.[28] Equally, the DWF has consistently programmed sessions devoted to the experiences of writers living outside literary metropoles: how to make it as a writer in Australia if based outside the twin poles of Sydney and Melbourne;[29] how established writers feel leaving the cosmopolitan inner cities to return to the suburbs of their childhood and adolescence;[30] and an interactive Google Maps visualization of the locations of Australia's best emerging writers (with the prize for registering being a free trip to Melbourne for the DWF).[31] For online-only writers festivals, place seemingly plays the role of the repressed that cannot help but return. These festivals desire to have it both ways: to celebrate the online-only festival's freedom from situated embedding, but at the same time to showcase the cultural aura and embodied habitus of specific literary locales.

Conclusion

Writing recently about the curious phenomenon of literary celebrity, Swedish academics Anders Ohlsson, Torbjörn Forslid, and Ann Steiner note that "better descriptions and analyses are needed of how authors stage themselves at live or mediated literary events, and how this contributes to the value negotiation process" (2014: 42). Some seventy years after the staging of the first annual writers' festival, and some four decades since the phenomenon's boom, we require less lamenting over festivals' alleged encroachment on the proper grounds of literature, and more analyses of how festivals function, as well as credible accounting for their resilient, and growing, public appeal. Festivals allow up-close-and-personal contact with authors, permitting readers and writers the rare experience of occupying the same spatiotemporal domain. But the mainstreaming of digital media in literary festival settings has prised apart the traditionally taken for granted spatiotemporal dyad to significantly complicate matters. It is now possible for a festival author and audience to communicate at the same time though occupying different places, as via a live feed or online-only writers' festival. It is even conceivable that reader-writer communion can occur in the same place though at a different time, such as when a particular literary locale accretes such talismanic associations that it becomes a draw for literary tourism, as with writers' house museums. The location of particularly long-running literary festivals with a set venue, such as the Edinburgh International Book Festival's Charlotte Square, or Adelaide Writers' Week's Pioneer Women's Memorial Garden, can see them transformed into semi-hallowed literary ground, with guests and audiences in attendance conscious of the parade of literary greats who have trod the same turf in preceding years. Digital media's increasing role in archiving and publicizing such past events only burnishes a particular location's literary aura.

The fissuring of spatiotemporal simultaneity under the pressure of digital media should come as no surprise; some twenty years after the rise of "new media" we have grown accustomed to digital technology initiating changes that are rarely straightforward and frequently appear contradictory. Accordingly, the grafting of digital media onto the literary festival model has prompted both atomizing of geographic place while simultaneously promoting the fetishizing of particular literary locales. Digital technologies both invite broader participation under the banner of democratic inclusiveness, while maintaining festival organizers' right of veto over the general public's contributions. On one hand, digital media enables mass participation in festival events on a virtual basis but, on the other hand, foregrounds what non-metropolitan audiences are missing and thereby increases the coterie frisson of the live event. The exclusivity of witnessing an event live increases in direct proportion to the number of people who know of it but were not there in person. Thus mass-mediated spectatorship lends the embodied experience the ground against which to define itself.

In the midst of this complicated and multiplying media environment sits the book, the first means of disembodied communication, rendered simultaneously more embodied through the phenomenon of meet-the-author culture, and more geographically transcendent by digital media. This makes literary festivals key forums at which to reflect upon contemporary literature's multiply-mediated state, and how literature has come to be defined by the interplay between communication mediums. It has been academic orthodoxy for some time that literature exists transmedially, as evident by the inclusion, for example, of a CD of poets reading their work with the seventh edition of the undergraduate-standard *Norton Anthology of English Literature* (2000), or by the gradual inclusion since at least the mid-1990s of born-digital literary works into more innovative literary curricula. But it has been less readily acknowledged up to this point that the various institutions that collectively broker literary culture *also* exist transmedially. Reconceptualizing twenty-first-century literary culture as sited at the dynamic overlap of oral, print, and digital domains allows us to examine the real-time workings of the literary system in a now richly multimedia environment. All those who seek a role in curating the public life of literature should embrace this fact.

CHAPTER FOUR

Consecrating the Literary

Book Review Culture and the Digital Literary Sphere

Some guy on the net thinks I suck

And he should know

He's got his own blog

NICK HORNBY (2010)

The ideal of democratizing book reviewing turns out to have surprisingly deep historical roots. At the very inception of the public sphere in the eighteenth century, expanding political rights were seen as concomitant with a broadening conception of cultural authority. This was, according to Habermas, a logical progression, "since within a public everyone was entitled to judge" (1989: 40).[1] Fantasies of an egalitarian reviewing future have often been fueled by firsthand knowledge of deeply flawed existing book reviewing structures. George Orwell, numbly familiar with the hand-to-mouth existence of freelance book reviewers, wrote in his 1946 essay "Confessions of a Book Reviewer" of an imagined alternative whereby penniless hacks dishing up trite review copy to order might be replaced by a crowd of enthused, novel-reading amateurs: "Nearly every book is capable of arousing passionate feeling, if it is only a passionate dislike, in some or other reader, whose ideas about it would surely be worth more than those of a bored professional. But, unfortunately, as every editor knows, that kind of thing is very difficult to organise." From Orwell's mid-century standpoint, the democratic spirit may have been willing but the technological flesh was weak, so to speak. Writing some fifty years later near the century's close, Australian publisher and cultural commentator Ivor Indyk bemoaned the erosion of a public literary sphere of the kind idealized by Habermas through the combined forces of late-twentieth-century economic rationalism, corporatization and marketing:

> There is virtually nowhere now where readers can engage publicly in the business of criticism. They can pay for the pleasure at a university, and be examined for their skills. The best creative writing classes are surely creative reading classes under another name. But otherwise, it rarely happens nowadays, not at festivals, not in bookshops, not at public seminars or meetings. . . . It is in the conversation about

literature, the recommendation and the debate, that the literary community really exists. (1997: 40)

Ironically, Indyk's essay appeared in 1997, the very year that online book retailer Amazon pioneered what is still the Internet's best-known and largest forum for amateur reviewing: Amazon's customer reviews. Grappling with the need to fill white space on the young company's website and to do so on the cheap, while also wanting to prolong potential purchasers' time on the site, Amazon championed a democratic discourse of amateur reviewing (Spector, 2000: 141–42; Miller, L. J., 2009: 106; Packer, 2014). Amazon's own customers, not anointed literary critics, would vote on the worth of individual titles via their one-to-five-star rating system. The cumulative rating for a title, easily calculated by Amazon's proprietary algorithms, would thus represent the real-time judgment of "the people." According to Amazon founder Jeff Bezos, customer reviewing would thus "let truth loose"; it was to be veritable cultural democracy in action (quoted in Spector, 2000: 143).[2] Even had Indyk known of Amazon's innovation, it is unlikely to have quelled his disquiet at the literary world's allegedly parlous state of debate. Given his article's rather pessimistic, political economy–tinged analysis, it is probable he would have seen the book retailer's "customer reviews" as simply a further devaluation of book reviewing—indeed the logical outcome of the long-running eclipse of "criticism" by "hype" (between which two categories his essay maintains a very clear distinction).

These varying responses to the idea of cultural democracy in reviewing are interesting for the continuum they form. At one pole is found intense dissatisfaction with the book reviewing establishment: pompous professional critics; hack freelancers; a pervasive climate of back-scratching and favoritism; and the timid evaluative language indulged in by an inbred coterie fearful of payback. At the other pole, however, cluster fears of radical cultural relativism: kneejerk judgments by an ignorant, unqualified mass; the reduction of nuanced critique to crude quantitative measures; and the potential for online systems to be "gamed" in various ways. Typically, such analysis of contemporary trade book reviewing as exists—scant as it is—ricochets between these poles, lamenting both a world in which the mandarins maintain a stranglehold on cultural authority as well as the lawlessness of the emerging digital frontier where "everyone's a critic." Reading over such work, one has the impression that book reviewing's previous status quo may have been deeply flawed, but that the specter of an amateur free-for-all looks worse. Book reviewing's critics are indeed, as Gail Pool has remarked, a "self-critical, gloomy, hyperbolic" lot (2007: 3).

This chapter seeks to move discussion of literary reviewing on from these entrenched positions to consider ways in which the distributed structure of the Internet might in fact be reconcilable with ideas of cultural hierarchy. Some two decades on from the introduction of Amazon customer reviews, and contrary to the fears of both camps, the digital literary sphere has been steadily incubating its own systems of cultural evaluation. Through review-the-reviewer features, blog-roll mentions, and cooperatives of literary bloggers, quantitative and qualitative measures are combining to generate new structures of digital literary authority. Moreover, offline and online modes of consecration are blurring, as in the *Guardian* Books section's listing of the "Top 10 Literary Blogs" (2005),[3] or invitations for litbloggers to speak at writers' festivals.[4] Social media has certainly rendered reviewing more democratically accessible and interactive than the traditional print reviewing paradigm. Yet, contrary to allegations, these coalescing digital cultural tastemakers are not reducible simply to the logic of quantification—whereby Internet traffic equates to cultural worth. We are witnessing the literary critical equivalent not of an absolute monarchy nor a proletarian revolt, but something poised ambiguously in between. In undertaking detailed examination of online-born modes of cultural evaluation and consecration, we can observe the machinery of literary reputation in the process of being forged—not only that of authors, but also of reviewers and cultural outlets themselves. Attending to the mutating idea of literary-critical expertise at work in online environments provides insights into the theoretical compatibility of cultural expertise with network technologies. These insights are in turn transferable to other spheres of cultural activity, such as film criticism, music journalism, and restaurant reviewing, giving the issues canvassed in the present discussion salience beyond the digital literary sphere.[5]

The Traditional Book Reviewing Model

In order to comprehend the changes wrought in book reviewing by the digital literary sphere, it is first necessary to understand the traditional print-media book reviewing model against which more recent developments pit themselves. Print traditions in effect constitute a baseline against which we can plot digital variations. While literary academics might be expected to have some firsthand familiarity with the traditional book reviewing process, the dominance of textual analysis as the discipline's default methodology has tended to push such institutional practices to the periphery of critical concern.[6] Such a selective emphasis on literary texts themselves misleadingly underestimates how modes of literary consecration are profoundly social and the extent to which judgments are inflected by the institutional regimes through which texts move. It is thus pertinent to outline explicitly the print reviewing paradigm that literary academe habitually takes for granted.

In the world of legacy mainstream newspaper and periodical publications, a literary editor typically selects from the mass of submitted titles those works of fiction or nonfiction thought to be culturally important and of sufficient interest to a publication's readership and assigns them to a reviewer from the periodical's reviewing pool. There is intense pressure on publishers' marketing and publicity departments to get house titles reviewed positively and prominently, leading to literary editors having a huge oversupply of (free) titles (Sutherland, 1978: 92–93; Howard, 1992: 92; Curtis, 1998: 1–2, 11–12; Curran, 2000: 226–27; Gillieron and Kilgarriff, 2007: 10, 177; Delaney, B., 2014: 10). To reduce the submissions pile to more manageable size, self-published titles, e-books, and genre titles are automatically culled as the first step in a winnowing process of Sisyphean proportions (Curran, 2000: 221–22; Steiner, 2008; 2010: 482; Delaney, B., 2014: 10).

Once a title is earmarked for review, the literary editor must decide whether to accord it a feature, mid-length, or capsule review. Even if a title is selected for the industry-standard mid-length review, there is the further consideration of whether it will be reviewed on its own or in combination with a number of similarly themed titles. A named expert critic then reviews the work(s) in a piece of typically between six hundred and one thousand words—Orwell regarded one thousand words as "a bare minimum" (1946). More recently, "capsule" reviews of around one hundred words have become increasingly common in newspaper arts supplements squeezed for column space by the collapse of print classified and display advertising (Curtis, 1998: 6; Longley, 1998: 217). While representing a valiant attempt to maintain the number of titles "noticed" by an outlet, the length of these capsule reviews effectively prohibits quotation, let alone detailed engagement with the text.

Writing in 1963, Henri Peyre defined the critic's minimum job description as "to choose between the good and the bad, between the good and the less good, and to state his reasons for his opinions" (133). Few would dispute this as book reviewing's fundamental rationale, but the way in which this task is performed is profoundly inflected by the assumed critical authority and consecratory power of a given reviewing outlet. The status of the critic vis-à-vis the book under review is variable, running the gamut from reader surrogate to mouthpiece of cultural authority, with the status and reach of the reviewing outlet the best indicator of the stance a critic will adopt. For example, reviewers at smaller newspapers and periodicals frequently cultivate the tone of the reader's friend: scouting on the reader's behalf and advising honestly on which books are worth the reader's (presumably) limited time and budget. Lorna Sage, both a prolific book reviewer and a literary critic of distinction, termed this vicarious selection work "reading as surrogate and advocate" (1998: 263). The reviewer's "voice" is crucial in creating such a sense of reviewer-reader intimacy and the trust that sustains it, especially in longer-format reviews: "We readers *do* yearn to know the reviewer, yearn for a measure of levelling with us to establish credibility" (La Salle, 1997: 170).

At the upper echelons of the media hierarchy, by contrast, lead literary reviewers for major metropolitan mastheads have the power to make or break a new title or authorial career through a glowing front-page review or searing denunciation. The doyenne of such reviewerly consecration is Michiko Kakutani, for some three decades chief literary critic at the *New York Times Book Review*—"the outlet that has become synonymous with the very act of book reviewing in America" (La Salle, 1997: 173).[7] Kakutani's reviews, occasionally written in the voice of book or film characters, are treated as oracular pronouncements by many in the book business. Such a concentration of critical power has, unsurprisingly, bred dissenters and earned Kakutani her share of rebukes (Howard, 1992: 96–97; Woodward, 1999: 93; Teres, 2009: 243–44). Ben Yagoda in particular takes Kakutani to task as the apotheosis of "the enervated (or prissy) voice of an enshrined critic" (2006). The juridical critical posture—one favored by what former UK literary editor Anthony Curtis calls "omniscient reviewing clerisies"—can develop especially in smaller national markets with limited reviewing outlets (1998: 338). Edna Longley, for example, notes that the preeminent status of John Banville, Booker Prize–winning novelist and long-serving literary editor of the *Irish Times*, effectively puts "most of the eggs . . . in one editorial basket" (1998: 216), making reviews by Banville a high-stakes gamble for Irish authors and publishers alike.

In major metropolitan publications the critic pronounces on the artistic and intellectual worth of a new book as measured against a canon of great works of which the critic has an intimate knowledge assumed to be greater than that of the review's reader (channeling Matthew Arnold's storehouse view of culture as "the best which has been thought and said in the world").[8] Viewed from the perspective of twenty-first-century digital developments, most striking is how the affordances of print media themselves reinforced this concept of reviewing as incontestable judgment. The book critic's verdict was typically univocal, once-off, and ex post facto: a title was reviewed by a single critic once only, and usually only after the book's publication. The effect was decidedly not formative in intent—designed to feed into a project's ongoing development—but rather emphatically summative: a pronouncement on whether or not the writer's goals for the work had been achieved. The communication involved was also markedly unidirectional; differences in opinion or ripostes from disgruntled authors or fellow critics could be published only at the (rarely granted) discretion of the book review editor. Authors left seething at what they perceived as an unfair critical hatchet job had little option other than to hope for better treatment at another masthead or to plot elaborate revenge fantasies.

Critiques of Contemporary Literary Reviewing

The traditional book reviewing paradigm has had its detractors, drawn frequently from the ranks of reviewers themselves. But there has been surprisingly little academic consideration of book review culture as a whole, considering how familiar academics are with the practice, either as reviewers themselves or from having their own books reviewed, and how frequently academics comb historical book reviews to excavate initial responses to now canonical works (cf. Sutherland, 1978; Weisbard, 1995; Janssen, 1997; Murphy, 2005; Harvey and Lamond, 2016).[9] Systemic and empirically verified critiques of reviewing culture have more commonly been instigated by cultural-sector lobby groups based outside the academy, or sited at its creative-practice margins. Specifically, there has been a long-running trend in the Anglophone literary world critiquing the stranglehold over reviewing space and hence literary taste formation exerted by male writers. For example, the UK group Women in Publishing (WiP) in 1987 produced the report *Reviewing the Reviews*, crunching the numbers on over five thousand published book reviews. In the same spirit, the US publication *The Women's Review of Books* in November 1993 celebrated its tenth anniversary by convening a conference on "Women Reviewing / Reviewing Women" which "focussed on the art, craft and politics of book reviewing" ("'Women,'" 1994: 13). Selected papers from the conference were published regularly in the journal during 1994–1995.[10] More recently, US-based organization VIDA: Women in Literary Arts has secured significant publicity for its reviewing-by-gender breakdown of leading US and UK literary publications, beginning in 2010.[11] The VIDA count in turn helped to catalyze similar campaigns internationally: since 2012 the organization Canadian Women in the Literary Arts has produced its own review-by-gender count;[12] and in Australia a similar count demonstrating starkly unequal gender representation in book reviewing spurred the establishment of the Stella Prize for women's writing, first awarded in 2013.[13] This $50,000 prize, similar to the Women's Prize for Fiction (formerly the Orange Prize) in the UK,[14] is designed to attract publicity and drive sales of the best work of fiction or nonfiction by an Australian woman writer.[15] US book review analyst Gail Pool also alludes to a 1980s campaign for gender parity in reviewing led by high-profile feminist writer Marilyn French, demonstrating how far back such critiques of gender bias in book reviewing go, and how seemingly intractable the problem of female underrepresentation remains (2008: 9; see also Simons and Fullbrook, 1998: 8; "Who's Writing," 2011).

All these campaigns eschew mere anecdotal evidence as a matter of strategy, instead painstakingly verifying their claims of unfair treatment of women's books through detailed quantitative analysis. As Erin Belieu, co-founder of VIDA, articulates: "Actual data to point to" is essential for ensuring that critiques of systemic patriarchal bias cannot be dismissed offhand as individual grievance or authorial hypersensitivity (Belieu and Prufer, 2016: 102–3). The campaigns collate statistical data on the gender breakdown of both author and reviewer for book reviews published in major broadsheets and literary periodicals, as well as on the length and prominence of reviews. Overwhelmingly, all of these studies reveal a marked statistical skew toward male critics reviewing male authors. In the words of the WiP report: "The results of this survey show a pervasive discriminatory pattern that can only serve to heighten the second-class status of women's books in most general readership publications" (1987: 19). The allegation is that this constitutes homosocial back-scratching and buttresses a de facto male stranglehold on the most prestigious echelons of literary culture; "as *Women's Review of Books* editor Amy Hoffman has said, [it] 'guarantees that they'll find the same old guys to say the same old thing' " (Pool, 2008: 9). The critical esteem bestowed by such publications creates a beneficial ripple effect throughout the literary ecosystem, influencing decisions over marketing, prizes, residencies, subsequent book contracts and, at further remove, canon-making practices and curriculum design.[16] Literary editors at major newspapers and periodicals presented with such data frequently express shock and remorse. Tellingly, disputing the data or its method of calculation is a rarer response. The iterative nature of VIDA's annual tally is central to the group's aim to turn such espoused good intentions into demonstrable improvement.

But by concentrating their critique on the gender imbalance evident in the review pages of a limited number of "Tier 1" broadsheet newspapers and literary periodicals, feminist activists risk missing the point in a technological and cultural climate in which reviewing itself is radically altering.[17] Rather than fighting for equal representation within an admittedly prestigious, though undoubtedly shrinking, sector of print culture, feminist attention might be better focused on the potential of the burgeoning *digital* literary sphere—in which the majority of reviewers are typically female and in which a much broader cross-section of books published can be considered for review, and over a longer post-publication period (Rich, 2007; Moody, 2011: 51). This need not be reduced to an either/or choice

between storming the citadel of (male) literary prestige or retreating to a generally delegitimized (female) ghetto of online reviewing. Clearly, women's profile
in literary culture needs to be raised at both the high-visibility, high-prestige end
of the reviewing market, as well as in its multiplying online manifestations. While
as a feminist scholar I am broadly very supportive of the aims of existing feminist
campaigns for enhancing women's literary visibility, the near-complete omission
of online reviewing forums from even recent discussions is cause for concern.
For example, Belieu defends the VIDA count's focus on mainstream literary
publications by citing the potentially ghettoizing, preaching-to-the-choir effect of
women writers self-marginalizing in women-only outlets.[18] She also notes, legit-
imately, that online publications do not pay reviewers at rates comparable to print
publications (if they pay at all), nor are they cognizable in academic terms for
tenure or promotion (109; see also Pool, 2007: 98; Robinson, 2014). But neither
is most book review work for print outlets countable as research quantum; at best
it can be presented as evidence of an academic's social "outreach" or "impact."
Troubling here is not VIDA's primary focus on the already consecrated world of
print publication, but its implicit positing of the digital literary sphere as something other, rather than as a realm that significantly intersects with and profoundly influences "mainstream" literary culture: "I think it's clear we shouldn't
look to the internet to solve these problems. There will always be gatekeepers.
There will always be prestige publications. Human beings seem to want these
hierarchical categories in most things. I don't see that changing soon" (Belieu
and Prufer, 2016: 110). It would appear a better tactical decision simultaneously
to secure women's foothold in this emerging mass reviewing culture *as well as*
in legacy print reviewing. Belieu is certainly correct that hierarchy is an enduring
structural feature of all fields of cultural endeavor. But by staking a claim relatively early in the development of such digital reviewing spaces, feminists will be
better placed to influence coalescing hierarchies of reviewing credentialism and
distributed patterns of cultural authority as they emerge.

Online Venues for Amateur Literary Criticism

The most significant aspect of review culture as it manifests in the digital literary
sphere is its greatly broadened base of participation. This fact, rather than the
actual content of reviews generated by "amateurs," is the most salient feature of
twenty-first-century criticism.[19] As Pierre Bourdieu writes, the act of reviewing
always involves a twofold assertion of worth: "All critics declare not only their
judgement of the work but also their claim to the right to talk about it and judge it"
(1993: 36). The first of these evaluations, of the work itself, is explicit—forming

the content of the review. The second, the right of the reviewer to cast judgment, is almost invariably implicit, for to plead one's fitness to review is automatically to call into question one's authority. Genuine cultural authority, according to the rules of the consecratory game, is distinguished by its critical self-confidence, unburdened by any need to demonstrate its bona fides and brooking no challenge.

Since the advent of Amazon's customer reviews in 1997, the Internet has normalized the act of amateur reviewing, not only of consumer experiences (restaurants, hotels, tourist attractions) but, more controversially, of cultural products such as books. Caroline Hamilton has noted the magnitude of the shift perceptible in a mere two decades, observing that "now, of course, there is a place to review everything. We've gone from having specialist classes of people who could have opinions to this being a standard feature of modern life" (2012: 73). The democratization of reviewer expertise involves seizing of the critical mantle by millions of reviewers uncredentialed by any reviewing establishment—an establishment whose worth in any case they typically do not acknowledge, armed as they are with the certainty that "I may not know much about Literature but I know what I like." For Andrew Keen, recovering Silicon Valley entrepreneur and polemicist against the "flattening of culture," this equates to "ignorance meets egotism meets bad taste meets mob rule" (2007: 2, 1).[20] In particular, Keen decries Web 2.0's "belittling [of] expertise, experience, and talent," and its collapsing of traditional divisions between creator and audience through the eclipse of cultural gatekeepers such as "professional critics" by "amateur bloggers [and] hack reviewers" (15, 16).

The logic underpinning jeremiads such as Keen's is as flawed as the inverse which gave rise to it—the uncritical techno-utopianism of Web 2.0 "visionaries." Neither trades in nuance or subtlety. Rather than engaging in polemical point-scoring, academic research has the advantage of greater hindsight and the ability to explore shades of gray—even to the point of fixating on those shades of gray. Hence the compelling question for the present discussion in contemplating review culture's future in the digital literary sphere is: To what extent is the concept of cultural hierarchy reconcilable with the decentralized structure of the Internet? If the two are in fact compatible, what forms does such cultural expertise take online?

In posing such a question it would be mistaken to frame the mainstreaming of the Internet in the mid-1990s as representing some decisive democratic break with earlier hierarchical traditions. For questions of cultural authority have manifestly been in flux throughout the twentieth century. Cultural historian Michael Kammen, writing at the turn of the millennium specifically about US culture, has argued that the expansion and increasing commercial sway of mass culture from mid-century onward eroded earlier confidence that cultural taste could be neatly calibrated against levels of income, education, or class: "Ordinary people—the consumers of cultural artefacts—have steadily increased their own cultural authority, especially in the past forty years or so" (1999: 134). The adoption of user-friendly graphical Internet browsers such as Mosaic and Netscape Navigator from the early 1990s provided the technological means for ordinary people already rhetorically empowered by postmodernism's climate of cultural relativism to publish their views for a global readership. Hence the Internet did not trigger the mass democratization of reviewing culture, in technologically determinist manner, so much as showcase and thereby accelerate an existing populist tendency.

Prominent online venues for amateur literary criticism include:

- Book retailer websites (online-only, brick-and-mortar, and hybrid). The best-known of these, Amazon's "customer reviews," allows anyone to rank a book on a scale of one to five stars. Amazon also awards a variety of "badges": "Top Reviewers" (that is, "Top 1000/500/50/10 Reviewer"); "Hall of Fame";[21] plus the chance to review the reviewer through "Was this review helpful to you?" feedback.[22] There has been long-running discussion-board carping that former "Amazon Number-One Reviewer" Harriet Klausner does not actually read all the books she reviews (Marcus, 2004: 225; Harmon, 2004; Pool, 2007: 101; Reagle, 2015: 54–55).[23]
- Social cataloging sites (such as Goodreads or LibraryThing). These allow members to rate any book on a five-star scale, post reviews, seek recommendations, and share the contents of their bookshelves. Further, Goodreads (since 2016 incorporating former rival Shelfari) encourages users to "like" and comment upon the reviews themselves. Goodreads' "internal ranking system" for reviews appears to rank reviews algorithmically by the number of "likes" they generate from other users.[24]
- Literary or book review blogs (also known as litblogs or book blogs). (Some examples are *Bookslut, The Elegant Variation, The Complete Review, Reluctant Habits* (formerly *Return of the Reluctant*), *Beatrice.com, DoveGreyReader Scribbles, MaudNewton.com, City of Tongues*). These are websites run by bloggers who post on literary or more broadly bookish matters, and include reviews, features, interviews, competitions, and giveaways.[25] The prominence of a blog within the literary ecosystem can be assessed through blog-rolls (lists of other blogs read and recommended by particular bloggers) as well as results ranking on blog-specific search tools such as Technorati

(2002–2014), Google BlogSearch (2005–2011), or BlogSearchEngine.org. Search tools and directories specifically for book blogs also exist.[26]

- Online forums attached to mass-media book clubs. These include Oprah's Book Club (1996–2011); *Canada Reads* (2002–); the Richard and Judy Book Club (UK, 2004–2009); Radio National's *Books and Arts* book club (Australia, 2012–), and so forth.
- Booktuber channels (YouTube channels dedicated to amateur book reviews performed in audiovisual mode). Booktubing is a subcategory of the vlog (video blog) as practiced by authors such as John Green.[27] Typically the format consists of a talking head discussing book titles, often showing the books' covers and rating them. There are even booktuber videos listing favorite booktubers, the equivalent to Amazon's review-the-reviewers function or a blogroll.[28]

Writing a decade on from book reviewing's online migration, Gail Pool wrote, "Writing for the Web has yet to become the way for a book reviewer to establish a critical reputation" (2007). Exchanges of critical currency appeared to go only one way: "Critics who already have status have reviewed for such online magazines as *Salon* and *Slate*," but a reviewer gaining profile online cannot hope to convert this into print credibility (98). A further decade on this remains broadly true. Certainly evidence exists of publishers cultivating influential online reviewers for marketing and publicity purposes, especially in popular fiction genres long overlooked by the print reviewing establishment.[29] But in terms of developing its own independent modes of consecration, the digital literary sphere has struggled to emerge from the shadow of its print antecedents. While mainstream literary culture is by now indisputably digital, and much consecratory prestige flows from print to digital environments, born-digital consecratory agents still struggle to win approval in the print domain. More typical is the pattern of the print sphere bestowing some of its long-accumulated cultural capital on these upstart digital rivals through a slightly patronizing pat on the head. Much as Coco Chanel reputedly declared, "I like fashion to go down into the street, but I can't accept that it should originate there," markers of literary esteem are still most often forged in print-born environments (Mackrell, 1993: 73). In part this is because the typically algorithm-generated nature of online-only consecrators' rankings creates an air of quantification that breeds suspicion among word-oriented humanists. In part also it arises from the pervasively commercial settings from which many born-digital consecratory plaudits emerge (see below). But the division is relative, not absolute, and the variety of Internet-incubated modes of consecration emerging shows that it is a matter of time until cultural esteem won online is convertible into print capital.

Significance of Digital Interactivity for Review Culture

Social media environments come with a built-in right-of-reply: the comment function on blogs; the potential to tweet in response to a Twitter message or retweet it; the ability to reply to a previous reviewer on a social cataloging site or to post an immediate response on Facebook. In their very architectures, such technologies undermine earlier conceptions of the critic as lofty evaluator of aesthetic worth and unchallengeable arbiter of cultural standards. British novelist and cultural critic Will Self adeptly summarizes the shift, remarking that criticism in the digital era has become "more a conversation than a series of declarations" (2013). Interestingly, this category drift away from reviewing as pronouncement toward open debate was perceptible even in the early phases of the Internet—now retrospectively termed Web 1.0. Despite the fact that Internet content in the 1990s was, viewed from the perspective of the Web 2.0 era, a restrictively unidirectional affair from online entities to their web users, shakeups in the traditional dynamic of book reviewing were already perceptible. For example, writing in 1999 about the becalmed state of US literary reviewing, Richard Woodward pondered: "The future of reviewing may be more one-on-one interactions, like the *Slate* book club, where two critics trade fours about a new title" (131). The Internet's then very limited reader-feedback functionality necessitated that interactivity be demonstrated via the proxy of two critics exchanging views (a more dynamic format long preferred by televised film review programs).[30] Nevertheless, the medium's distributed structure seemed already to be forcing changes on traditional book reviewing's univocal critical norm.

Digital media permit readerships to engage critics in debate, potentially challenging their facts, lines of argument or—at the most diffuse level—grounding assumptions (Steiner, 2010: 489; Rettberg, 2014: 38–39). Professional book reviewers may, in turn, respond to reader feedback online—drawn into a conversation with readerships that could result in clarification, modification, or even retraction of a previous judgment. In a social media context, interactivity becomes not merely an occupational hazard for a critic—something to be endured for the sake of appearing in touch with the audience—but in itself a sign of a critic's bona fides. As Belgian researchers of online literary sociability Joachim Vlieghe and Kris Rutten observe, in such reviewing forums "Greater importance is ascribed to personal experience and social interaction in relation to literature, as opposed to professionalization and institutionally validated expertise" (2013). In a striking inversion of the previous critical status quo, online reciprocity here becomes the hallmark of authority.

Granted, such a scenario presupposes a rather rose-tinted, Habermasian conception of human behavior in digital environments, in which rational discourse is the agreed goal. Online anonymity and the trolling behavior it frequently encourages would seem to point in the opposite direction, emphasizing the use of distributed technology to abuse and harass those of contrary opinions. The result is frequently a demoralizing "echo chamber" effect whereby web users seek out opinions that merely reinforce their existing worldview (Rettberg, 2014: 172; Reagle, 2015; Frey, 2015: 92–93; Barnes, R., 2018). However, this is not a necessary corollary of moving cultural criticism to online spaces. Effective site-use policies, evident moderation of discussions and, possibly, affiliation with an existing offline community can preserve the democratic and participatory benefits of online reviewing and prevent it from degenerating into its worst manifestations.

Given the interactive affordances built into Web 2.0 media, it is surprising how little use of them is made by some literary reviewing sites born in the digital era. There have been criticisms from litbloggers such as Jessa Crispin that much online literary reviewing is merely an unimaginative application of the traditional print culture template: "The removal of the newspaper book review and the rise of the Internet literary culture gave us all absolute freedom. So we all just basically recreated newspaper culture, because it was easy to replicate and had worked for others for so long" (2016: 63).[31] An example of such deliberate shutting down of review interactivity is the *Sydney Review of Books* (established 2013) which, despite being founded well into the Web 2.0 era as an online-only outlet, has no comments function but only a "Correspondence" link displaying reader responses approved by the site's editorial staff, akin to newspapers' "Letters to the Editor" sections. Thus, when in October 2015 Melbourne-based academic Beth Driscoll published a joint book review of three new novels by female authors, grouping their work under the category of "middlebrow" fiction, the ensuing controversy broke not on the *Sydney Review of Books* website itself but on Twitter before being subsequently picked up by international literary media such as the *Guardian* (Jaffe, 2015).[32] Only ten days after Driscoll's review appeared did the *Sydney Review of Books*'s "Correspondence" column publish a jointly authored letter by the reviewed novelists refuting Driscoll's allegedly derogatory categorization of their work.[33]

Likewise, online-born book reviewing outlets may place significant limits on the degree of interactivity they permit their audience by aggregating reviews from print outlets, in addition to providing a limited amount of born-digital reviewing from website-approved sources. The effect is an oddly qualified championing of the digital literary sphere's potential: the site owners appear to embrace the Internet's low barriers to entry and global reach, but are intent upon reserving for themselves critical expertise by denying other reviewers the ability to post on the website. An intriguing example of such a hybrid print-digital reviewing website is the US-based *Complete Review* (established 1999), which typically collates reviews of a given book from mainstream print outlets, juxtaposes these with its own, online-born review, and then provides an overall "report card" on the work, with reviewer results averaged on an A+ / −, B+ / − (and so on) scale (F is the lowest grade, rarely awarded on the site) (Gillieron and Kilgarriff, 2007: 179–80). Hence the website's consciously contradictory self-description as: "A selectively comprehensive, objectively opinionated survey of books old and new."[34] In marked distinction to Amazon and social cataloging sites, there is no functionality for readers to add their own book reviews, making the website more a collation exercise and expression of a single amateur reviewer—the site's founder and managing editor, Austrian-born Michael Orthofer (Mahajan, 2016). *The Complete Review* thus maintains a contradictory position on critical polyvocality. On one hand, its aggregation of reviews from multiple national jurisdictions and in languages other than English demonstrates the inevitably wide variety of critical responses to an individual work. The website's Editorial Policy is at pains to emphasize this innately subjective and variable nature of its own, and others', reviews, stating:

> The editors of this site are not objective in their judgements, and they also have an agenda (we like to think it is one that insists on high standards, clear vision, creative strength, but it is probably much more mundane than that).
>
> Compare reviews, compare your opinions to that of the *complete review*, compare them to other reviews.
>
> Always ask yourself why these people are passing these judgements.[35]

However, the website itself stops short of permitting users to record their own, innately subjective, infinitely variable responses to books, at best offering a smorgasbord of credentialed critics' opinions, supplemented by its own judgment (attributed to the corporate identity of the website rather than to Orthofer personally).[36] Thus, in line with film scholar Mattias Frey's verdict on the Rotten Tomatoes website (which similarly accords privileged status to mainstream print reviewing) we could say that *The Complete Review* "remains entirely anachronistic in its *veneration* of critics and criticism" (2015: 88).

Reclamation and Celebration of Affect

It is a fair bet that what online review sites that severely curtail reader participation are trying to prevent is undue overflow of affect: gushing, insufficiently rational-critical responses to literary works that mistake the emotional intensity provoked by a particular book for its cultural value. Such site administrators seek to differentiate their own, specifically "critical" responses from the customer reviews ubiquitous on Amazon, or the effusive reader posts thronging social cataloging sites such as Goodreads and LibraryThing.

Certainly, the characteristic tone of digital book-review culture *is* personal, intimate, conversational, resoundingly and unembarrassedly *affective* (Steiner, 2008). Reviewers' most valued qualities, in fiction especially, are typically relatability of the plot, character exemplarity (specifically role-model potential), and the narrative's overall power to stoke emotional engagement. Cultural historian Joan Shelley Rubin (2009) associates this therapeutic approach of reading for personal growth with offline (especially women's) book clubs, citing the research of cultural sociologist Elizabeth Long (see also Hartley, Jenny, 2001; Farr, 2005: 41–42, 47–48, 51; Steiner, 2008; Ramone and Cousins, 2011: 5–7; Moody, 2011: 48, 51–53; Allington, 2016: 258). The "empathic" reading mode's most influential interpretive community has surely been the phenomenally successful Oprah's Book Club and the imitators it inspired across the broadcasting systems of numerous countries (Farr, 2005: 42; Aubry, 2011). Importantly, however, the affective turn is not the *creation* of digital or even broadcast media, but rather a long-standing "underground" form of demotic literary criticism now massively amplified through its archiving and discoverability on the Internet.[37]

In this spirit, Goodreads trumpets its reviews as "the best and most authentic in the world," implying that professional book reviewing devalues emotional resonance.[38] But this is not necessarily the case: Lorna Sage wrote that "what literary editors like is an excited, vivid, dramatized response, whether it is positive or negative is less important than its power to arouse interest, to make the book in question twitch and show signs of life" (1998: 262). Likely the real target of Goodreads in trumpeting its "authenticity" is actually literary academe: university-generated literary criticism has virtually expunged emotion from authorized literary responses (from New Criticism right through to postmodernism, despite all their other differences) (Moody, 2011: 48).[39] Peter La Salle, writing about the cultivated impersonality and ennui-inducing bloodlessness of US academic literary criticism, alleges, "The Scholar, no matter what critical school he or she has subscribed to in the long rotation of them, has made it an ethic not to reveal self in this great

Nation of Selves" (1997: 172). Certainly literary academe has, from its inception, registered palpable unease with literary affect, as too woolly and subjective (and feminine) a criterion to ground a discipline already struggling for academic respectability—unable to rely upon the difficulty of a foreign or (even better) dead language to validate its object of study (Littau, 2006). The situation has changed somewhat with the humanities' comparatively recent rediscovery of long-re-pressed affect with "the affective turn."[40] Yet the demonstrations of affect most valued by these scholars tend to be those translatable into the psychoanalytic vocabulary and theoretical frameworks favored by academe. If unembarrassedly emotional responses to books can be written by amateurs and communicated directly to other amateurs, who then write back reinforcing them, what need is there for a literary clerisy to document, interpret, and validate such responses? Cultural studies critics Michael Bérubé, Hester Blum, Christopher Castiglia, and Julia Spicher Kasdorf remark on the literary academy's disdain for the kinds of demotic criticism carried out in digital forums and embodied book clubs: "When the [general] community finds such [inventive and imaginative] language in sup-posedly non-literary sources—*Amazon.com* reviews, Web forums, *Goodreads*, blog book events, and library resources online—professionals of the 'reading class' are quick to dismiss the activity as wrong reading" (2010: 420). Already fighting a rearguard action against hostile economic rationalist governments and a voca-tionally oriented population often alienated by or indifferent to the humanities, literary academe has been intent on defending what remains of its hard-earned role as cultural credentializer. If Amazon or Goodreads reviews constitute valid arbiters of cultural worth—of the people, by the people, for the people—what need is there for academic literary criticism at all?

Such debates about the role of the critic in an era of digitally accelerated cul-tural democratization concentrate primarily on questions of textual specifics, hierarchies of value, and readerly dispositions. As a consequence they tend to overlook the larger economic context whereby affect is pressed into service in the Web 2.0 economy. The commercial logic of social cataloging sites depends upon user "stickiness": the time users remain on the site and the nature of their activities while there. This may variously drive revenue from user subscriptions (LibraryThing), third-party advertising (book blogs), or links to book retailing (Amazon, Goodreads). Hence impassioned emotional responses to books are not only perhaps most intuitive for readers outside the academy but also most likely to generate heated online debates, which themselves increase user stickiness. Time spent on the website thus encourages creation of more content, at no cost to the site's owners, and increases the likelihood of purchases (whether from the site itself or via affiliates). At a bare minimum it adds to the pool of data about site users that is Web 2.0 companies' primary, rapidly appreciating asset. "Authentic" emotion is thus put to work commercially in the social-cataloging site, a fact that undercuts such sites' championing of ostensibly democratic literary reviewing.

Debates Generated by Online Book Review Culture

Online book review culture raises issues related not only to the tonal qualities and aesthetic preferences of reviewers but also to the structural conditions of review culture itself. The following section examines in turn three pressing debates: status rivalries between variously credentialed book reviewers and literary bloggers; the slippery nature of reviewer identity in virtual environments; and the commercial drivers of many online reviewing "communities."

"Accessories to the Real Literary Discussions":[41]
"Professional"/"Amateur" Reviewer Distinction

In May 2007, in the wake of the *Atlanta Journal-Constitution* eliminating the position of literary editor and in the process letting go long-serving incumbent Teresa Weaver, an online flame war erupted between litbloggers and traditional print periodical book reviewers. The online world's self-appointed, uncredentialed book bloggers were, the National Book Critics Circle (NBCC) implied, an ill-mannered rabble whose substandard digital books chatter undermined the precarious viability of "real" newspaper and periodical book reviewing. The bloggers did so by giving newspapers' bottom line–fixated corporate owners an excuse to cut costs by claiming that books coverage was already freely available online (Rich, 2007; Getlin, 2007; Birkerts, 2007). Reviewer Richard Powers, writing (somewhat ironically) on the NBCC's blog *Critical Mass*, cautioned, "We are in danger of drowning in an ocean of liking or disliking" (2007).[42] Accusations that much online books "coverage" was merely opinionated, ill-informed drivel, produced by attention-seeking egomaniacs indifferent to the larger cause of Literature, added fuel to the fire (Getlin, 2007). Predictably, the blogosphere gave as good as it got, hitting back at print media's defenders by pointing out that if print reviewing was so ossified by pretension, self-regard, and indifference to the opinions of "real" readers that they had been abandoned in the rush to interactive alternatives, they had only themselves to blame (Rich, 2007; Gomez, 2008: 60). The dispute produced the unedifying spectacle of literary review culture in the act of cannibalizing itself. Many of the rhetorical missiles being lobbed may well have been designed more to drive online traffic to a particular antagonist's website than to throw light on the future of book reviewing. Nevertheless, the moment is significant in that it publicly foregrounded book review culture's internal conflicts and identity crises at a pivotal point in the mainstreaming of social media.

Combatants in the bloggers-versus-reviewers flame wars were eager to present the conflict as essentially two-sided, an opposition that lent itself with wearying predictability to media presentations of a war between old and new media (see Getlin, 2007). Conservative cultural commentator and self-declared print loyalist Sven Birkerts framed the dispute in precisely these terms: "It's the difference between amateur and professional. What we gain in independence and freshness we lose in authority and accountability" (2007). But, on closer examination, the spurious distinction between "professionals" on one hand and "amateurs" on the other fails to hold up. Print periodicals' "professionals" are in fact typically freelancers with jobs in other sectors who are paid token amounts to pen book reviews. Conversely, the so-called "amateur" bloggers, allegedly motivated solely by a love of literature, were by 2007 finding themselves increasingly absorbed into the publicity and marketing strategies of multinational publishers, and in some cases actively sought to turn their blog's viewer traffic into hard currency via advertising or affiliate links. Rather than two armies facing off against each other, the metaphor that comes most readily to mind is fish fighting each other in an ever-shrinking pond. The false dichotomy masks the fact that there are more than two adversaries in this dispute. At a key transitional moment in the history of book reviewing, "amateur" bloggers and "professional" reviewers sought not only to define themselves against each other but also in opposition to a third party: academic literary criticism. Addressing the triangular nature of book reviewing's contemporary identity thus requires first critiquing the "professional" status of print reviewers, then investigating the creeping professionalization of blogging "amateurs," before explaining literary academe's telling absence from the 2007 dispute.

The 2007 shakeout in contemporary book reviewing was triggered by a wave of closures of print reviewing outlets, of which the *Atlanta Journal-Constitution*'s was only the most recent. The identity crisis among professional literary critics had for many years been exacerbated by shrinking review space in broadsheet newspapers as arts and culture supplements had been merged with op-ed sections or scrapped altogether. The long-running structural driver of these changes was the collapse in advertising revenue triggered by the Internet.[43] Such a "nightmare scenario" had been forecast by Gerald Howard as far back as 1992, before accessible browsers had made surfing the World Wide Web a routine feature of mainstream life. Howard in fact predicted newspapers' competition would come from the then modish media of "hypertext, interactive television and virtual reality" rather than the (then still very embryonic) Internet (106, 90). But while he may have misjudged the causes, he was spot on in recognizing that loss of advertising revenue undermined the whole economic rationale for newspapers' cultural offerings. Journalist and leading Australian book reviewer Gideon Haigh observes: "Newspapers publish books pages with a grudging air, regarding them as a financial burden because they attract little advertising support" (2010). Arts supplements, where they do survive, are typically justified along perversely economic rationalist lines as attracting a desirable upper-middle-class professional reader demographic to the newspaper, which indirectly drives advertising for noncultural products (cars, watches, jewelry, alcohol) among readers with high disposable incomes (Sutherland, 1978: 101). It is a model of cultural reviewing as media loss leader, with books lending a tony gloss to publications that elsewhere increasingly pander to mass readerships in both format and content. More pervasively, there is a detectable category drift in book reviewing to diffuse lifestyle items, as authors are profiled in weekend magazines, book reviews are merged with author interviews and restaurant reviews in hybrid "Lunch with . . ." columns, and all avenues are pursued to turn book notes into news proper (for example, via prize announcements or literary scandals) (Sage, 1998: 264; Woodward, 1999: 93; Curran, 2000: 217, 234–35).

Within this context of an industry forced by digital disruption to reexamine its fundamental economic logic, the "professional" status of the majority of print publications' book reviewers is still more precarious. Book reviewing is typically performed on a poorly remunerated "piecework" basis, and often as more of a hobby or sidebar to another literary-sector activity (for example by academics, authors, publishers, editors, and journalists) than as a profession in its own right (Sutherland, 1978: 90; Sage, 1998: 262, 266). Media sociologist James Curran rightly noted in 2000 that book reviewing, like so many other spheres of late-twentieth-century cultural work, "has become more casualised" (229). Railing against the work conditions of book reviewing has a decades-long history: Orwell damned it as "a quite exceptionally thankless, irritating and exhausting job" ([1946] 2003). Decades later, with the hegemony of print under siege in ways that Orwell could only dimly have imagined in *1984*-ish dystopian mode, the situation had become, if anything, worse. Books editor Gail Pool, writing near the century's close, lamented: "We [reviewers] are held in very low regard. The issue isn't only pay—though I doubt there is any work more poorly paid—but also disparagement, the dismissal of reviewing's importance, the dismissal of it even as real writing" (1994: 16).

Yet Pool, probably book reviewing's leading analyst, was sufficiently clear-eyed in her subsequent monograph *Faint Praise: The Plight of Book Reviewing in America* (2007) not to idealize the digital literary sphere as offering a reviewer haven from economic necessity. Online reviewing and book blogging may have rescued literature-loving reviewers from the economic exigencies of newspaper managerialism, but they substitute a new variety of economic concerns for these old-style concerns. Relatively early in the first flush of blogging's new-millennial novelty, Pool sounded a note of caution: "As bloggers try to establish an economic foundation for their sites, as they seek financing and good relationships with publishers who, after all, provide books, they will face many of the same pressures print publications have confronted" (2008: 9). Pool's prescience has been well borne out in the decade since. High-profile litbloggers are frequently courted by book publishers and retailers, who for example send them advance proofs or review copies to stoke pre-release publicity (Gillieron and Kilgarriff, 2007: 11, 18; Steiner, 2010: 482–83). Already by 2007, Rebecca Gillieron and Catheryn Kilgarriff in their *Bookaholics' Guide to Book Blogs* were having to temper their rather impressionistic celebration of book bloggers as radical outsiders to the literary system, beholden to no authority other than their own eclectic tastes, with the parenthetical concession that "as bloggers begin to sell advertising space and/or books from their sites this may well be changing already" (30). Blogger Angela Meyer (*LiteraryMinded*) confirms the trend: "I am seeing publishers are beginning to notice bloggers and are proposing them to write reviews of books that fit their audiences," adding the perhaps unintentionally revealing coda, "They are beginning to treat me like a conventional media outlet" (Henly, 2011: 34).[44] As the incremental drift toward commercial co-optation of blogging continues apace, it becomes increasingly fraught—if not downright implausible—to insist on the blogger's original, defiantly outsider perspective (Rettberg, 2014: 12, 56). For example, media writer Martin Taylor, analyzing "how book marketing changes when it's digital," advises book retailers to launch a charm offensive of blogger cultivation: "Include VIP invitations to your events, help to distribute their reviews by linking to them on your site, or offers of guest posts on their blogs when you do reviews. This will also give you much wider distribution for your reviews and will win points with bloggers who will appreciate some good quality reviews" (2013: 15). Moreover, many bloggers receive incremental commission payments from "affiliate links" (websites that readers of a blog can click on to purchase a book title mentioned in the blog) (Calvani and Edwards, 2008: 108, 113; Orthofer, 2010: 70, 72; Ray Murray and Squires, 2013: 15–16; Taylor, 2013: 15; Mayo, 2016: 3). In commercial terms, the blogger is acting as a referral service for online retailers, with the likes of Amazon indifferent as to where a book recommendation comes from so long as it results in a firm sale.

Into this increasingly blurry distinction between who is actually a professional and who an amateur we can introduce a third, hitherto largely silent, party: the demonstrably professional academic literary critic. Credentialed with multiple tertiary degrees and accorded indisputably professional status by virtue of full-time salary and job tenure, academic literary critics reframe the dynamics of the ostensibly binary blogger-versus-reviewer debate, triangulating demarcation lines in the dispute. It is through such a zooming-out to reveal the broader contours of the book reviewing debate that we can better capture the forces and motivations driving parties in this existential tussle over the future of reviewing.

Literary academe's silence in the heated 2007 dispute between book bloggers and print reviewers illustrates the vast gap between theory-focused academic literary criticism and the world of mass-oriented "book talk," whether in print or online. This chasm at the heart of literary discussion was alluded to earlier in this chapter's treatment of affect and its role in reader response, and the possible narrowing of this gap with the academy's recent "affective turn" which appears to valorize popular emotional responses to books. How and precisely when the disjunction between literary criticism and literary reviewing arose is itself a matter of dispute. Henri Peyre, writing in 1963, dated the emergence in the US of "a beehive of ponderous critics" to the post–World War II era, specifically to 1945 (128). Similarly, Harvey Teres identifies the 1950s as the era that saw a shift away from a largely unified (albeit highly cosmopolitan and male) US literary culture in which the major figures were typically New York public intellectuals to a literary criticism dominated by academic professionals: "The tendency was to retreat from the broader audience of educated readers that had previously sustained a largely non-academic (and sometimes anti-academic) public critical culture. These developments changed the language of criticism, which on the whole became more self-reflexive, specialized, and obscure" (2009: 235). (Paradoxically, this narrowing of contributors to cultural debates occurred during the exact period that UK cultural studies scholars such as Richard Hoggart and Raymond Williams were radically expanding the ambit of what counts as a text worthy of academic analysis.) The sense that exclusionary specialist vocabulary and extreme textual formalism delegitimized everyday book lovers and their often primarily emotional investments in literary texts became stronger as Continental post-structuralist theory entered the Anglophone academy during the 1970s, hardening to become literary studies' governing paradigm by the early 1980s. Mattias Frey, paraphrasing Ronan McDonald, dates the public intellectual / academic rupture somewhat later than Peyre and Teres (to the early 1970s), but diagnoses the same bifurcating effect on cultural criticism: "The 'death of the critic' entailed the end to a communicative mediation between a learned authority and a willing, engaged reader; since then scholarly and journalistic criticism have increasingly diverged, and the vacuum of authority has been replaced by a host of nonexpert bloggers and a dispersive field of reviewing that fails to capture the public imagination" (2015: 6). Leading media scholar and social scientist James Curran, exponent of a discipline that gained increasing prominence in academe during the same period, sees the reviewer/academic dichotomy as an effect of the increasing professionalization of the academy in the second half of the twentieth century, and the incremental pressure on scholars exerted by university managers to demonstrate their research performance according to subject-specific journal hierarchies: "Universities as communities of learning ceased to be comprehensible even to their own members . . . , still less to a wider public. . . . By and large, academics chose voluntary internal exile by writing books, with tiny print runs, for narrow niche publics" (2000: 232–33).[45]

Statements are frequently encountered from book reviewers seeking to distinguish themselves from both academic literary criticism *and* amateur online criticism. As with the 2007 US reviewing dispute, they walk a precarious tightrope, however. On one hand they set themselves up in opposition to the academic credentials, specialist theoretical vocabulary, and bone-dry prose style of tenured academics, positing themselves as more authentically close to the common reader (a notoriously vague construct, even in decades gone by). On the other hand, they typically seek to draw a clear distinction between their own expertise, as demonstrated by a newspaper or magazine byline plus a CV of past reviews, and the mass amateurism of Amazon-style customer reviewers. Such print reviewers despair at amateur critics' lack of familiarity with landmark works and authors of the past, the intemperate and/or personal nature of online reviews, and the banality of reducing aesthetic and intellectual response to a five-star or A/B/C high school-essay–style rating (Stinson, 2017). Journalist Gideon Haigh closely echoes the NBCC in lamenting "a world in which 'liking' and 'not liking' are the only options" (2010). For reviewers such as Haigh, old-school broadsheet book reviewing represents a valuable social service being eroded simultaneously from above by an overly rarefied academy *and* from below by an army of self-appointed lit-bloggers. Yet his defense of non-academic literary discussion, intriguingly, deploys the vocabulary of *academic* specialization: "Reviewing is a discipline, a form of argument demanding logic and evidence as well as 'taste' and 'opinion.' And it is a discipline in barely acknowledged decline" (2010). The discourse of the print book reviewer is shot through with contradictory attitudes to cultural authority: both iconoclastic skewerers of academic "expertise" and staunch defenders of their own; at once the tribune for the common reader and decrier of the vox populi.[46] Small wonder then that, in the disintermediated climate of the Internet, traditional book reviewers have been among the first to sense their own redundancy.

Amazon "Sock-Puppetry" Scandals

Wikipedia, that indispensable guide to Internet terminology and digital mores, defines a "sock puppet" as "an online identity used for purposes of deception."[47] The chief characteristic of the sock puppet is that, like its children's television namesake, it lends the appearance of a conversation between various parties whereas in truth they are but the one person. The rather morally bankrupt practice of anonymous self-reviewing has a long and—if it is possible to use such a word in this context—eminent history. Gérard Genette records how literary notables such as Stendhal and Barthes penned laudatory pseudonymous (or in Barthes's case signed, third-person) "auto-reviews" as part of a raft of publicity tactics (1997: 352–53). In the world of traditional print periodical reviewing, literary appraisals were for many decades published unsigned, or with only the reviewer's initials (potentially themselves also pseudonymous) placed at the bottom. However, the global reach, lack of editorial filter, and seemingly consequence-free nature of online communication has taken fake reviewing to a new level.

In the early years of Amazon customer reviews, when the novelty of globally published evaluations from "real people" was yet to wear off, Bezos's response to the threat of sock-puppet reviews was dismissive. In an interview with *Playboy*, Amazon's founder flattered the reader that their own critical antennae were sufficiently attuned to detect a fake review: "When people have a vested interest, they often say so. . . . Of course there are exceptions, but you can usually tell whether a review is thoughtful, flippant or biased. There are going to be a few people who are sophisticated enough to organize campaigns, but that will be the exception" (Sheff, 2000). In the scholarly realm, analysts of reader response were fascinated with Amazon reader reviews from the website's early years, compelled by the prospect of a freely available, globally compiled database of real reader hermeneutics, classified by date and in many cases also providing the reader-reviewer's geographic location. However, veracity was an immediate, niggling academic concern; Paul Gutjahr, in one of the earliest scholarly considerations of Amazon customer reviews from the perspective of reading theory, sounded a note of caution about this new empirical treasure trove: "There is no way to confirm either the content or the identity of those who write these reviews" ([2002] 2011: 394).[48]

The first major public revelation of how tainted Amazon's "authentic" customer reviews in fact were occurred in 2004 when a technical fault on the firm's Canadian website revealed the user names of reviewers who had chosen to remain anonymous. The mass unmasking of reviewer identity showcased literary reviewing at its most base and self-serving: authors puffing their own books, viciously taking down those of their rivals, and engaging in quid-pro-quo backscratching with literary friends (Harmon, 2004; Pool, 2007: 100; Steiner, 2008). The still most infamous case of Amazon sock puppetry occurred six years later. Orlando Figes, a professor of Russian history at the University of London's Birkbeck College, published damning online reviews of two rivals' works on Soviet Russia under the online moniker "orlando_birkbeck." These titles were in competition with his own most recent book on the topic, which he effusively praised as "a fascinating book . . . [that] leaves the reader awed, humbled, yet uplifted. . . . I hope he writes for ever" (Lea and Taylor, 2010; Kermode, 2013: 207). After a series of increasingly damaging evasions, denials, and claims that his spouse had written the reviews, Figes eventually admitted authoring the posts and was ordered to pay legal damages to the two historians whose books he had slammed (Dodd, 2010; Topping, 2010). Also in 2010, media commentary in the UK claimed that public relations firms were setting up fake reviewer profiles to heap praise on clients' books (Fagge, 2010). In 2012, crime writer R. J. Ellory was caught using sock puppets on Amazon to praise his own "magnificent" books and slam those of prominent crime-writing peers (Flood, 2012; Kermode, 2013: 207). Crime writers interviewed for a *Guardian* story on the contretemps alleged sock puppetry was "absolutely rife," to the extent that the Crime Writers Association was drafting a Code of Ethics condemning the practice (Flood, 2012). Again in 2012, Jeremy Trevathan, head of publisher Pan Macmillan's Adult Division was revealed as having given five-star Amazon reviews to numerous of his own writers. He defended his behavior with the claim that "this is about talking and engaging with readers."[49]

By this point, the integrity of Amazon's customer reviews was clearly in crisis, with waves of increasingly damaging media reports compounding the public impression of a system so thoroughly gamed as to be nearly worthless. The issue widely discussed at the time was whether repeated sock-puppetry scandals and various websites' failure to eradicate the practice had so debased the currency of amateur reviews that the public no longer regarded them as credible consumer feedback (Vinjamuri, 2012).[50] For Amazon in particular, a firm that—in the absence of a familiar storefront presence—had elevated customer service to a corporate mantra, this threat to brand integrity was existential. If cumulative customer reviews did not in fact reflect the wisdom of the crowd, Bezos's democratic daring in removing the fusty critical middlemen to "let truth loose" would stand revealed as a catastrophic abrogation of corporate quality control.

In the years since, Amazon has worked hard to restore public confidence in the reliability of its customer reviews, characteristically favoring technical, quantitative fixes. There is some irony in this because sock puppetry and the broader problem of "objective" evaluation endemic in all cultural reviewing stem from the battle between agents over various forms of capital structuring the Bourdieusian field. Quantitative measures would seem a blunt instrument with which to address what are, at their root, knock-on effects of status differentials and prestige scarcity. Nevertheless, Amazon's Conditions of Use current at the time of writing (last updated June 2016) prohibit reviewers from engaging in defamation, "commercial solicitation," or impersonation.[51] Additionally, Amazon's slightly less draconically titled "Community Guidelines" disallow "creating, modifying, or posting content regarding your (or your relative's, close friend's, business associate's, or employer's) products or services" as well as "posting content regarding your competitors' products or services."[52] (The "Review Guidelines" of Amazon's now subsidiary Goodreads also prohibit this species of "self-promotional reviews.")[53] Amazon has instituted various technical checks, such as linking reviewer identity with purchaser credit card records, marking reviews from those with a buyer record for the item as "verified purchase," and appearing to elevate these up the hierarchy of review listings. Similarly, reviews posted by a celebrity or other well-known person are marked with a "*THE*" badge, indicating that credit card records indicate that the poster of the review is the person commonly associated with that name.[54] Such cross-linking of transaction records makes the setting up of multiple false identities for the purpose of sock puppetry significantly more difficult, though not impossible.

Located at the borderlands of quantitative and qualitative remedial measures is Amazon's "Was this review helpful to you?" function, which effectively allows readers to review the reviewer. The feature puts faith in the ability of Amazon's customer base to distinguish between self-interested puffery and vicious takedowns on one hand and genuine, informed, arm's-length feedback on the other, much as Bezos had originally claimed. Reviews with the most favorable reader votes are algorithmically sorted to appear higher in the reviews listing, and positive votes also increase a reviewer's chances of earning a "Top Reviewer" badge.

Reflecting on the significance of this feature for DVD reviewing in particular, professional film critic Mark Kermode expresses himself as, at least initially, impressed by this "very commendable system": "Perhaps this really could be the dawn of 'reliable' customer reviewing, a new way of sourcing criticism boasting the immediacy of social media, the back-up of democratic verification, and the efficiency of automatic editing" (2013: 212). While still manifestly fallible and vulnerable to being gamed in ever more sophisticated ways, the revised Amazon review-the-reviewer function nevertheless provides an example of Internet-generated modes of cultural hierarchy emerging independent of offline critical authorities.[55] Clearly the facility is not provided principally as a public service; Amazon has a direct commercial interest in ensuring the integrity of its customer reviews. Moreover, such algorithmically based solutions, while boasting the benefits of automation and systemwide implementation, nevertheless return the onus of labor and verification to an unpaid volunteer customer base. Amazon's Conditions of Use make it clear that the firm has the unilateral right to remove any review content that it finds undesirable, but that it has no countervailing obligation to monitor Amazon-hosted reviews or message boards.[56] In turning the task of critical evaluation over to "the people," Amazon has also outsourced to this unpaid voluntariat the responsibilities for quality control, reviewer bona fides, and editorial standards formerly assumed by publishers of print reviews. Hence online-born forms of cultural hierarchy are certainly evident, but the labor and time costs associated with servicing them are borne by users themselves.

Interpenetration of Cultural and Commercial Motivations

As noted at the start of this chapter, Amazon's early championing of democratic reviewing was primarily opportunistic: in exchange for providing free content to populate Amazon's then stark website, reader-reviewers were flattered that their opinion mattered, and were invited to broadcast their verdicts on individual books to a global audience. All this occurred at a time when (and also because) digital interactivity was still novel. Prior to the introduction of customer reviews in 1997, Bezos had hired an in-house editorial staff gleaned from existing book-world organizations to create the content that would demonstrate Amazon's trustworthiness as a site for readers' literary investment and credit card details (see chapter 2). James Marcus's memoir *Amazonia* (2004) records how, in subsequent years, Amazon's center of gravity gradually shifted away from such externally credentialed literary expertise to the more cost-effective alternatives of customer reviewing and automated recommendation software. By the end of Marcus's five-year stint at Amazon, the firm's technological wonks were able to track site users' behavior in minute detail, incrementally strengthening the "gravitational tug of the marketplace" (24). While adamant that he was never explicitly told to "make nice" to a particular book title, Marcus details how Amazon's developing suite of IT tools allowed the company to track whether or not a particular piece of editorial content had led to a purchase (24). Specifically, staff reviews that did not lead to click-through sales were labeled "repels," and in-house editorial staff, Marcus included, were admonished for too high a repel rate (196; see also Packer, 2014). The anecdote highlights how Amazon's website has, from its inception, comprised a thorough intermeshing of cultural and commercial motivations, with the community-building aspects strategically harnessed to maximize commercial benefits. Nor is Amazon alone in this. John Palattella, writing about Amazon's book-retailing archrival Barnes & Noble's online publication *Review*, judges it "better edited than any newspaper books section, but it also happens to be owned by the country's largest corporate chain bookstore. Neither the quality of its reviews nor the generosity of its writers' fees can expunge from its pages its innate commercialism" (2010). Across the online reviewing sector, the uneasy hosting of "criticism" on book retailing sites contributes to what Richard Woodward memorably termed "the smiley-face policy towards books that prevails at Amazon, Barnes & Noble, and [now defunct chain] Borders" (1999: 131).

On Amazon's current website, commercial inducements are touted at every turn: from the ever-present lure of the bottomless shopping cart, through the proffering of individual book titles in myriad print and digital editions, to expedited delivery options. On Goodreads, each book title's web page includes links to over a dozen online retailers (the alphabetical listing ensures that site owner Amazon appears first), as well as various prominently displayed "sponsored books" advertisements which vary, Google-style, according to the individual web user's search history. This last lure hints at such websites' less obvious, though commercially more lucrative, product: the data users actively contribute to the site or leave unconsciously. Each user's record of titles viewed, reviews read, and forums visited leaves a trail of digital footprints which can be tracked, compiled, and exploited internally or sold to third parties hungry for potential consumer profiles. When combined with the user data derived from now Amazon subsidiaries Goodreads, LibraryThing, and Shelfari, this constitutes a massive cache of online book user information unrivaled in its scope and detail.[57] As Lisa Nakamura astutely notes, "By submitting our favourite book titles, readerly habits, ratings, comments, and replies . . . to our social network of readers, we are both collecting and being collected under a new regime of controlled consumerism" (2013: 241). The Amazon site user thus browses commodities in an endless virtual bazaar while offering up their own tastes, judgments, and social connections for corporate commodification.

From among this general community-cum-consumer-base, online retailers select key groups of early adopters, consecrating them with opinion-influencer status, and supplying them with pre-release or otherwise "special" content in exchange for posting reviews to their highly active bookish micro-communities. Amazon's "Vine™ Voice" self-describes as "an invitation only program that gives Amazon reviewers advance access to not-yet-released products for the purpose of writing reviews."[58] It is also one of the prestigious "badges" displayable under selected reviewers' user names. Similarly, Goodreads offers its inner sanctum of "First Reads" reviewers giveaway books for prepublication comment, as does LibraryThing through its "Early Reviewer" program offering free book copies in exchange for reviewing on users' blogs (Pinder, 2012: 70; Miller, L., 2013).[59] The various websites are hazy about the criteria by which one is invited to join such programs or how specific titles are matched to individual reviewers. The suspicion hovers that favorable coverage of previous or generically similar titles ups one's odds of receiving free books and other preferential titbits.

To say the least, such commodification of reading as a social practice complicates simplistic assumptions about ostensibly "democratic" forms of criticism and mass engagement in online literary culture (Miller, L. J., 1999: 311; 2009; Gardiner, 2002: 167; Pool, 2007: 99; Wright, 2012: 112–13). Nowhere is this spelled out more starkly than in Amazon's Conditions of Use, located by clicking on "Help" at the bottom of its home page and then navigable only by inputting the specific phrase into the search box.[60] There, in the two paragraphs dedicated to "Reviews," Amazon spells out unambiguously the profoundly lopsided relationship the firm enjoys vis-à-vis its reader-reviewers in intellectual property and contract law. By posting reviews and other content to the site, reviewers assume full responsibility for any damage that may arise from their reviews, but in return retain no rights whatsoever to benefit financially from the content they create. Amateur reviewers automatically grant Amazon "a nonexclusive, royalty-free, perpetual, irrevocable, and fully sublicensable right" to use their content in a vertigo-inducing range of ways: Amazon may "use, reproduce, modify, adapt, publish, perform, translate, create derivative works from, distribute, and display such content throughout the world in any media." Furthermore, Amazon and its sublicensees reserve the right to use the reviewer's name in relation to their content, should they so choose. The intricate bibliophilic reading notes and social maps freely offered up by bookworms on social cataloging sites can thus be commercialized ad infinitum by the sites' owners, whereas users have no enforceable legal ownership over their often laboriously created profiles. As chapter 2 explored in relation to book publicity and marketing, and as chapter 5 proceeds to analyze in relation to online reading, the ever-porous division between the book's identity as cultural artifact and its status as commodity has here collapsed entirely. Not only that, but the sequential model of a book's progress from creation, through distribution, to eventual consumption, in the style of Darnton's "communications circuit," has here fused into a single entity in which all online interactions potentially contribute to each process simultaneously. In a final act of digital disintermediation and disruption, formerly distinct industry roles have become interchangeable, as readers morph into hybrid reviewer-marketers, and retailers promise to convert them further into self-published authors, distributing and selling their works in turn. So hydra-headed is Amazon's presence in the digital literary sphere that attempting to stand outside of its systems is tantamount to swearing off online bookish engagement altogether.

Conclusion

Controversy over online reader reviews represents an instance of broader debates over the Internet's erosion of established cultural arbiters, and these debates in turn form part of a much wider field of research on the relationship between technological and social change on one hand and literary authority on the other (Long, 1985–1986; Radway, 1997; Miller, L. J., 1999). Precisely what makes analyzing the nature of contemporary online reviewing so fascinating is that we are witnessing a moment of profound cultural flux, where the economy of media scarcity and barriers to entry that once circumscribed reviewing authority within closely guarded confines have dissolved, and a new mass of amateur reviewers, not credentialed according to existing schemas of cultural authority, are entering and influencing public discourse around books.

As contemporaries of these developments, we need to rethink ingrained assumptions that the flat architecture of the Internet is incompatible with cultural rankings. Colin Robinson, co-publisher at digital press OR Books, similarly argues for a midpoint between book reviewing's exclusionary ancien régime and an Internet-induced critical free-for-all: "To express discomfort at the attrition of expert opinion is not to defend the previous order's prerogatives. Nor is it elitist to suggest that making the values and personnel of such professional hierarchies more representative is preferable to dispensing with them" (2014).[61] In the digital literary sphere critical authority has been distributed; it is less inherent in a clearly ranked reviewing clerisy than demonstrable through voluntary communities of loose affiliation. Readers seek out and attach themselves to critical subgroups that appear to share their taste in books. Accordingly, the authority of an individual critic is now less assumed ex officio than won through an ongoing process of readerly wooing and persuasion, maintaining the reviewer-reader relationship through posting of material that sustains and develops this rapport.

Assuredly, these emerging hierarchies of cultural authority incubated by the digital literary sphere are far from perfect. Vulnerable to being gamed by self-interested participants, infused with commercialism, and at times betraying a fast and loose attitude to fact checking and English grammar, they nevertheless constitute important and growing loci of contemporary literary culture. Recall too that the traditional print periodical model of reviewing was replete with accusations of back-scratching, self-interest, and pandering to publisher advertising or the proprietor's editorial line. Accordingly, binary approaches to contemporary literary culture that force participants to nail their colors to either a print or digital mast(head) manifestly miss the point. By the second decade of the new millennium, literary culture has become a complex hybrid of print and digital outlets that exist in a state of mutual dependence. Emerging from a period of radical egalitarian rhetoric, in which every participant's view was deemed as valuable as any other's, the literary web has long since entered a period of critical rationalization in which digital-born finding tools, recommendation mechanisms, and evaluative hierarchies are emerging to assist readers to sort and classify the deluge of book-related information generated daily. From this voluminous output have emerged ratings systems, review-the-reviewer functions, and coalitions of allied parties in the form of blogroll listings and blogger cooperatives. Each represents an attempt to reconcile the traditionally hierarchical concept of cultural authority with the ostensibly flat communication architecture of the Internet. Through all of this, traditional print-media outlets have not stood aloof but attempt to leverage their inherited consecratory role by anointing the best of the online-born efforts, imitating their successes, and debating their pitfalls with ill-disguised glee. Literary culture in the twenty-first century is still characterized by hierarchies, but they are notably plural, more loosely defined, and demonstrably more in flux than in the pre-digital era.

CHAPTER FIVE

Entering Literary Discussion

Fiction Reading Online

In an affecting passage in the second volume of Karl Ove Knausgaard's monu-
mental six-part novel-cum-memoir *My Struggle* ([2009] 2014), the narrator recalls
a particularly memorable Christmas visiting his uncle Kjartan. Then an adoles-
cent, the author recounts that his maternal uncle worked the family farm in rural
Norway, as well as being employed offsite as a ship's plumber, undertaking back-
breaking manual labor all day before returning home to care for his elderly parents. Somehow, in the midst of this constellation of unceasing demands, he has
developed a passion for reading Heidegger, despite the inconvenient fact that "no
one within a radius of several kilometres had even heard of Heidegger, and no
one wanted to either" (158). Laboriously deciphering the text in his high school
German, Uncle Kjartan is set aflame with the philosopher's ideas. When his
university-educated relatives come to visit, he pours forth for hours on end an
entire year's worth of pent-up intellectual infatuation with Heideggerean philosophy; in Knausgaard's words "his sluice gates opened" and it was "*Dasein*" this
and "*Das Man*" that—"the sole topic of conversation was Heidegger" (159).

As Christmas-break small-talk goes, this is heavy stuff. The intensity of Uncle
Kjartan's intellectual engagement with these difficult philosophical texts is coun-
terpointed by a total absence of fellow enthusiasts with whom he can discuss
such works year-round. The effect is something like the intellectual equivalent of
an immense weight concentrated upon a tiny surface area—every moment his
educated relatives are in the house becomes of heightened significance because
there will be no other intellectual peers or sparring partners for many long months
to come. Intellectually, Kjartan lives the feast-and-famine pattern of a hunter-
gatherer; when it comes to readerly discussion, it is all or nothing.

It is impossible to read this moving account of a committed autodidact's ob-
sessive reading during the mid-1980s and not to wish he had been able to prolong
and expand such intellectual exchanges through some kind of university distance-
learning program. Or, in less formal, more contemporary terms, that he had been
a member of an online book club. For it is precisely this kind of highly motivated,
intellectually committed but geographically isolated reader who has most to gain

from the sociable reading practices and interpretive communities made possible by the Internet. Online reading communities facilitate the entry of enthused but typically amateur readers into public literary discussion, fostering communities of interest that can be as geographically inclusive as they are selective in their preferred reading material. For participants without ready access to the formal structures of a university seminar, the camaraderie of a suburban reading group, or even the proxy discussion of a television book club, online book clubs bring to the reading act a crucially interactive dimension. A reading group adds an encompassing social dimension to an individual's intense intellectual and emotional engagement with a text and has the potential not only to add to the reader's hermeneutic experience after reading is complete, but also subtly to alter the very moment of textual encounter itself. In online reading environments, textual interpretation becomes an implicitly—sometimes explicitly—social experience from the very moment a reader encounters a work. Whether this might be viewed as the ultimate liberation from readerly isolation, or as a nightmare of enforced groupthink, the phenomenon has no equivalent in embodied settings.[1] For this reason, scholars with an interest in the future of reading (which should, by definition, include all humanists) need to be cognizant of reading's new manifestations in the twenty-first-century digital literary sphere.

This chapter's chief concern is to examine how online reading environments prompt book history to rethink some of its core tenets regarding reading. Because I wish to keep discussion focused on theoretical and methodological principles transferable to other examples, I group together a number of case studies that combine reading and online environments in different ways. I employ the umbrella term "online reading formations" as a suitably capacious designation to encompass digital platforms of various kinds exhibiting a degree of collective identity, facilitating participant interaction, and evincing a bookish self-conception or point of common interest. That said, there exist significant differences between the various online reading formations examined here. The Kindle and Kobo, for example, are e-reader devices with online hosting services that allow some degree of reader interactivity, albeit often at aggregate level. The online mass-reading experiment Infinite Summer, by contrast, is closer to a single-text book club, presupposing readers consuming David Foster Wallace's *Infinite Jest* (1996) in codex versions, or on non-networked e-readers, before convening for online discussion over a preset, delimited period. Finally, the book-exchange network BookCrossing differs again in that actually analyzing books gifted by other readers appears to be of lesser importance than logging the same copy that has passed through previous readers' hands. Hence the case studies evince a wide variety of participant motivations, degrees of community cohesion, and shades of commercial affilia-tion. Given this variation in my chosen case studies and their technological bases, the title of my discussion has been deliberately chosen: not "online reading" (in the sense of reading that necessarily takes place online) but "reading online" (con-veying the idea of reading moving online in multiple forms to explore the various affordances of digitally networked environments).

Equally, this chapter's focus is primarily on fiction reading, as the dominant sector of contemporary leisure reading. While all Internet usage involves read-ing to some degree (even increasingly image-dominated social media), fiction re-mains the book sector that best cultivates a certain practice of long-format, linear, immersive reading in which emotional investment by the reader in the text is avidly encouraged—even, in the subsector of literary fiction, culturally sanctified. For this reason, the manner in which the innately interactive affordances of dig-ital technologies upend many previously settled assumptions about reading re-veal themselves in especially pronounced form in the realm of fiction.

Characteristics and Benefits of Online Reading Groups

What would motivate someone to eschew the face-to-face conviviality of an em-bodied book club in favor of its virtual counterpart? Importantly, for an isolated reader like Knausgaard's Uncle Kjartan, online book clubs are free from geo-graphic, time zone, and scheduling limitations in a manner characteristic of Internet sociability (Chelton, 2001: 33, 35; Rehberg Sedo, 2002: 16; 2003: 79–80, 82, 85; 2011a: 8; 2011b: 105–06; Long, 2003: 208–11, 214–16; Fister, 2005: 303, 305; Starkey, 2005: 50; Maclaran and Masterson, 2006: 130–31; Foasberg, 2012: 44; Pinder, 2012: 75, 78). They have the related virtue of being unconstrained by limited local bookish infrastructure such as brick-and-mortar bookshops or li-braries because they are able to piggyback on online book retailers' inventories, and increasingly on their hosting services as well (cf. Long, 2003: 211). More than this, virtual book clubs facilitate a "purer" form of book talk: semi-anonymity means participants' age, sex, race, appearance, social class, and accent are largely unknowable unless a reader chooses to (mis)represent them through personal disclosure, a pseudonym, or an avatar (Chelton, 2001: 33; Rehberg Sedo, 2002: 16; 2003: 75; Long, 2003: 209; Fister, 2005: 305; Starkey, 2005: 50; Fitzpatrick, 2012: 196; Vlieghe and Rutten, 2013; Delaney, B., 2014: 12; Walmsley, 2016: 75). Compare this to resolutely embodied book-discussion settings such as a univer-sity seminar or suburban book club where the value of a participant's contribution is inevitably (albeit perhaps subconsciously) filtered through a range of socioeco-nomic assumptions made by other participants (Long, 2003: 211; Rehberg Sedo,

2011b: 102). Some social markers persist of course in the digital literary sphere: a certain degree of affluence to afford computer equipment or smartphone and Internet connectivity; IT savvy and knowledge of appropriate netiquette in navigating online forums; competence in written expression; sufficient leisure time; and possibly also familiarity with literary-critical terminology (Long, 2003: 209; Rehberg Sedo, 2003: 74; Gruzd and Rehberg Sedo, 2012; Pinder, 2012: 85). But these represent markedly lower barriers to entry than those operative in most embodied book clubs.

Furthermore, an online forum's asynchronous communication and unlimited space facilitate lengthy, reflective responses rather than kneejerk, on-the-spot replies (Chelton, 2001: 33; Rehberg Sedo, 2003: 82; 2011b: 105; Fister, 2005: 306; Walmsley, 2016: 73–74). This allows participants perhaps unfamiliar with "book talk" environments and the cultural capital required to pass in them to revise, edit, and even spellcheck their responses. They can thus assiduously craft their preferred book-club persona. The purely digital medium also permits a level of readerly control over self-presentation unparalleled in physical settings. Online book clubs, especially those of the social cataloging variety represented by Goodreads and LibraryThing, offer a range of tools for detailed online self-curation. Through the posting of one's library, books recently read, to-be-read lists, reviews, interactions with other readers, and the like, readers can construct a multifaceted—frequently aspirational—portrait of themselves as avid bibliophiles. The website's algorithmic tools can then suggest new books based on other members' collections and match readers with other users who have similar tastes, thus reinforcing a trend toward micro self-categorization. In digital terms, such online profiles echo the sixteenth-century vogue for trick paintings of people who turn out, on closer inspection, to be in fact artfully arranged assemblages of bookish paraphernalia: codices, bookmarks, quills, and the like.[2] Online, the readerly persona can be, quite literally, built out of books.

This is not to posit online and face-to-face (F2F) book clubs as mutually exclusive entities. Many online book club members expound in their posts on how a certain book was received in their F2F book club, suggesting that avid bibliophiles are aware of and appreciate the different affordances of the two media (Rehberg Sedo, 2003). Insatiable bibliophiles may even belong to multiple online book discussion forums simultaneously and differentiate between the tone, depth, and format of discussions on each, preferring Goodreads, for example, for its range and diversity and (the now defunct) Shelfari for its committed community and the in-depth analyses facilitated by its "nested" discussion threads.[3]

For such reasons, online book clubs function, counterintuitively, both to diver-

The Librarian (c. 1566) by Italian painter Giuseppe Arcimboldo

sify as well as to rarefy bookish culture. Their ease of use and affordability make them porous groupings with culturally democratizing potential to draw in "broader constituencies" than have typically characterized public book discussion (Long, 2003: 216; see also Vlieghe, Muls, and Rutten, 2016: 35). Yet their tools for self-display encourage ever more elaborate rituals of literary self-fashioning on the part of committed bibliophiles already well ensconced within the consecrated sanctuaries of literary culture (academe, newspaper and little-magazine review-ing, creative writing programs, librarianship). Readerly egalitarianism and literary one-upmanship appear, paradoxically, to coexist unproblematically in the digital literary sphere. There is precedent for such a dynamic of simultaneous broaden-ing and deepening of readerly culture. Book history has long been fascinated with the reading experiences of socially marginalized groups—peasants, the semiliter-ate, religious dissenters, working-class autodidacts, women. Yet the discipline's origins in Annaliste social history have gifted it a keen awareness that patterns of literary adoption are often wildly uneven across territories and even within individual communities.[4] Especially given this intellectual heritage, the variability of online reading communities represents a compelling, socially intriguing development in the "late age of print" or incunabula period of digital literary culture.[5] And yet, such analyses of digital reading as have emerged over the last two decades have yet to fundamentally reconstruct how the discipline of book history conceives of itself.

Online Reading Communities: Demonstrably Vibrant but Academically Elusive

Online reading communities go by various names: "virtual book clubs" (Chelton, 2001), "virtual reading communities" (Collins, 2010: 78), "digital social reading" (Rowberry, 2016: 212), "socially networked reading" (Barnett, 2014: 143), and "Internet-mediated reading" (Allington and Pihlaja, 2016: 206). In practice their manifestations range from the widely known Amazon customer reviews and Goodreads-hosted book clubs, to more esoteric web arcana such as the 2009 mass-reading experiment Infinite Summer[6] and the book-gifting website Book-Crossing.[7] Among scholars of the contemporary book world there is consensus that virtual reading groups are proliferating and culturally intriguing phenomena, but have yet to be the subject of substantial academic analysis. Frequently the phenomenon is labeled as ripe for future research, even by those whose central academic concern *is* contemporary reading, who might therefore be expected to give us a handle on it. The leading scholar in this area, DeNel Rehberg Sedo (2002, 2011a, 2011b; Fuller and Rehberg Sedo, 2012, 2014; Gruzd and Rehberg Sedo, 2012), noted in 2003 that "There are no studies of online reading groups" and that her article sought to fill that gap (66), but it concludes by adding that further qualitative research is needed and begging "the academy [to] pay attention" (86). For Claire Squires, writing in 2007, "The Internet and the way in which it has allowed readers to express their responses to texts in a public forum" still represents a new frontier for reading research—"a rich research tool for scholars, and a potential testing-ground for various theories of the popularity (or otherwise) of books and the uses to which they are put" (412). The editors of the curriculum-defining, seemingly tautologically titled, *The History of Reading: A Reader* (2011) note in their introduction that "the sheer scale of the evidence of reading and response to published (both printed and electronic) texts in archived emails, the blogosphere, computer hard drives, and social networking sites is only now beginning to be comprehended, let alone scrutinised" (Towheed, Crone, and Halsey,

4). And as recently as 2014, Australian researcher Tully Barnett continued the trend of noticing online reading research's conspicuousness by its absence: "The new ways people are using books in digital environments is [*sic*] worthy of continued study," but "thus far, scholars in book studies have not provided much analysis of digital reading" (143, 145).

Why is the intellectual work of understanding reading online seemingly always still to be done? Partly the resistance is logistical: because online phenomena are constantly mutating, they are hard to capture in the kind of lapidary analyses favored by academe. For the discipline of book history, which announces its preferred retrospective orientation in its very name, online reading phenomena are also insistently, unsettlingly, of the present. Perhaps the field is better surrendered to the disciplines of media studies and communications, with their fascination with digital phenomena and oft-criticized tendency toward presentism?[8] Equally, the thoroughly commercialized nature of many online reading sites, and the phenomenon's increasing dominance by corporate behemoth Amazon through product innovation and acquisition of rivals, problematizes claims of resistant reading of the kind book historians and cultural studies theorists have long valorized. But book history's toying with, rather than wholehearted embrace of, digital reading to date is also, I suggest, because reading online disrupts some of the orthodoxies about reading that book historians have established through such dogged, painstaking research. It is only since the 1980s that book history has normalized the study of reading as an academically credible and methodologically feasible undertaking—wresting it from literary criticism's sweeping generalizations about a putative idealized Reader to substitute empirically verified, historically specific examples of individual and collective reading practices. Online reading phenomena entice book historians with their promise to provide more democratically dispersed reading data than ever before available, but they simultaneously disrupt some of the things we thought we now knew. Robert Darnton in 1986 encapsulated book history's understanding of reading as historically and contextually variable in a phrase that book historians now take to be axiomatic: reading, he wrote, "has history. It was not always and everywhere the same" (24). Discomfortingly though, socially networked reading highlights that some of the characteristics of reading we in book history have long been postulating may indeed stand revealed as specifically *historical* practices, only tangentially applicable, if at all, to the present. For a discipline that has prided itself on paying attention to the fine-grained nature of historical variability—even elevating this to a touchstone—it is disconcerting to find that one has been confusing the specific with the universal.

The History of Reading: From "First Steps"[9] to "The State of the Discipline"[10]

It is appropriate at this point to synthesize from the last forty-odd years of book history research some key tenets of the history of reading. At the risk of oversimplification, I have distilled the current disciplinary state of play to five key principles which, taken together, form a baseline against which we can assess the disruptive theoretical and methodological impact of online reading formations.

· Most importantly, even heroically, the history of reading has wound back assumptions about reading as a silent, solitary, private, and passive activity to establish that **reading is an *active*, transactional engagement with a text to construct meaning** (Iser, 1974; Long, 2003: xvi; Rehberg Sedo, 2003: 67; Price, 2004: 311). Similar principles had emerged earlier from the parallel traditions of French post-structuralism and German reader response theory. But book history's innovation was to ground these largely universalist, textually derived philosophical assertions in historical evidence. The resulting confluence of these various traditions, and their progressive braiding together through academic institutionalization, has made it a veritable orthodoxy across the humanities that meaning is not inherent in a text, and that no text is ever completed until it is consumed by an individual reader (Darnton, 1986: 20; Bennett, 1987: 70–71; Chartier, 1994; Cavallo and Chartier, 1999: 1).

· Secondly, in a demonstration of its ancestral line back to bibliographical studies,[11] book history insists that **material format is a crucial influencer of textual interpretation**: in the words of pathbreaking book historians Guglielmo Cavallo and Roger Chartier, "forms produce meanings" (1999: 2; see also Bennett, 1987: 72, 75; McGann, 1991; McKenzie, [1986] 1999). This assertion of literary history's fundamental materiality placed the burgeoning book history movement of the 1980s in marked opposition to the dematerialized tenor of mainstream literary criticism and, in particular, to the then booming field of literary theory. For the book historian, literary interpretation was also irreducibly situated in specific social contexts; in the words again of Cavallo and Chartier, "No text exists outside of the physical support that offers it for reading (or hearing) or outside of the circumstance in which it is read (or heard)" (1999: 5).

A third, equally intellectually revolutionary, proposition is the aforementioned one that **reading as an activity is historically and geographically spe-**

cific, dependent upon particular protocols, acts, and material supports. Epistemic shifts from public recitation to silent reading, and from intensive to extensive reading are often cited in support of this contention. But book historians, again true to their Annaliste roots, have been chary of any simplistic, clear-cut transitions: their research substantiates much readerly variation along class, gender, racial, generational, educational, and religious lines at the same time and place (Darnton, 1986: 12; Bennett, 1987: 74; Chartier, 1994; Cavallo and Chartier, 1999: 2–3; Eliot and Rose, 2007: 59).

- Fourthly, **theoretical postulations about the nature of the reading act require empirical substantiation.** Historical reading practices can be partially recuperated through extant sources, on both macro-analytical (library borrowing records, publishers' catalogs, sales records) and micro-analytical levels (diaries, memoirs, correspondence, legal records, marginalia, oral histories, even furniture design and depictions of reading in art) (Darnton, 1986; Finkelstein and McCleery, 2006, 2013; Eliot and Rose, 2007; Rehberg Sedo, 2011a: 15). In their efforts to preserve, collate, and disseminate such scarce historical reading records, book historians have been pioneering adopters of digital technologies. The UK's Reading Experience Database (RED), along with its mostly British Commonwealth offshoots, compiles textual evidence of individual acts of reading across five centuries (1450–1945), using the crowdsourced labor of volunteers for much of its data input.[12] On the other side of the Atlantic, the "What Middletown Read" database of borrower records from a midwestern community library over a period of eleven years, beginning in 1891 and concluding in 1902, has enabled book historians to precisely map the circulation of texts across subsets of readers, as well as to reconstruct with rare exactitude the reading diet of specific individuals.[13]

- Finally, book history has established that **"all reading is rooted in the social"** (Rehberg Sedo, 2011a: 16). All texts may be capable of generating an infinite range of interpretations, including by the same reader at different life stages (Barthes, [1968] 1986; Cavallo and Chartier, 1999: 1). However, in practice the range of acceptable readings is narrowed by socially and epistemologically powerful "interpretive communities" (Fish, 1980; Rehberg Sedo, 2003: 68–69; 2011b: 113; Collins, 2010: 44). These are social institutions (principally literary critical in Stanley Fish's original formulation but, by extension, also religious, educational, professional, political, domestic) whose interpretive protocols and practices intervene between a text and an individual reader to strongly encourage certain forms of ideologically charged interpretation. An interpretive community's preferred readings are rarely mandatory but *are* coercive, or at a minimum highly persuasive, for members wishing to be seen as competent, or worthy of advancement, within the interpretive community.[14]

Fish's interpretive communities tend to exert their hermeneutic pressure once reading of a work is complete (it helps that he was discussing the New Critics' preferred genre of poetry), not while reading is ongoing. That reflected the reality of codex-dominated literary studies in 1976 when the ideas in his *Is There a Text in This Class?* were first published in article form. But the concept of ex post facto interpretative community influence cannot be automatically assumed in the networked reading environments of the twenty-first century. Contemporary readers may actively seek out (or be involuntarily subjected to) the opinions of multiple interpretive communities at any time during the course of their reading. These opinion influencers may even include the author, as the preceding chapters' discussions of authorial blogging, tweeting, and myriad digital promotional activities bear out. Whether seeking affirmation, illumination, or contestation from co-readers, the contemporary reader is always enmeshed in a demonstrably social web. Resiliently individualistic readers may need to resort to actively disabling the default settings of their reading platforms to prevent information inflows from other readers or, conversely, the automatic publicizing of their own reading activity to others (Nelles, 2013).

Digital Media's Challenges to Book History Conceptualizations of Reading

The Internet's precisely time- and date-stamped archives of digital reading are enticing to book history researchers in that they represent a much more geographically and socially dispersed readerly catchment than previously available sources for the history of reading. They largely put to rest previous scholarly disputes over the representativeness of those readers whose rare accounts of reading survive, and by extension also the merit of databases such as the RED that attempt to compile these accounts (Darnton, 1986: 7, 19). Reading was for a long time the poor cousin within book history's peak scholarly body, the Society for the History of Authorship, Reading and Publishing (SHARP),[15] because of the difficulty of reconstructing reading's often private, solitary, and ephemeral nature. Finally, with the mainstreaming of reading online, it would appear that reading is enjoying its time in the academic sun. But the new avalanche of readers' self-documentation in online spaces raises the question of whether book historians' existing research methodologies and theoretical models are adequate to account for reading formations characterized not by paucity but by plenitude.

Transitioning from Source Scarcity to Overabundance

Specifically, there is the issue of the quality of reader accounts. The sixteenth-century millers and industrial-age, working-class autodidacts who loom large in the history of reading may not have been representative of their larger social groupings, but at least their earnest quest for intellectual self-improvement guaranteed diligent crafting of thoughtful responses to works read (Darnton, 1986; Rose, 2001). Can this be equated with the thrown-off, ill-punctuated, and syntactically garbled one-line Amazon customer review? Or a reader review that fundamentally misunderstands the aims or genre of a particular book?

By extension, the sheer scale of data about online reading forces scholars to rethink their default reliance on textual analysis in dealing with evidence of historical reading practices and to explore the potential of alternative research methodologies. This transition has already occurred among scholars of late twentieth-century reading, who have capitalized on the fact that their reading subjects are still alive, and hence potentially available for interrogation. Such scholars have made extensive use of social science research methods such as surveys, focus groups, interviewing, participant observation, and discourse analysis to give greater nuance to studies of reading groups, mass reading events (MREs), and literary festivals (Radway, 1984; Hartley, 2001; Long, 2003; Crone and Towheed, 2011; Fuller and Rehberg Sedo, 2012, 2013; Weber, 2015; Murray and Weber, 2017). Yet such social science methods, while innovative for book history, themselves come with built-in limitations. While MREs such as those based on the "One Book, One Community" model frequently incorporate a digital component, they are nevertheless primarily live and embodied in their conception (Fuller and Rehberg Sedo, 2012: 246). This fact makes them different in kind from solely digitally based reading formations. Interviewing and surveys transfer awkwardly to such born-digital environments and, faced with a body of readers as vast as Amazon's customer reviewers pool, such tools may prove impossible to implement. Equally problematically, bulk accounts of reading experiences online may either not warrant close textual analysis (too brief, too poorly expressed) or the sheer scale of records is beyond the capacity of any individual researcher to close-read.

With the preferred research methods of both comfortably historical and late twentieth-century "contemporary" reading researchers coming up short in attempting to adequately comprehend digitally based reading, digital humanities (DH) research methods and tools seem the natural alternative. What larger patterns might "distant reading" of online reading data reveal?[16] Possible DH tools include data visualization software (network diagrams, word clouds, graphs of user traffic, sentiment-analysis programs) which have the advantage of being often largely automated, off-the-shelf products (Gruzd and Rehberg Sedo, 2012; Finn, 2012, 2013; Driscoll, 2015). There are also the various cumulative overview functions built into commercial reading platforms themselves (Amazon's mean number of star-reviews for a title; Kindle's average pages of a title actually read; the Kobo "Reading Life" app's reading-rate calculator, and so forth) (Rowberry, 2016, 2017).

However, there is an inherent risk of naïve positivism in any rush to adopt DH methods and tools to comprehend new reading formations—as though the social sciences allure of quantification automatically generates a higher truth claim than the more traditional humanities mode of qualitative analysis. A second concern is the various weaknesses in the design of the DH tools themselves, such as sentiment-analysis software's tin ear for irony or sarcasm (Driscoll, 2015: 865). Finally, humanities scholars should be wary of unconsciously internalizing what James Marcus has termed Amazon's "Culture of Metrics."[17] Certainly we want to avail ourselves of the various measuring systems that the online migration of reading makes possible, but while retaining a critical perspective on them. Undue focus on metrics is still, after all, a form of textual analysis—just on a mass scale and looking at big-picture trends rather than the individual reader's detailed account. It does not question the institutional structures that shape reading online, nor the culture of minute self-surveillance and rendering of personal data for corporate ends which is hardwired into the design of such interfaces. In corporate-hosted online reading ventures, surveillance is rendered so normative as to be virtually invisible. Book historians may well want to make use of such rich datasets, but not to the extent that we passively accept how they have been generated or acquiesce in the culture of corporate data mining. Even in the age of putatively paperless reading, we need to watch that we don't lose sight of the forest in our scrutiny of the trees.

Moreover, we need to be alert to the degree of readerly performativity involved in online reading reports. Granted, marginalia or diary notes, and certainly discussion of one's reading in correspondence, were also acts of self-fashioning and literary display, but these are dwarfed in scale by the potentially global audience for acts of readerly performance in digital media. As in all online identity debates, the disembodied nature of the medium raises doubts as to the authenticity of reader self-descriptions and responses to texts (Smith and Watson, 2014). Have the books displayed on a Goodreads member's on-site bookshelf even been read or have we reached the virtual equivalent of the apocryphal nouveau-riche businessman furnishing his library with books ordered by the foot? Rumors have long abounded on Internet message boards that Amazon's top-ranked book reviewers do not actually read all the works they review or are merely pseudonymous smokescreens for a veritable factory of drone reviewers. Former Amazon Literary Editor James Marcus's memoir *Amazonia* (2004) is again illuminating on the subject of online readerly performativity, specifically on how gaming the system has been evident from virtually the inception of the "authentic" Amazon customer review in 1997. Marcus, as a professional literary critic, was clearly not predisposed to support Amazon's celebration of amateur "expertise." He notes that Harriet Klausner, for many years Amazon's highest-ranked reviewer with an astonishing thirty-one thousand reviews, excelled in producing bulk reviews rather than insightful ones, and he decries this mistaking of quantity for quality: "A reminder: art is not a popularity contest. Taste, talent, and discrimination have nothing to do with numbers. Case closed" (226).[18] In book historians' justifiable enthusiasm to embrace troves of online data promising to reveal what real readers, en masse, actually think of their reading material, we need to guard against credulously accepting reader accounts at face value.

Finally, there is the problematic issue of such sites' cultivation of data for commercial purposes. Reading historians often convey the excitement of unearthing the hitherto neglected archive of a particularly active and eloquent reader, giving the sense of earlier sources for the history of reading having lain largely untouched—virgin academic territory (Darnton, 1986: 6). Compare this to the situation of the scholar of digital reading who is often working with data sets with the admitted advantages of being both freely available and globally accessible, but which have been curated and frequently designed from inception for commercial purposes, and whose continued existence depends to a greater or lesser extent on their continued financial utility (Barnett, 2014: 160). In this sense, commercial considerations permeate not only production and circulation of books (as book historians have been reminding literary critics for decades) but also saturate the responses of contemporary online readers. It is an uncomfortable realization, as book historians have, perhaps unconsciously, often regarded reading as the least commercially inflected phase of the communication circuit: once a book is actually sold to the reader, literary communication was thought to largely retire from the commercial realm to that of private communion. Yet, there can be no bracketing off of readers' aesthetic responses from commercial considerations when emotional rapport (between book and reader, between reader and author, or between readers) is itself the currency of most online communities, and hence invests such websites with commercial value.[19]

Intervention of Interpretive Communities or Other Readers during the Reading Act

In their attempt to dislodge commonsense assumptions that reading is a solitary affair, book historians have seized upon evidence of inter-reader textual negotiation and sociability such as glossing in medieval manuscripts and marginalia in printed codices. Marginalia may have been comparatively rare in the print-culture era, usually confined to one or at most a handful of prior readers' interventions as recorded in annotated secondhand or library copies (Barnett, 2015: 11). But inter-reader communication was almost the norm in pre-Gutenbergian Western manuscript cultures through practices of scribal marginalia and monastic glossing (Finkelstein and McCleery, 2013: 108). The fact highlights yet another way in which digital culture more closely resembles pre-print textual affordances. Media historian Thomas Pettitt has popularized this idea of digital culture revitalizing a preexistent, collaborative mindset through the phrase "the Gutenberg parenthesis," with its understanding of print protocols as medium-specific, not transhistorical, bookish norms (2007). The appeal of such material evidence for book history has lain in its demonstration that readerly interpretation is not formed in isolation and *then* communicated, but is itself constituted dialogically. Debate over interpretation stands revealed as ongoing throughout the course of reading, making interpretation a more thoroughly socialized process for participating readers.

In networked reading, the interactive exception represented by marginalia becomes the new norm; online readerly interpretation is not formed in relative isolation and *then* communicated, but is itself formed dialogically at the moment of encountering the text (Tosca and Pedersen, 2015: 194). The difference here between print or manuscript reading cultures, on one hand, and networked reading cultures, on the other, is thus one of degree rather than of kind. Mass readerly annotation of digital texts takes the readerly intervention associated with codex marginalia and amplifies it immeasurably by the scale of digital-hosted reading communities (Rowberry, 2016: 215). As Ted Striphas points out, one's marginalia and annotations have always been visible to other readers with access to individual physical books in one's library, but with the advent of reading online "a reader's private scrawl is no longer secreted away in the odd corner of a random volume but is instead archived in third-party databases, where it is identifiable and accessible" (2010a: 311). The socialized reading experience of an embodied, intimate

community passing around a book in sequence is here scaled up to global proportions. Potentially, it holds out the analytically enticing prospect of a multilayered,
palimpsestic archive of readerly discussion around a given text.

Online book clubs make the social determination of textual meaning traceable
in ways not readily available even to researchers of in-person book clubs. For example, the social networking site Goodreads hosts over twenty thousand book
clubs, which a member joins only after reading the group's description, aims,
preferred genres, and community rules (Kaufman, 2013).[20] Members may vote
on which book to read next or a work may be selected by the group's moderator,
but before a reader has even encountered the first page of a particular text an entire filter of attitudes, assumptions, and preferred reading protocols has already
been communicated by the interpretive community. This is in addition to the
more diffuse filters of authorial reputation, cover design paratext, and publisher-
generated publicity, which typically intervene in a reader's first encounter with a
book, and which in all likelihood have already influenced the book club's own
anointed opinion influencers.

The social nature of online interpretation even threatens to become intrusive.
With digital reading devices and their proprietary software, the interpretive community morphs from cheerleading squad and periodic interlocutor to potential
pest, with individual readers perhaps having to chisel away previous readers'
annotations and encrustations of the text to clear some space for their own textual
encounter. For example, the market-dominating e-reader, Amazon's Kindle, has
since 2010 promoted socially interventionist reading through its Kindle Highlights function, which enables readers to bookmark, highlight, and annotate the
digital text as well as to consult a built-in dictionary. Kindles now by default display other readers' ten most popular highlights and notes in a given text (the
feature can, however, be turned off).[21] Further, by signing up for "Public Notes" a
reader makes their annotations accessible to anyone who "follows" them, Twitter-
style (Barnett, 2014: 151–52).[22] The two features have been combined for an even
more precise rendering of mass reading practices: "Amazon displays Popular
Highlights and Public Notes by combining the highlights and notes of all Kindle
customers and identifying the passages with the most highlights and notes."[23]
These are displayed on each Kindle book's home page, thus forming part of each
e-book's paratextual wrapping. The Highlights function's noting that "[X number
of] other people highlighted this part of the book" calls to mind that subgroup of
codex readers who have long resented a previous reader's marginalia tarnishing
the purity of their initial reading encounter, but here amplified massively by the
scale of networked communication.

One commentator has described the Highlights function as "intellectual voyeurism (at least at the aggregate level)" and an active disincentive to read the whole book, instead encouraging skipping from one much-annotated passage to the next (Tucker, 2010; see also Baron, 2015: 114). It is reminiscent of a character in Whit Stillman's droll filmic comedy of manners *Metropolitan* (1990), who claims to prefer reading literary criticism to the classics themselves because "that way you get both the novelists' ideas as well as the critics' thinking." By analogy, Kindle Highlights facilitates readers skipping to the most highlighted and annotated sections of a work (typically in a book's first half) and eavesdropping on other readers' interpretations as substitutes for reading the text in its entirety.

Clearly, there are also significant privacy issues in terms of Amazon knowing not only which books individuals have purchased, and read, but exactly which sections they have highlighted and even the contents of their annotations (Alter, 2012; Di Leo, 2012: 2, 30; Striphas, 2010a: 302–04, 308; Baron, 2015: 130; Barnett, 2015: 16–17; Davis, 2015: 515, 521; Tosca and Pedersen, 2015: 197; Rowberry, 2016: 213). Beginning in August 2016, Kindle Highlights could additionally be synced with Goodreads book clubs (also Amazon-owned) so that members of the same book club could read each other's notes and highlights simultaneously.[24] This opens the possibility of real-time discussion of the book *within* the book itself, rather than (as previously on Goodreads) via an ancillary platform, thus binding interpretive commentary and the original text into an ever more intimate relationship.

A text that has been much studied as part of educational curricula, whether at high school or college level, can thus collectively become massively annotated and highlighted, and the reading preferences of dominant interpretative communities consequently web the text, even for readers who are not reading for formal educational purposes. Equally, there is immense potential for long-running hermeneutic conflict around particularly charged texts—such as foundational religious texts, Charles Darwin's *On the Origin of Species*, *The Communist Manifesto*, or *Mein Kampf*—to play out in the digital reading domain. This could be to the extent that a reader wanting a "fresh" encounter with the text cannot help but be aware of the webs of interpretative politics and rhetorical conflict that surround a particular text and its authorized meaning. Such webs manifest not, as previously, at a diffuse socio-rhetorical level but concretely and immediately in the display of the text itself. While all texts come packaged with hermeneutically influential paratext (even in e-book editions),[25] it is another order of intervention to be badgered by highly invested interpretative communities at the very moment of trying to decipher a book's content for oneself.

Advertisement for Kobo's "Reading Life" app showing various reading metrics offered as well as a range of "award" badges.

Taking social reading still further is e-reader rival Kobo's "Reading Life" app, also launched in 2010. This allows users to post directly to their Facebook and Twitter accounts what they are reading, their favorite passages and reviews, as well as generating "Reading Stats" (such as the percentage of books in one's Kobo library read; peak reading times; page-turns per hour, and so forth).[26] Various "awards" are also on offer: "Deep Thinker" (for adding notes to a book); "Inverted Comma" (for adding highlights); "Social Butterfly" (for adding ten shares to Facebook); as well as "secret" awards, the criteria for which are undisclosed. The interface design closely resembles those of wearable fitness-tracking devices. These similarly proffer various badges for achieving a certain step-count or number of active minutes per day, and dangle these at strategic intervals to keep users engaged with the device once the initial novelty of self-tracking has worn off. It is therefore no exaggeration to cast Reading Life as a sort of Fitbit for the life of the mind. Both utilize the dashboard display that gives users an overview of their interaction with the device, and both encourage at every turn sharing of one's personal data with others in one's social network of fellow device owners. This sharing is usually encouraged along aggressively competitive lines, introducing a clear element of rivalrous social display. Indeed, Reading Life's tagline—"Read.

Discover. Connect. Share"—implicitly posits digital sharing as the logical end-point of any reading experience:[27] reading undertaken in isolation and without the approbation of an audience appears almost not to have been worth the effort.[28] There is a crucial shift discernible here between the social group to which the reader reports back at the *end* of reading a work (such as a F2F book club) or at preset intervals (such as a university tutorial discussing a lengthy Victorian novel over several weeks), to the interpretive community which is ever-present during the act of reading itself—metaphorically perched on the reader's shoulder reminding them to note this, be wary of that. It looms as the literary equivalent of the backseat driver from hell.

Various commentators have rightly pointed out that social reading apps of this kind are "'gamifying' the reading experience" (Ray Murray and Squires, 2013: 14; see also Barnett, 2014: 159). Such technologies also draw reading into a particularly Web 2.0 mode of minute self-management and data generation, whereby the smallest details of one's daily routine are recorded, calibrated, and offered up for data mining by commercial entities who are then free to sell this data to third parties, such as publishers.[29] Despite the clear commercial intent of the device creators, and the manifold privacy implications of deeply personal data being made widely available, such micro self-surveillance is continually presented as personally liberating. An individual's leisure activity is thereby converted into voluntary labor, adding value to corporate interests (Nakamura, 2013: 241–42; Nelles, 2013: 51–52). After all, a tool such as Goodreads' book recommendation algorithm increases its accuracy ("user-friendliness") in direct proportion to the number of users entering vast amounts of personal data relating to their libraries, book lists, and social networks. Such unpaid labor constitutes an individual's performance of self-improvement, whether intellectually or physically, for a presumably admiring audience.

Distributing Critical Authority in "BOOK CLUB 2.0"[30]

"Intra-group communication" between readers on a mass scale is clearly a key characteristic of online book clubs and has also been core to the appeal of mass-media–sponsored book clubs with affiliate websites, such as the industry-changing Oprah's Book Club and its UK counterpart, Richard and Judy's Book Club (Long, 2003: 202; Rehberg Sedo, 2011a: 7; Baron, 2015: 123). Online literary culture has "reconfigured traditional notions of cultural authority" through the democratizing impact of Web 2.0 technologies and their associated dispersal of cultural capital from the few to the many (Rehberg Sedo, 2011: 7). In fact, the single most striking aspect of socially networked reading is that ordinary readers feel entitled to cast critical judgment, for a global audience, on what they are reading. This, rather than the content or prevalent tone of particular judgments passed, is the most significant characteristic of the online reading phenomenon.

The distributed cultural authority on display in online book clubs is dramatically illustrated by the 2009 mass-reading experiment Infinite Summer (IS). This online book club was established by blogger Matthew Baldwin to support readers through David Foster Wallace's critically acclaimed, sprawling, infamously labyrinthine postmodern novel *Infinite Jest* (1996). Over twelve weeks of the (northern-hemisphere) summer, readers were invited to tackle the thousand-plus-page tome at a rate of seventy-five pages per week (plus endnotes, plus footnotes to the endnotes) and to report back to the website on their progress. Established in part as wry acknowledgment of *Infinite Jest*'s status as an all-too-frequently-unread bookshelf marker of aspirations to cultural capital, the project was conceived also in tribute to Wallace, who had committed suicide the previous year (Peltz, 2009).

Striking within IS is the emphasis on readerly egalitarianism and the implicit demotion of interpretive-community authority figures; no attempt is made to lay down the law about interpreting Wallace's signature work. In fact, Baldwin flatly states under the online heading "The Rules" "there ain't none" and then happily undercuts this with a proviso about not posting spoilers, conceding "So, apparently, there *is* at least one rule."[31] This scrupulously non-hierarchical stance persists despite the fact that there *are* clearly hierarchies built into the project's design. An initial four organizer-selected "Guides" were appointed "to promote and facilitate discussion" by providing weekly progress reports,[32] in addition to a diverse array of around twenty one-off commentators and essayists (for example, young adult author John Green, digital literature scholar Kathleen Fitzpatrick, and Wallace's editor at Little, Brown, Michael Pietsch). The non-prescriptive choice of terminology is apt, as the Guides, all Wallace novices, frequently confess their sense of intimidation and even bafflement at the book's virtuosic vocabulary, multilinear plot, and (in)famously proliferating endnotes. The effect is to add to the rather appealingly disorganized, improvisational, anti-authoritarian "we're all in this together" tone pervading the whole interpretive undertaking.

IS became, to the delight of its originators and Wallace's editor,[33] a transmedia event with manifestations that quickly escaped the loose confines of the online forum to spawn "all over the web":[34] organizers, but also self-starting participants, established an official Facebook page, Tumblr blog, LiveJournal community, Goodreads and Shelfari groups, and Twitter hashtag (Fitzpatrick, 2012: 193). The archived webforum remains, however, the best encapsulation of this dynamic online reading experiment, with reader posts on their progress, sorted by

page counts and helpfully auto-generated percentage-completed tallies, plus discussion threads about particularly intriguing or confusing aspects of the text.
Despite the seventy-five-pages-a-week chronology built into the original project
design, Infinite Summer persists as an online reading resource: Baldwin stated,
"Someone could read 'Infinite Jest' a year or five years from now, following along
with the site as they do so, and feel as if they are part of the community despite
the temporal separation" (Coscarelli, 2009). This, six years later, is precisely what
I did in order to begin writing this chapter. Striking is how many people partici-
pated in the discussions and the relatively high level of readerly engagement with
such a challenging text. Rank-pulling and importation of academic literary-critical
authority are noticeably minimal. In the second week of discussion participant
"Rich C" introduced the work of Jean-François Lyotard, complete with a lengthy
quote, into a discussion of whether Wallace's work can be considered "postmodern," but this very postgraduate-sounding intervention was more the exception
than the rule in the forum, and was taken up by only one of the week's many
other participants.[35] Similarly, a passing reference by participant "Miguel" to Der-
ridean deconstruction in week four was elaborated upon at length (complete with
suggested further reading), but only after an explicit request from another forum
participant to "please either explain or post a link to a good explanation-page."[36]
Thus, while reading online renders the presence of interpretative communities
more intrusive than previously, the authority of such communities is comparatively diluted by the networked structure. Other readers become more insistently
vocal, but their dictates are simultaneously more open to dispute.

The modes of readerly interpretation on display in IS are various. But a recurrent motif is reading the novel through the lens of Wallace's then recent suicide.
Such an interpretative bent has the potential to lend the mass-reading exercise a
rather ghoulish, Kurt Cobain-esque quality, as though reading the work might
bring a reader closer to its author, for whom many IS participants express near-
veneration. Repeatedly, participating readers confess to having felt sadness upon
learning of Wallace's death, although they did not know him personally.[37] This
might be easily dismissed by academically trained readers as naïve biographical
fallacy, and a product of this particular online reading group's establishment in
conscious homage to Wallace. However, reading *Infinite Jest* through the guise of
authorial biography has become almost inescapable given that the text dwells at
such length on the topic of suicide. Aside from the teasing allusions to *Hamlet*,
particularly in the title but also sprinkled obliquely throughout the text, there is
the fact that several of the novel's main characters have either committed suicide
and are presented in flashback or appear as ghosts/hallucinations (for example,

the protagonist's father James O. Incandenza, aka Himself or The Mad Stork, as well as minor character Eric Clipperton), or they attempt suicide (Joelle van Dyne, aka Madame Psychosis, aka the Prettiest Girl of All Time, or P.G.O.A.T.), or they are in the grip of addictions to various substances that blur the line between willed erasure of one's map (to adopt Wallace parlance) and indifference as to the consequences (such as Don Gately and Gene Fackelmann). The book's core thematic preoccupations led IS participants to discuss addiction and suicide at length, not only in relation to *Infinite Jest* and its author's biography, but also in their own lives. In a week four post on the topic of suicide, one of the regular Guides confessed to having "some experience with the whole horrible concept,"[38] and in week five guest "infinitedetox" posts about using *Infinite Jest* to help him through drug withdrawal.[39] Such acts of personal sharing generated waves of empathetic and affirmative responses from forum participants.[40]

These contributions illustrate the common reading-group mode of reading fiction as therapy. Much analysis of Oprah's Book Club has focused, usually critically, on her positing of literary fiction as an emotional archive through which one might rifle for role models in overcoming personal adversity (Travis, 2003; Farr, 2005; Farr and Harker, 2008; Striphas, 2009; Fitzpatrick, 2012). The application of the bibliotherapy model to *Infinite Jest* is ironic, given that so much of the novel is taken up with describing and fondly skewering the group-therapy model of Alcoholics Anonymous, the original twelve-step program. In fairness, forum participants using the book as a biblio-therapeutic exemplum are keenly aware of this irony: the title of infinitedetox's post is a direct reference to the Boston AA group frequented by character Don Gately. Intriguingly, the IS webforum as a whole displays a notable lack of condemnation of such readerly protocols from forum participants more schooled in the typically Olympian distance and theoretical self-consciousness of academic literary studies. Despite *Infinite Jest* being a book more readily taken up in academe than the selection of a typical suburban book club, in Infinite Summer a plurality of reading strategies and interpretative protocols were simultaneously on offer, with participants seemingly disinclined to dictate which modes of readerly interpretation were legitimate and which were intellectually beyond the pale. Guide Kevin Guilfoile, while declaring himself in no way a "radical relativist when it comes to critical theory," acknowledged the multiplicity of readerly interpretations in his first post, in this sense establishing the rule that, on IS, there *are* no interpretative rules: "Readers bring their intellect to the page just as the author does and each reader brings different knowledge and experience and history and bias. Each reader understands the book a bit differently."[41] Self-reflexively, and presumably unconsciously, IS thus came to mirror uncannily *Infinite Jest*'s description of Boston AA as "a benign anarchy": "No regs, no musts, only love and support and the occasional humble suggestion born of shared experience. A non-authoritarian, dogma-free movement" (1996: 356).

The mass-access architecture of the IS webforum finds its critical reflection in such ecumenical reading strategies: authority is distributed both technologically and discursively, in a mutually complementary and self-perpetuating dynamic. In online book clubs the idea of a singular valid interpretation of a work appears to have been thoroughly delegitimized, not only by several generations of post-structuralist-educated readers coming online but also by the self-evident fact that an abundance of competing interpretations for any given work is available at a keystroke. Even were singular interpretations of literary texts to become once again intellectually fashionable, imposing them would be a practical impossibility in a networked world.[42]

De-/Re-Materializing of Text

Digital media always seem to carry material undertows, however much they disavow them. Even in Infinite Summer where there was no stipulation about which edition of *Infinite Jest* readers should consume, many readers reminisced, unprompted, about the material characteristics of the work as they first encountered it: its place on their bookshelves; the sun-faded spine; whether read in hardback or paperback; the way their arms ached from holding the mammoth book while reading propped on their elbows. In an online reading environment, readers seem driven to introduce these talismanic corporeal and material experiences in spite of the forum's uniquely disembodied format—perhaps even because of it. Such observations underline Danielle Fuller and DeNel Rehberg Sedo's contention that "there is a special place that reading occupies—and that the codex book maintains—in an era of media digitization" (2014: 18).

With IS, readers were typically reading *Infinite Jest* in codex format or on standalone e-readers and *then* convening online. Yet digital reading also increasingly takes place entirely in digital environments, as explored in the preceding discussion of Kindle and Kobo e-readers. These "purely" digital reading environments are also irreducibly material: the haptic qualities of the reading device, the format and interface of the screen display, the interactive affordances of particular e-readers, and aural possibilities such as text-to-speech read-aloud functions all profoundly influence a reader-cum-listener-cum-audience-member's consumption of a text. This unavoidably material and situated nature of reading in digital environments has been noted by media and cultural studies scholars, as where Lisa Nakamura notes of Goodreads that "the virtual form of these literary conversations seemed to invite information about where and how the book had been consumed" (2013: 241). Yet the connection with foundational work in book history, like that of Roger Chartier, has rarely been drawn. This false disciplinary divide wrongly suggests a semi-invisible line populated on one side by book historians who investigate print culture or digital tools for examining print-born artifacts, while on the other side media, communication, and cultural studies scholars, along with electronic literature experts, freely lay claim to born-digital texts.[43] Such an intellectual dichotomy impoverishes both disciplines and needs bridging: digitally enabled reading is a profoundly, if perhaps counterintuitively, *material* process, and book history's insights into the technological and social consequences of the moment of textual consumption are more, not less, relevant in the digital literary sphere.

The most dramatic manifestation of the return of the materially repressed in the digital literary sphere is the online community BookCrossing. Here the particular thrill is that readers are holding the very same copy of a book that has passed through numerous prior readers' hands and hence exerts unique, auratic power. The online book exchange-cum-reading group BookCrossing was established by software developer Ron Hornbaker in 2001 and describes itself as "the world's library."[44] A book is registered with the site and receives an identifying code ("BCID"). The "owner" then gifts it by leaving it in a public place (typically in a protective Ziploc bag) with a note about BookCrossing, inviting others to read the book and add their thoughts to the volume's online journal so that previous readers may track the progress of "their" copy across cities and countries. Typical identifying slips read "I'm Free! I'm not lost! Please pick me up, read me, and help me with my journey! (See inside)." Once a finder ("catcher") logs into the site and leaves a journal entry, the original book donor is automatically notified of a "successful release" (bird metaphors appear pervasive).

BookCrossing's organizers avidly stoke this desire for material connection with embodied readers in an increasingly dematerialized, virtual world (even though the website's very concept of course depends upon networked technology). One way in which this is achieved is by providing templates for BookCrossers to customize their own unique BookCrossing labels so that finders will be able to identify a book as released by a particularly prolific BookCrosser.[45] This works to reinforce the site creators' claim that the ultimate "mission" of BookCrossing is to initiate and sustain conversations among bibliophiles worldwide: "The site remains a fun way to track and share books while connecting people at deeper levels using books as the architecture and glue to facilitate the Great Conversation."[46] The claim has some justification: the website boasts around 1.7 million users and over twelve million registered books.[47] The book with the most "hops" has over six hundred entries, though numbers fall off sharply to over one hundred immediately after that.[48]

Membership is markedly international, especially in Continental Europe and outside the Anglosphere; the website claims activity in 132 countries and the site is readable in fifteen languages.[49] The BookCrossing community's most active member, "countofmonte," has registered a jaw-dropping eighty-five thousand–plus books, putting even the implausibly prolific Harriet Klausner in the shade.[50] Unusually among online reading formations, BookCrossing sponsors international face-to-face conventions (non-official "UnConventions" are also publicized on the site).[51] At these events BookCrossers get together socially, attend workshops, and stage mass book releases.[52] There is an echo here of Lynne McNeill's concept of "real virtuality" (a piquant inversion of the more familiar "virtual reality") whereby online networks manifest in real-world occurrences, such as flash mobs (2012: 90, 96). In the realm of real virtuality, the boundaries between physical participant, traveling object, and the virtual domain in which the object's itinerary is recorded become increasingly blurred. McNeill states that, in Book-Crossing, "the object has become an avatar for the participant" (2007: 290). In a manner reminiscent of the contemporary writers' festivals examined in chapter 3, BookCrossing posits the respective virtual and embodied domains not as separate spheres so much as permeable, complementary forums for socialized literary activities.

BookCrossing contains links to book retailers but not advertising and is minimally commercial, in marked distinction to Amazon. Yet even on Amazon, where ostensibly dematerialized Kindle versions of books are touted at every turn, customer reviews frequently evince a conception of the literary work so resolutely embodied as to gladden the heart of book historians. To take as an example the book with which this discussion began, Karl Ove Knausgaard's *A Man in Love,* several of the reviewers discuss the material form of their book copy: lamenting the UK paperback as "sadly a typical example of current British book-making, ugly airport novel, bulky, cheap paper, horrid meaningless design, with a catchpenny title and huge 'international bestseller' headline,"[53] or bemoaning like a persnickety bibliographer the "cheap binding (glued not stitched on a 500 page novel)."[54] One customer reviewer of the fourth volume in Knausgaard's *My Struggle* series goes so far as to post pictures of his US hardback's detached spine and miscut pages under the heading "Archipelago Books=Poor Quality Control" so that potential purchasers are forewarned.[55] The virtual book club, always threatening to float dematerialized into the digital ether, has responded by insisting upon the physical, material, and bodily incarnations of the reading act. Paradoxically, it underscores to amateur readers the specificity of reading encounters at precisely the point in time when this key tenet of book history might, at first glance, appear to have been rendered technologically redundant.

Commodifying Reading Community

Book history's gadfly role vis-à-vis mainstream literary studies has been to remind colleagues that literary culture is pervaded by commercial concerns and that, far from tarnishing our encounters with books, such commercial contexts have often proven enabling, or at least they warrant analytical scrutiny. But the reader's commercial utility has generally been seen as stopping at the point of purchase: whether a book was actually read has long been a matter of publisher indifference, largely quarantining the act of reading itself from commercial scrutiny and leaving the book historian free to postulate about interpretive communities and resistant reading practices. Compare this to the era of online book clubs, which range along a continuum from reading communities grafted onto primarily commercial concerns (like Amazon), through reading groups that differentiate discussion and commercial agenda with varying degrees of strictness (such as Goodreads, though it is now Amazon-owned), to avowedly non-commercial book blogs which trumpet the freedom of opinion underpinned by their independence from advertiser and publisher revenues (such as *DoveGreyReader Scribbles*).[56] At the commercial extreme of this reading spectrum stands the website BookMovement, established in 2003 as an international book-club clearinghouse. Readers are encouraged to register their book club with the site via the lures of reading-group scheduling software, discussion guides, and online forums. The site then sells user data to third parties, such as publishers interested in connecting with specific reading demographics, whether for market research or advance publicity purposes.[57] Banner advertising, "sponsored books" giveaways, and "buy" buttons for multiple market-dominating book retailers reinforce the website's thoroughly commercial orientation. Publishers and retailers are here offered valuable mass data on a title's or genre's popularity, demographic appeal, geographic uptake, and rate of book-club adoption.[58] As with the conscientious self-tracking encouraged by Kindle and Kobo reading apps, readers' participation in BookMovement represents voluntarily rendered labor in the service of a commercially constituted and corporate-maintained community. For scholars of the digital literary sphere, ethical questions about utilizing mass reading data again rear their head: need a researcher using online reading data be an active member of that online community, and should they gain the informed consent of other members to participate in any research project utilizing their content (Rehberg Sedo, 2011b: 104–5)? What evidentiary status should we accord such reader comments given that they have been elicited, curated, combed, and sold within a thoroughly commercial environment, and will cease to be available should their commercial utility fade? In crunching such data for elaborate visualizations are we distracting ourselves from the urgent task of crafting political economy–informed critiques of how such websites elicit user data in the first place? A particularly unsettling characteristic of the digital literary sphere is that its very porosity leaves us unable to study it at arm's length.

Conclusion

Regardless of the exact proportion of reading that takes place in offline and on-line environments, the overall trend is clear: reading has become thoroughly en-meshed with digital culture, and this pattern is only set to continue as the twenty-first century unfolds. My aim here has not been to somehow pit book history and media and cultural studies against each other but, rather, to catalyze intellectual exchange between them and to demonstrate cross-pollination across disciplinary, institutional, and departmental boundaries. The burgeoning world of digitally enabled reading is too fascinatingly complex to do without either the materialist orientation and knowledge of historical precedent brought to the table by book

Christophe Vorlet's 2010 cartoon accompanying the *New York Times* article "Yes, People Still Read, but Now It's Social" by Steven Johnson. Reproduced by permission of Christophe Vorlet

historians, or the familiarity with networked architectures, transmedia exchanges, and cultural theory characterizing media, communication, and cultural studies.

For book history as a discipline there is the exciting prospect of masses of new data about readers, generated by readers, becoming freely and globally available. However, this material cannot simply be appended en masse to the discipline's existing theoretical and methodological schemas. Online reading environments fundamentally challenge several of book history's most closely held and hard-won precepts: in digital reading formations interpretive communities are more intrusive than ever before, yet their hermeneutic authority is more open to question; texts become, counterintuitively, *more* rather than less materialized; and the quality of ballooning readers' reports is rendered newly suspect by self-conscious, real-time performance, competitive logics, and commercial utility. For book history to do justice to these transformative changes it will be necessary to overcome the discipline's default retrospective orientation. Too often book history has been like one half of a rather delightful 2010 *New York Times* cartoon by Christophe Vorlet encapsulating current reading practices: on one side a gleefully multi-tasking octopus uses its various tentacles to simultaneously read a book, peruse a Kindle and an iPad, tap on a laptop computer, write a letter in longhand, watch television, and listen to an iPod—while surrounded by a flurry of Post-it Notes. Meanwhile, a neighboring octopus, his attention and all eight tentacles ascetically focused on a single codex volume, looks on in eye-rolling disdain.[59] This latter stance has too often been ours, book historians and literary scholars alike: tolerant of rather than embracing digital reading developments. Such an attitude does a disservice to the epoch-changing significance and intellectual piquancy of the era through which we are living. In sum, it is through cross-disciplinary research that we will fully test the implications of Robert Darnton's discipline-founding claim that "reading has history. It was not always and everywhere the same." Logically, reading thus also has a *present*, with its own particular characteristics and dynamics, and this present deserves the full scholarly energies we can bring to understanding it.

Accounting for Digital Paratext

In 1999, US electronic literature author and theorist Robert Coover delivered a keynote address to the Digital Arts and Culture conference with the rather elegiac title "Literary Hypertext: The Passing of the Golden Age." In it Coover appeared to encourage his audience of fellow hypertext enthusiasts, somewhat bruised from the failure of their early-1990s predictions to find mainstream acceptance and buffeted by successive waves of technological obsolescence, to shift their critical gaze from the diminishing number of avant-garde electronic literary texts being produced to the electronic literature movement's successful "embodiment in institutions" (1999): "So, does this mean that literature is dying on the Web? On the contrary. If anything, true to the nature of silver ages, we are into a mini-boom as electronic magazines and prizes proliferate, new electronic publishers emerge, organizations spring up to develop online readerships and bring them into contact with the new writers. No, though most of the world's literati continue to shy away from this new, increasingly dominant medium, and so continue to drift further and further from the center, the new literary mainstream is being carved here."[1]

The transcript of Coover's speech reads as a beautifully written clarion call for literary scholars to embrace online manifestations of literary culture with the curiosity and open-mindedness they deserve. If it was so intended, it was premature and remains to this day unanswered. For literary studies as a discipline has, in the almost two decades since, displayed a distinctly standoffish and tepid response to digital literary phenomena. Perhaps it is the very nature of the digital literary sphere—so large, so amorphous, so protean, and chaotically decentralized—that discourages academic scrutiny. Certainly, mainstream critics concede, bookish culture exists online, but it seems presently too hard to get an analytical handle on to have registered at the center of literary studies.

Faced with this current technological and academic state of play, the present study in its introduction opted to structure its investigation using a matrix model. This was designed to synthesize a vast range of phenomena and actors into dual axes of literary processes (authorship, publishing, cultural policy outreach, reviewing, and reading) and specific digital platforms (websites and other digital tools adopted by interested agents). With a nod to Bourdieusian "field" theory, this matrix model attempts to combine a degree of intellectual scaffolding to enhance analytical clarity while allowing for the uncertain, constantly mutating nature of its object of study.

The key constitutive element of the digital literary sphere as analyzed throughout the chapters of this volume is what I collectively term "digital paratext." The range encompassed by this term is enormous, but its various manifestations have in common a focus on literary interests and their existence in a digital environment. Thus we can include in this category the various authorial blogs, vlogs, podcasts, Twitter messages, and Facebook and Instagram posts circulated by writers as part of their public performance of authorship, as examined in chapter 1. These activities complement and at various points intersect with more marketing- and publicity-focused texts such as the book trailers and blog tours examined in chapter 2, which may be more often publisher-generated. Chapter 3 broadened its analytical remit to examine the public life of literature as concretized in the phenomenon of writers' festivals, with their plethora of digitally archived author talks, panel sessions, digital storytelling experiments, and audience commentary. The participatory audience was also front and center in chapter 4's examination of digital reviewing culture, where readers' reviews, social cataloging profiles, litblogs, and booktuber videos attest to an insatiable hunger to engage esteemed creators and fellow bookish enthusiasts in global literary conversations. This consumer-oriented view of literary culture finds its fullest manifestation in chapter 5's concentrated focus on online reading formations, the publishers' websites that cater to them, and online businesses springing up specifically to convert readers' interactive enthusiasm into commercially serviceable buzz-generation.

Doing justice to the range and analytical implications of such a broad empirical domain has obliged this volume to range equally widely across differing humanities and social sciences frameworks: foremost book history (and especially its subset examining twenty-first-century developments), but also literary studies (including its outlier electronic literary studies),[2] (new) media studies (in particular the subfield of political economy of media), film and television studies, the loose mélange that is cultural studies, cultural sociology, and cultural policy, and even, in chapter 3's discussion of the implications of "liveness," theater and performance studies. Employing such diverse disciplinary approaches eclectically and on an as-needed basis accurately reflects the convergent nature of the digital literary sphere—in fact the digital literary sphere demands such an interdisciplinary mindset. But that is not to overlook the stark, and in many cases deeply entrenched, divisions that exist between these disciplines. Various of the traditions mentioned have histories of significant animosity; most have inherited separate institutional structures, disparate publication outlets, and divergent conference circuits, and—especially between literary and media studies—there exist deeply internalized preferences for the study of, respectively, text versus context. Thus the present volume attempts to straddle tectonic rifts between the humanities and social sciences over appropriate theoretical and methodological procedures.

It is to a large extent true that later twentieth-century tensions between literary studies and media and cultural studies over questions of cultural value have mostly subsided, but institutional and methodological differences, because less often clearly articulated and subjected to debate, have proven harder to overcome (Murray, 2016b). Given its relatively recent emergence and explicitly interdisciplinary self-conception, book history is the field within which this book would, if pressed, primarily locate itself. But this discussion aims to be in dialogue with developments across the range of humanities and social sciences disciplines mentioned above. At the most fundamental level, the present study questions whether these should in fact remain separate disciplines—a question to which this conclusion returns at its close.

There is a risk of any work analyzing the digital literary sphere beginning to date almost immediately (as this study surely will). In order to futureproof its analysis to the greatest extent possible, this book has deliberately focused not upon specific technological platforms (however modish) but on key literary processes: creation (regardless of whether the authorial figure is singular or plural); circulation (whether approached programmatically or virally serendipitous); and consumption (whether that stands at the endpoint of a communicative chain or is only fodder for further fan-fictional iterations of a text). These formerly discrete processes have become undeniably blurry at their boundaries in the Web 2.0 era, with much feedback and crossover between nodes, and certainly there is evidence of role elision. Nevertheless, some legacy book-industry structures remain and are likely to do so for the foreseeable future and hence retain analytical utility.

To return to Coover's rather preemptive announcement of a new literary mainstream online, we might ask whether the relative paucity of subsequent academic analyses of the digital literary sphere is attributable to academics fearing that any work on the topic will rapidly become obsolete in the face of technological change. Better, arguably, for one's professional prospects and citation rate to adopt a more cautious stance vis-à-vis the new developments. But such a protracted wait-and-see approach risks the academy as a whole being sidelined in a techno-social context in which the status of traditional cultural authority figures and the relative weight of their critical judgments are very much in play (as examined in chapter 4).

Literary academe (and the humanities more generally) cannot afford to sit this game out, wait until the dust settles, and then retrospectively consecrate a new canon of writing that has somehow emerged. By then our self-assumed role in the cultural conversation may well have been usurped and, worse, we will have ceded the opportunity to help shape an emergent literary environment. Given that a key theme of this volume has been the incremental commercialization and data harvesting of digital literary sphere activity, the academy may be one of the few places from which such a critique can still be mounted. The project of understanding the workings of the digital literary sphere is thus an urgent one with far-reaching implications.

"Mediated Paratext—A Use Inevitably Destined to Spread":[3]
Genette and Since

As the present conclusion places significant weight on the concept of digital paratext as an umbrella term for digital literary sphere phenomena, it is worth tracing the term's intellectual origins and current deployment. Gérard Genette was the first, in his groundbreaking study *Seuils* (1987), to bring sustained attention to the crucial role that paratextual "wrappings" play in mediating a literary work's initial reception and subsequent interpretation. This landmark study focused precisely on those bibliographical elements that mainstream literary scholars and historians, intent upon accessing the "wheat" of the text, had habitually disregarded as so much bookish "chaff": cover design, book series, dedications, prefaces, notes, and so forth. Paratexts constitute "a zone between text and off-text, a zone not only of transition but also of *transaction*: a privileged place of a pragmatics and a strategy, of an influence on the public, an influence that . . . is at the service of a better reception for the text and a more pertinent reading of it" (2; italics in the original). Genette's key concept of "paratext" was (in fine Structuralist style) itself taxonomically subdivided into *"peritext"* (encompassing the previously mentioned paratextual elements bound into the book copy) and *"epitext,"* denoting the broader social discussion of a book via printed reviews, broadcast interviews, in correspondence, and so forth (4–5, 344–45). In book history's avid uptake of Genette's peritextual elements—particularly since the work appeared in English translation as *Paratexts* in 1997—the more diffuse textual penumbra represented by epitext has been comparatively ignored. Adoption of the term by mainstream literary scholars or even by book historians has been infrequent. Rare exceptions to the general rule include Alexis Weedon, who notes that in online book retailing Genette's thresholds of interpretation (cover designs, front matter) find digital equivalents in features such as Amazon's "Look Inside" function (2007: 122). Similarly Laura Dietz classifies authors' statements about their motives for adopting a digital media presence as "epitext": "This statement of motive is a key tactic in the authorship of authorship" (2015: 202; see also 210). But it is curious that Genette's handy term has been so infrequently employed in book history or literary studies to date, as it is within the domain of epitext that we might usefully locate the constitutive elements of the digital literary sphere.

Intriguingly, Genette's paratextual ideas have recently become influential in a field almost unmentioned in his own work: screen studies. Jonathan Gray's monograph *Show Sold Separately* (2010) takes up Genette's concept of paratext to analyze the myriad additional, semiotically significant materials generated by the contemporary film and television industries: DVD bonus features, director's cuts, film trailers, TV promos, fan films, spoilers, and the like. Gray explicitly invokes Genette's own metaphor of the "airlock" to describe how such screenic paratexts function; constituting a liminal zone that is neither entirely within nor wholly outside the screen text, paratexts assist viewers in transitioning between one and the other "without too much respiratory difficulty" (hence the original title of Genette's book: "thresholds") (40; see also 25, 35, 117, 140). Their purpose is to habituate and acclimatize potential viewers to the creative content proper by cultivating appropriate viewing dispositions—communicating genre expectations, star billing, and critical plaudits (3, 6–8). Gray argues persuasively that screen studies must broaden its traditional object of analysis to account for the cultural pervasiveness of such screenic paratexts and their mediating role in preconditioning audiences' encounters with a screen text, particularly viewers' frequently decisive first encounter. In this argument Gray has been joined by fellow film and television scholars Paul Grainge and Catherine Johnson, whose *Promotional Screen Industries* (2015) similarly recuperates the traditionally disparaged category of promotional screen content for academic analysis. Such seemingly banal texts as advertisements, film trailers, television promos, credit sequences, station identifiers, and corporate showreels surround the screenic text proper, mediating its relationship with prospective audiences, advertisers, and reviewers. Formerly distinct demarcation lines between programming and advertising have grown increasingly blurred since the advent of digital media technologies (Jenkins, 2006). This blurring of categories renders the academy's hitherto overly neat valorization of one and denigration of the other unsustainable: "Derision of promotional forms like trailers and mobisodes can limit understanding of paratextual creativity, both in the function these objects serve in constituting the films and television programmes they surround, and in the way they have become a more commonplace component of audiences' media diets" (Grainge and Johnson, 2015: 5). With promotional culture entities commanding high budgets, awarding prizes for exceptional achievement, and cultivating their own fanbases, creative and commercial interests have grown so intermeshed as to be practically indistinguishable.

Especially valuable for understanding the digital literary sphere is Gray's awareness that such screenic paratexts are not created solely by authorized producers but equally by technologically empowered audiences (20). Viewer motivations in devising such paratexts may range from the laudatory to the outright parodic. Yet, regardless of where amateur creators fall along this spectrum, the widespread availability, low technical barriers to entry, and abundant online channels for circulating user-generated content lay to rest previous conceptions of audiences as passive recipients whose resistance ran only to devising semiotically subversive readings. Digital paratexts for screen content are now designed by media corporations precisely to catalyze consumers' co-creative aspirations, hoping through "affective economics" to convert fans' voluntary creative labor into greater reputational and commercial value for screen brands (Jenkins, 2006: 20, 59–92). Digital screenic paratexts are thus of interest not only in their own right (as quirky pieces of text on which we might practice close-reading) but for their role in foregrounding competing claims for meaning-making authority in the screen industries at large (Gray, 2010: 23).

Implications of Digital Paratext for Disciplinary Self-Conception

It is worth pondering why digital paratexts have to date remained at the very margins of academic study, even of book history, the (inter)discipline whose commitment to examining all manifestations of written communication might have predisposed it to eager interest.[4] Let us consider in turn some potential objections to digital paratexts' inclusion in book history's scholarly project.

Too Trivial

Compared to the incontrovertible cultural value of an illuminated medieval manuscript, a Gutenberg Bible, or a first edition Penguin Classic, digital paratexts may appear simply too small-scale to reward academic attention. Yet are we to accept such a contention from a discipline that finds interpretative significance in a printer's ornament? Since when did book historians discount so much as the smudge left by a reader's thumb as hermeneutically insignificant?[5]

Too Commercial

Here the reservation might be that a book trailer or authorial blog-tour post are principally marketing, rather than creative, texts. But book history emerged from bibliography during the 1970s to remind mainstream literary studies (besotted as it then was with highly dematerialized post-structuralist theory) that books are *always* irreducibly physical and commercial objects. Indeed, book history's international scholarly association, the Society for the History of Authorship, Reading and Publishing (SHARP), itself arose out of the 1991 "Masterpieces in the Marketplace" conference, the aim of which was to rematerialize readings of the nineteenth-century Anglo-American canon by reconstructing the material, institutional, and economic contexts of such works' publication and survival.[6] So SHARPists who insist upon viewing Dickens's novels through the lens of their print serialization or repackaging for three-decker editions can hardly claim that a publisher-created book trailer or other promotional paratext is too irredeemably tainted by commercial interests to warrant academic attention.

Too Ephemeral

This is perhaps a more serious reservation about admitting digital paratexts to the book history fold, as the rate of content generation in digital environments and the current relatively haphazard archiving of the Internet present difficulties in preserving the objects of twenty-first-century book historical study. These factors thus jeopardize the longevity of analyses drawn from digital paratexts, perhaps producing disincentives for scholars to enter this domain (Burdick et al., 2012: 21). However, projects such as the Internet Archive's Wayback Machine (recovering previous versions of the Internet) make evanescence a relative, not an absolute, problem.[7] Consider also book history's long championing of the historical and social importance of *print* ephemera: the broadsheets, chapbooks, playbills, authorial correspondence, and publishers' files that provide essential interpretative context for analysis of print communication. If these materials can be declared worthy of preserving for posterity in depositories such as the University of Reading's Archive of Publishing and Printing, how much more so should digital paratexts be preserved?[8] This is especially so when not-for-profits' webcrawlers and other commercially available tools automate so much of this archiving and make records universally and freely accessible.

Too . . . Other

This is where we get to the nub of book history's sidelining of digital paratexts to date: they appear, at first glance, simply too "other"—too new, too Internet-based, too close to what media, communication, and cultural studies might consider *their* analytical home turf.[9] The irony here is that each of these comparatively recently emerged disciplines is yet to pay the digital literary sphere much detailed

attention either: their marked preference for screenic culture has largely relegated digital *literary* paratexts to the "too bookish" basket. Thus, a whole terrain
of contemporary online bookishness remains up for disciplinary grabs.

Perhaps we can trace this unfortunate disjuncture between book history and
media studies to *our* founding figure Elizabeth Eisenstein's academic take-down
of *their* founding figure Marshall McLuhan. Late in her life, long after McLuhan's
death, Eisenstein baldly stated an opinion she had first put more diplomatically
in her magnum opus *The Printing Press as an Agent of Change* (1979): "His [Mc-
Luhan's] ideas didn't work."[10] Eisenstein, as an empirically trained historian, took
pains at the time of her book's appearance to distance herself from McLuhan's
sweeping generalizations about shifts in medium effecting transformative psy-
cho-social change (Baron, Lindquist, and Shevlin, 2007: 10). She admonished,
"We need to think less metaphorically and abstractly, more historically and concretely, about the sort of effects that were entailed and how different groups were
affected" (1979: 129). Rather than the Canadian media theorist's catchy "probes,"
frequently nonsequential lines of argument, and highly allusive prose style, Eisenstein strove to reconstruct the impact of printing through verifiable contemporary evidence and extensive secondary sources (McLuhan, 1962; McLuhan and
Carson, 2011).

Blame for the failure of book history and media studies to make common
cause over digital paratexts ought, however, to be shared by both sides. Media
scholars, for their part, appear willing to cite the work of Eisenstein in passing,
but almost always as part of a broad historical survey of communication technologies in which Gutenberg is of interest chiefly for how he leads to the main game
of, say, Google (Briggs and Burke, 2009: 18–19; Gleick, 2011: 399–401; Stokes,
2013: 38; Ouellette and Gray, 2017: 116).[11] The myopia of presentism is pervasive.
Yet, despite most media theorists disavowing any simplistically supersessionist
conception of media technologies—in which newer media eclipse and make redundant older media—most media, communication, and cultural studies work
overlooks the vital contemporary life of books and literary culture online. It is as
though the codex imparts some intellectual fustiness which would cramp the
style of digital media researchers.[12]

But if the disciplinary fault line represented by McLuhan on one hand and
Eisenstein on the other once existed, there have long been those willing to traverse it. D. F. McKenzie's *Bibliography and the Sociology of Texts* ([1986] 1999)—as
close to an urtext as book history has—defined "texts" broadly to include "verbal,
visual, oral, and numeric data, in the form of maps, prints, and music, of archives
of recorded sound, of films, videos, and any computer-stored information, every-

thing in fact from epigraphy to the latest forms of discography" (13). Refusing to cede what in 1986 were the latest media technologies to the claims of a then emergent "communications studies," McKenzie saw that such formats lay on an unbroken continuum with the oral, manuscript, and specifically print traditions which book history regards as its core objects of study (12): "Until our own times, the only textual records created in any quantity were manuscripts and books. A slight extension of the principle—it is, I believe, the same principle—to cope with the new kinds of material constructions we have in the form of the non-book texts which now surround, inform, and pleasure us, does not seem to me a radical departure from precedent" (1999: 14). To update McKenzie's position for the twenty-first century, no intellectually defensible distinction can be drawn between studying an author's correspondence and a writer's tweet; between a book retailer's display poster and a virally disseminated book trailer; between a fan letter sent via a publisher and an Amazon reader's review.

Pedagogical Challenges Presented by Digital Paratext

But if these reservations about including digital paratexts within the ambit of book history fail to hold up under close examination, the nature of digital paratexts themselves does present some seriously destabilizing features for book history pedagogy as it has come to be practiced.

Teaching Time-Based Media

Book historians are habituated to what Toronto School media theorist Harold Innis termed print communication's spatial-, as opposed to time-, bias: print excels in communicating across geographic distance but rarely achieves simultaneity, as with broadcast media ([1950] 2007). When setting an audiovisual literary paratext for our students, such as a video of a writers' festival panel session, should we stipulate reading (or rather viewing/listening) for a certain time period rather than a certain page count (Pressman, 2007)?[13] If teaching a potentially voluminous authorial blog, how exactly do we demarcate the confines of the work under analysis? Should every hyperlink and reader comment be construed as part of the work? Further, if blogs and podcasts are liable to be updated frequently, when is the text sufficiently "finished" for critique? Used to a print regime of scholarly control over a known text, how are book historians to deal with a "live" text that constantly updates and may do so again before the seminar studying it is even finished (Rabkin, 2006: 137; Burdick et al., 2012: 14–15)? And what are the implications for the pedagogical balance of power if our students are onto these latest mutations before we as educators are? Book historians, given the discipline's bibliographical origins, have been quick to remind mainstream literary scholars and historians that all texts are mutable—but not *this* mutable.

Dealing with Textual Instability

This characteristic instability of digital texts takes us to a second complication arising from digital paratexts' incorporation into the book history curriculum: it seems book historians have, in spite of protestations to the contrary, been subconsciously conceiving of a text as a series of "snapshots" rather than as an unfolding process. Book history has been quick to remind digital pundits that the protean nature of texts in digital environments does not represent a radical break with an eons-long tradition, but marks rather a return to the greater textual mutability that characterized manuscript culture (Finkelstein and McCleery, 2013). Thomas Pettitt's piquant phrase "the Gutenberg parenthesis" has been eagerly taken up because it puts into perspective the roughly five hundred years of print culture dominance as one particular socio-technological communicative formation rather than an inevitable state of existence (2007).[14] In this light, the "typographical fixity" ushered in by the Gutenbergian revolution is properly viewed as a specific interlude, not a permanent state of affairs, in human communication (Eisenstein, 1979: 113). Nevertheless, the speed of textual alteration in an era of widely disseminated social media means that a book trailer, for example, may be no sooner released than it is reedited, parodied, subtitled, redubbed, and recirculated as an Internet meme.

Furthermore, the parties to such textual manipulation have expanded from a circle of book-industry insiders (publishers, editors, printers, retailers, agents) to include virtually anyone. The boundaries of digital paratexts are not so much porous as nonexistent: the comments section on a writer's blog; the trail of replies to and retweets of a Twitter message; the cacophony of voices revealed on an authorial Facebook page. As Genette remarked of print literature's epitexts: their potential for "indefinite diffusion" marks them as "a fringe of the fringe" (346). *Digital* paratexts' even fringier status evidences a radical democratizing of the agents of literary culture with which book history—for all its championing of voices from below[15]—is yet fully to come to terms.

Extent of Audience Co-Creation

This leads to a final point about recalibrating the book history curriculum to account for digital-era practices: namely, our conception of "the reader." Robert Darnton's "communications circuit" ([1982] 1990) famously distributed authority for book creation away from Romanticism's traditional author-god to a range of intermediaries, including the reader. The digital literary sphere's ease of content creation by audiences demands that we radically extend Darnton's circuit model into a distributed network. Here the reader's role exceeds that of avid decoder or even resistant textual adversary, as book historians have documented since the "discovery" of reading in the 1980s by figures such as Roger Chartier, and which has been hardwired into the design of research tools such as the Reading Experience Database (RED).[16] Self-publishing, wikinovels, crowdfunded publication, and remix fiction fundamentally undermine book history's lingering author-reader binary distinction (Ray Murray and Squires, 2013). If we go the whole cultural-relativist hog and include fan fiction, with its culture of beta readers giving volunteer feedback on writers' drafts, we can further witness the merging of creator, consumer, *and* critical functions (Pugh, 2005; Thomas, 2011a, 2011b; Murray, forthcoming). Any hard and fast tripartite division of communication into sender-message-receiver categories is rendered fundamentally unworkable in digital environments (Hanrahan and Madsen, 2006: 2; Rabkin, 2006: 136–37). Not only does this necessitate wholesale expansion of the principally receptive role previously accorded the "reader." Book historians need moreover to reconsider whether the position of disinterested critic can be maintained in an environment where academics may be interacting with a given author online, reviewing a book on Goodreads, or appearing "in conversation" with an author at a literary festival. When every book users purchase—or even view—on Amazon affects that title's display via the company's Amabot recommendation algorithm, can scholars continue to regard themselves as somehow outside that which they—we, and our students—study?

Engaging with Digital Paratext: Opportunities and Threats

The foregoing discussion is not meant to suggest that book historians have had nothing to say about digital developments. That would clearly be false; to take only one example, the second edition of David Finkelstein and Alistair McCleery's eminently teachable *Book History Reader* (2006) contains a closing section focused on "The Future of the Book." The point is rather that digital paratexts are yet to register at the heart of what book historians do. Digital tools have been eagerly adopted by SHARPists to examine works of previous eras, but born-digital texts, whether creative or more obviously commercial, remain largely addenda to the discipline's core print-based object of study. Most fundamentally, digital humanities' theoretical insights are yet to register in book history's self-conception. We have lingered long with the idea of the social text, without fully understanding that that text has become socialized: radically distributed and subject to amendment with each reader, and that those readers' "produserly" efforts are themselves value-creating for the new Internet behemoths who dominate the book trade: Amazon, Google, and Apple.[17] The current evidence suggests that, just as with the unfortunate book history / media studies divide, book history / digital humanities scholarly exchange needs to go both ways. (The disciplinary interface is nicely encapsulated by the acronymic title of a 2017 conference convened by the Center for the History of Print and Digital Culture at the University of Wisconsin–Madison: "BH/DH.")[18] Leading DH figure Alan Liu, in a 2006 chapter sketching areas for future research, asks: "What and how did people 'know,' for instance, when cultures were dominated technically by orality, manuscripts, or print?" (21). Given that such concerns have constituted book historians' analytical bread and butter since at least the 1970s, Liu's omission of book history scholarship is startling. Similarly, electronic literary scholars N. Katherine Hayles and Jessica Pressman in 2013 proposed a new field of "comparative textual media" (CTM), given that "investigations of textual media *from a media standpoint* remain relatively small subfields within humanities disciplines, relegated to specialties such as bibliographic studies and textual studies" (ix–x; italics in the original). This would seem an unjustified and outdated view of the field. Where DH work, even in the dedicated subfield of digital literary studies, acknowledges book history, it predominantly takes the form of namechecking rather than extensive engagement. Thus the body chapters of Amy E. Earhart's *Traces of the Old, Uses of the New: The Emergence of Digital Literary Studies* (2015) focus exclusively on how digital tools have been used to examine pre-digital artifacts in the form of digital editions, archives, and data visualization. Her conclusion's passing acknowledgment that "textual studies and book history have given us theoretical structures and methodologies by which we might understand technologies of production" is the volume's sole reference to the book history discipline (119). In its last pages Earhart's study signals, enticingly, that DH's analytical gaze might also take in the contemporary era and that "we may bring our traditional methodologies and theories to bear on technologically produced humanities materials" (125). But this functions mostly as an envoi and prospect for future research. DH practice cannot be merely a one-way street, furnishing scholars with digital tools with which to better analyze the literary past. It can, and should, equally involve bringing traditional critical humanities analytical mindsets to bear on the institutions of contemporary digital literariness to illuminate—and influence—our unfolding literary present.

Such a process of mutual familiarization between book history and the digital humanities is all well and good. But book history's welcome ongoing parleys with the DH scholarly juggernaut should not preclude intellectual exchange with pre-existing disciplines with which SHARP has traditionally had little academic traffic: specifically media, communication and cultural studies, film and television studies, as well as the more bookish end of cultural sociology. Terrifically stimulating work on the interface of book retailing and algorithmic culture is appearing, for example, from cultural and media studies–identified scholars (Striphas, 2010a; McGurl, 2016; Rowberry, 2016). Failure by book historians to put our stamp on analyzing digital paratexts will see this territory claimed by such longer-established and (dare I say it?) more institutionally secure new humanities disciplines.

All this tracing of academic fiefdoms and their respective claims on the digital literary sphere is not, ultimately, an end in itself. The goal is not reducible to some squabble over academic spoils. In the end, it matters far less which disciplinary space stakes a claim on contemporary digital literariness than that such work is undertaken, with scholars appropriating and reworking whichever theoretical and methodological toolkits lie serviceably at hand. At the present moment, it appears that the most conducive of these spaces might be DH, if only for the capaciousness and lack of hard and fast boundaries stemming from its comparative newness. But even DH has its blind spots, with its recent beguilement with data too often sidelining questions of how and why (commercial) institutions create, maintain, and exploit data. This is where scholars affiliated with a range of other disciplines have much of value to bring to the table. Analysis of the digital literary sphere demands thorough familiarity with the book as a resiliently material object and knowledge of book-world infrastructure that only book history can contribute. Media studies, particularly its political economy strand, offers invaluable perspectives on how economics and culture are mutually constitutive. Like the increasingly converged media environment in which books exist, these disciplines may themselves be blending into a converged super-discipline in which it matters less where scholars come from intellectually than that they are committed to examining the contemporary digital literary sphere and, through dissemination of their scholarship, influencing it.

Introduction · Charting the Digital Literary Sphere

1. One admittedly crude comparison of Habermas's adoption in literary studies versus the social sciences can be made by performing a keyword search on his name in the MLA International Bibliography database (resulting in 1,372 entries since 1884) compared with the Web of Science database (3,279 entries since 1900). It's worth bearing in mind that many of the MLA hits are for German-language or German literary scholarship, inflating the impression of Habermas's take-up in departments of English literary studies.

2. A rare exception to this general rule is French academic Lionel Ruffel's uses of Habermas to explore the contemporary "literary public sphere," although by this phrase he signals not digital literary manifestations but instances where literature steps off the page into the physical world: live author readings, performances, and graphic and audio adaptations (2014: 111). For detailed analysis of literature's public incarnations via the phenomenon of writers' festivals, both embodied and virtual, see chapter 3.

3. The parallels here between the book and screen industries are striking. Consider this observation from film and television scholars Paul Grainge and Catherine Johnson (2015): "Industrial sectors such as film and television, advertising and marketing, and digital design have become more porous in their practices, interactions and claims of market territory. Indeed . . . the promotional screen industries are not a clearly defined sector, but a fluid, fast-moving site of industrial collaboration and competition, with promotional intermediaries from different fields moving into each other's territory" (8).

4. Jessica Pressman and Lisa Swanstrom implicitly make a similar point in their introduction to a special issue of *Digital Humanities Quarterly* on "The Literary" by asking, "What kind of scholarly endeavors are possible when we think of the digital humanities as not just supplying the archives and data-sets for literary interpretation but also as promoting literary practices with an emphasis on aesthetics, on intertextuality, and writerly processes?" (2013).

5. N. Katherine Hayles and Jessica Pressman, in their introduction to the edited anthology *Comparative Textual Media* (2013), note the importance of avoiding technological determinism in assessing the impact of media changes, as "media are always embedded in specific cultural, social, and economic practices" (xxvi). But this fairly standard media studies caveat against the fallacy of technological determinism is heeded more in the volume's section focusing on past eras than in the essays with a contemporary focus. The cultural, social, and economic practices prevailing in past eras may be more apparent to us because they are denaturalized, but they are no more powerful than those operative in our own era.

6. Scholars who *do* productively think through cultural formations by means of political economy methods, such as media historian Lisa Gitelman, tend to be explicitly interested in undermining the hallowed distinction between "literature" and mundane, often ephemeral manifestations of print culture (2014).

7. https://txtlab.org/about/

8. The most recently published English-language work Piper refers to explicitly is F. Scott Fitzgerald's *This Side of Paradise* (1920) (79).

9. https://www.hathitrust.org/htrc_sp17acs_awards

10. Cf. John B. Thompson's *Merchants of Culture* (2010), which devotes the ninth of its ten chapters to "The Digital Revolution," while structuring other chapters principally around residual print-culture categories such as book retailers, literary agents, and publishers. Thompson's gaze over trade publishing is also exclusively sociological, without delving into the specifically "literary" subfield of trade books, let alone examining how the digital revolution might be affecting the nature of contemporary literary writing.

11. See Patrick, 2016.

12. http://lbc.typepad.com/

13. https://www.netgalley.com/

14. Number of followers as of June 2017. For most recent follower count, see https://twitter.com/JoyceCarolOates.

15. http://margaretatwood.ca/; https://twitter.com/MargaretAtwood; http://www.fanado.com/

16. https://www.youtube.com/user/vlogbrothers; http://effyeahnerdfighters.com/post/11662391433/an-abundance-of-covers-contest

17. For example, https://www.youtube.com/user/penguinbooks.

18. https://www.pinterest.com/penguinbooksusa/

19. See, for example, Melbourne-based independent chain Readings, whose online masthead pointedly proclaims "Australia's Own Since 1969": http://www.readings.com.au/.

20. Amazon acquired online book-traffic rivals Shelfari and Goodreads outright in 2008 and 2013, respectively. Amazon had earlier taken a 40 percent stake in Library Thing (2006). In January 2016 Amazon announced that it would be "merging" Shelfari with Goodreads as of June 2016.

21. See for example, http://www.amazon.com/gp/help/customer/display.html?ref=footer_cou?ie=UTF8&nodeId=508088.

22. Examples include the #TwitterFiction Festival (started in 2012) and the Digital Writers' Festival (started in 2014). Interestingly, the inaugural Digital Writers' Festival, organized from Melbourne, remained keenly attuned to the significance of place in literary activity, hosting a live meet-up between representatives of all the (then) seven UNESCO Cities of Literature (https://www.youtube.com/watch?v=o8RlKouykBc).

23. Hallinan and Striphas aptly observe of this process that "questions of cultural authority are being displaced significantly into the realm of technique and engineering" (2016: 122). See chapter 2 for in-depth analysis of these issues.

Chapter 1 · *Performing Authorship in the Digital Literary Sphere*

1. Ewen's novel is one of a number of fictional satires on the twenty-first-century publishing industry to appear, all of which take aim in part at the cult of the celebrity author. See also Will Ferguson's *Happiness™* (2002), Steve Hely's *How I Became a Famous Novelist* (2009), and Peter Barry's *I Hate Martin Amis et al.* (2011).

2. http://www.rap.ugent.be/

3. Though, to their credit, the RAP project's lead researchers acknowledge that authorship in these periods is no less worthy of scholarly attention, but simply beyond the already broad chronological remit of their own project: "We assume that, even today and in the future, questions of authorship—in many different guises, and subject to new technological and economic pressures—will continue to have a social and cultural impact" (2012: 21).

4. There are rare precursors of this critical trend, such as John G. Cawelti's article, "The Writer as a Celebrity: Some Aspects of American Literature as Popular Culture," which appeared as long ago as 1977.

5. Kathleen Fitzpatrick oversaw the creation of the *Literary Studies in the Digital Age: An Evolving Anthology* (2013–) collaborative writing and editing experiment on the MLA Commons website as part of her former position as the Modern Language Association's director of scholarly communication.

6. J. Yellowlees Douglas dubs this essay "the single article that arguably has made more readers aware of hypertext fiction and inflamed more critics than any other" (2000: 7).

7. See also the remarks of former *Salon* editor Scott Rosenberg: "If anyone can 'publish' by forking over a few bucks to produce a paperback or e-book, then doing so won't be any more special than, say, printing out the manuscript on your Deskjet and running off a few copies at Kinko's" (Miller, L., 2010).

8. See https://www.kickstarter.com, http://www.pozible.com/ and https://unbound.co .uk/.

9. http://www.youwriteon.com

10. http://www.apub.com/imprint-detail?imprint=4

11. http://www.authorsguild.net/

12. For similar denunciation of transparently self-promoting corporate bloggers as "overbearing bores," see Baverstock, 2008: 169; as well as Groskop, 2010b; Driscoll, 2013; and Weiner, 2013.

13. John and Hank Green in 2010 leveraged their *vlogbrothers* experience to become co-directors of VidCon, an annual international convention advising would-be YouTube celebrities on the finer points of self-presentation, fan liaison, and search engine optimization (http://vidcon.com/).

14. https://www.youtube.com/watch?v=Roy5hc87-Mo

15. Atwood follower numbers are accurate as of the time of writing (June 2017).

16. At the present time Fanado is still in its beta-testing phase, and its aspirational but thin-on-details website suggests it is still seeking capital through crowdfunding.

17. The first of these scenarios has indeed come to pass: the sixth season of *Game of Thrones* (2016) was the first to move beyond the narrative of Martin's published books in the series. However, as Martin is jointly writing the screenplays for this and the slated seventh season, the narrative will broadly match that of the still-to-be-published volumes (Ward, 2016; Paskin, 2016).

18. *Hearts, Keys, and Puppetry* (2010) was a 2009 collaboration between Gaiman and BBC Audiobooks America to curate a mass-written Twitter novel for which Gaiman tweeted the opening sentence. Responses tweeted by the general public were then chosen to continue the narrative.

19. https://twitter.com/JoyceCarolOates

20. King had inflamed Twitter controversy through an observation that sexual abuse accusations against Woody Allen by his adopted daughter Dylan Farrow might reflect "an element of palpable bitchery." King subsequently issued a full apology for the "sad and painful mess" his tweet provoked (http://stephenking.com/news_archive/article429.html).

21. While Franzen has striven, from the beginning of his public career, to write socially engaged fiction, his advocacy of a rather Proustian withdrawal from the technologies of

modern life makes him easy to strawman as simply opposed to contemporary pop culture. Comments such as "the ineluctable superficiality of film" and "the pop-cultural narcosis" don't help (1996: 42, 53).

22. https://twitter.com/SalmanRushdie/status/379518868571435008

23. Franzen made a nearly identical point regarding literary agents requiring aspirant writers to demonstrate a minimum social media "platform" in an interview with the *Times* (UK) the same month (Pavia, 2013).

24. Shteyngart's book trailer—his second after the viral success of the trailer for *Super Sad True Love Story* (2011)—was posted on YouTube in December 2013, two months after Franzen's BBC Radio interview. In it, "Dr. Franzen's" sotto voce diagnosis of Shteyngart as a "little narcissist" seems particularly on point. "I'm so sorry," Dr. Franzen continues, "I've got to stop speaking the truth out loud."

25. Cannold, 2011: 15.

26. For more on book history's discovery of the reader, and the implications of this discovery for considering reader behaviors in the digital literary sphere, see chapter 5.

27. Such catering to readers' desire to go behind an author's printed words and to access the "real" person has, of course a much longer history, encompassing the nineteenth-century lecture tours of writers such as Mark Twain, Charles Dickens, and Oscar Wilde (Glass, 2004), the "writer on holiday" genre of magazine soft profiles analyzed by Roland Barthes in *Mythologies* ([1957] 1972), and, most recently, the *Guardian* newspaper's 2007 "Writers' Rooms" portrait series of authors' workspaces (Battershill, 2014).

28. https://twitter.com/stephenfry. Fry announced in February 2016 that he had deactivated his Twitter account because the increasingly shrill and pugnacious tone of "debate" in the Twitterverse had led him to the realization that the early thrill of the new technology had worn off and "too many people have peed in the pool." He felt, he wrote at the time of his decision, "massive relief, like a boulder rolling off my chest. I am free, free at last." (http://www.stephenfry.com/2016/02/peedinthepool/).

29. This makes a "following"/"followers" ratio of 1:1,060. The disproportion in Atwood's Twitter feed remains roughly the same even as her follower numbers have grown exponentially since 2011. As of June 2017, although Atwood has over 1.65 million followers she follows only 1,307 others (a ratio of 1:1,262).

30. The website of the Society for the History of Authorship, Reading and Publishing hosts a large number of such book history syllabi: http://www.sharpweb.org/main /teaching/.

Chapter 2 · *"Selling" Literature*

1. Amazon has since opened physical bookstores in a dozen US cities, and in May 2017 opened its first outlet in the literati heartland of Manhattan situated in the Time Warner Center at Columbus Circle (Morris, 2017; Gapper, 2017).

2. Amazon's virtual browsing tool was dubbed at its inception in 2003 "Search Inside the Book" but is now known as "Look Inside!"

3. The conclusion of the present volume considers how this disciplinary disjuncture between book history and the hybridized media/communication/cultural studies discipline has arisen, what its effects are, and how it might be overcome.

4. See, for example, Forsyth with Birn (1997) and Baverstock (2015).

5. The term "critical code studies" was first proposed by Mark Marino in his *Electronic*

Book Review article of the same name (2006). In it, he argued that new media and electronic literature scholars need to "begin to analyze and explicate code as a text, as a sign system with its own rhetoric, as verbal communication that possesses significance in excess of its functional utility. . . . I am proposing that we can read and explicate code the way we might explicate a work of literature in a new field of inquiry that I call Critical Code Studies (CCS)." This was to take the familiar Electronic Literature Organization form of textual analysis of born-digital artifacts: "close readings" and "direct analysis of specific source code." The practice has been pursued (including by Marino himself) at the level of a single line of code, or even of a specific typographical character. As such it represents an extreme extension of Katherine Hayles's concept of "media-specific analysis" and differs from the more cultural studies–style, contextually oriented methodology adopted in the current volume (2004). Marino, granted, hints at the larger contextual frame in which computer code's effects might be analyzed: "Through CCS, practitioners may critique the larger human and computer systems, from the level of the computer to the level of the society in which these code objects circulate and exert influence," promising that "the treatment of the cultural history and meaning of these languages will help contextualize analyses of specific programs." On balance, though, it is the former level of close readings of critical code that his article predominantly advocates.

It was thus left up to leading new media theorist Lev Manovich to more fully explore the contextual potential of code studies, first in his landmark *The Language of New Media* (2001), which called for "a new stage in media theory. . . . *From media studies we move to something that can be called 'software studies'—from media theory to software theory*" (italics in the original). More specifically, his subsequent book *Software Takes Command* ([2008] 2013) questioned media studies' traditional subdivision by specific media platforms to ask what happens when all mediums are running on the "metamedium" of software (4). It is Manovich who in practice more fully explores the cultural and social implications of software earlier hinted at by Marino: "Software studies has to investigate the role of software in contemporary culture, and the cultural and social forces that are shaping the development of software itself" (2013: 10).

6. Ed Finn, a researcher also interested in "the social forces influencing books and readers at their intersection with literary production," similarly credits Striphas with coining the term "algorithmic culture" (2013).

7. Julian Pinder (2012: 76) makes a similar point: "Online recommendations and algorithms . . . rank and order what is already out there, and thereby channel and amplify consumer behaviour rather than trying to predict it (or even to preempt it)." His subsequent discussion, however, is unsettling in its faith in the transparency of algorithmic tools, demonstrating how pervasive the view of algorithms as neutral measuring devices is even among literary academics trained in suspicious reading strategies.

8. Yung-Hsing Wu points out that the cultivation of bookishness was similarly apparent in Bezos's subsequent selling of the inaugural Kindle e-reader (2007) which, from its size, portrait orientation, and text display to the series of glyphs on its rear case, everywhere sought to remediate the codex form and to translate books' inherited cultural resonance to Amazon's new, digital-born object (2013).

9. This grew out of Amazon's previous in-house books blog, *Omnivoracious* (2007–), which called itself "the place for Amazon Books editors to talk about *our* passions for fiction, nonfiction, cookbooks, kids' books, mysteries, romance, and science fiction. Here *you'll* find

interviews with your favorite authors, Best Books of the Month announcements, reviews, and occasional essays on books, reading, and quirky trends" (http://www.omnivoracious .com/; italics added). The use of first- and second-person address is typical of the site's rhetorical ploys to sustain interpersonal rapport. The *Review* is also emailed daily direct to subscribers, a long-standing marketing tactic which, Marcus records, prompted many readers to "write back, as if they had received a personal letter. . . . It was . . . a direct-marketer's wet dream, since you could address an unlimited audience without paying a dime for postage or printing" (2004: 247). Earlier discussion of Amazon's "Editor's Service" email newsletters as community-building tools, though this time from a distinct business management perspective, can be found in Kotha, 1998: 216–17.

10. See also Striphas, 2015: 407.

11. Mark McGurl in a recent article makes a similar point about Amazon's positing of "the reader as customer, a quasi deity" (2016: 457).

12. Cf. author and independent US publisher Matthew Stadler, who draws a "sharp contrast" between the communitarian "culture of reading" and an atomized "culture of shopping," deploring "an age-old confusion of publics with markets" (2016). Predictably, the work of Jürgen Habermas is alluded to in his discussion. Stadler's closing analogy, whereby independent, print-on-demand publishers are to Big Publishing as the "slow-food" movement is to Monsanto-style agribusiness, would seem to overlook the parallel commodification of the health food movement and farmers' markets by upscale supermarket chains such as Whole Foods Market (in a delicious irony, since the time of writing Whole Foods has been purchased by Amazon). Teasing out such ethical consumerist ambiguities comprises the focus of book retailing and cultural sociologist Laura J. Miller's current research.

13. Kati Voigt (2013) dates the book trailer's emergence to 2002, when a US patent application for the term was filed (673). But newspaper database and Internet searches reveal that the term came into modest circulation only in about 2006.

14. See, for example: https://www.youtube.com/user/RandomHouseInc; https://www .youtube.com/user/PenguinGroupUSA; https://www.youtube.com/user/SimonSchuster Videos; https://www.youtube.com/user/panmacmillanbooks.

15. http://www.youtube.com/watch?v=RjWKPdDko_U

16. There has been some largely empirical work from educational and marketing researchers about book trailers aimed at young adult readers (Davila, 2010; Basaraba, 2016). Among the bare handful of humanities or social science considerations of the book trailer are Johanson and Freeman (2012), Voigt (2013), and Murray (2016). The first of these devotes a scant half-paragraph to the phenomenon.

17. Also appearing in recent years is the survey-based project, website, and blog *Watching the Trailer* (2013–), established by academics Fred Greene, Keith Johnston, and Ed Vollans (http://www.watchingthetrailer.com/). See also Greene, Johnston, and Vollans (2014).

18. Shteyngart's first book trailer was for the hardback edition of *Super Sad True Love Story* (2010): http://www.youtube.com/watch?v=EfzuOu4UIOU. The book trailer had garnered over three hundred thousand YouTube views at the time of writing. His second, featuring himself and actor Paul Giamatti as roommates attempting to pick up middle-aged "cougars" at a Brooklyn Heights book club, was released for the book's paperback publication: https://www.youtube.com/watch?v=DwWToVgnCCw.

19. *Little Failure* (2013) http://www.youtube.com/watch?v=sowt9Wq7zYU. Despite the

titillation, the video trails Shteyngart's first foray into book trailers with a comparatively modest sixty-nine thousand YouTube views at the time of writing.

20. http://www.youtube.com/watch?v=3xtcB457jq. Text's book trailer has far surpassed the success of US publisher Akashic Books's trailer for the same title, featuring Samuel L. Jackson reading the book aloud. At the time of writing, the US trailer had scored only forty-eight thousand YouTube views, despite the far larger domestic market and Jackson's Hollywood name recognition.

21. The award's name is a nod to the publishing house's Herman Melville namesake, not the musician. Winners of the top Golden Whale award receive a gold spray-painted whale statuette. Publisher Dennis Johnson has lamented that "We couldn't find a sperm whale, it's a beluga whale but it's close enough. . . . Or if you want to get your own, they're $14.95 at Toys 'R' Us" ("Honoring," 2011).

22. The book in question is the paperback edition of Cass's *Head Case: How I Almost Lost My Mind Trying to Understand My Brain* (2008), although the book is not mentioned or pictured in his popular book trailer—rather a marketing oversight (http://www.youtube.com/watch?v=yxschLOAr-s).

23. Rachel Arons, writing about Jonathan Franzen's halfhearted, talking-head book trailer for *Freedom* (2010), winner of the 2011 Moby award for Worst Performance by an Author, asks rhetorically: "What other writer would make a book trailer about being reluctant to make a book trailer?" (2013). The answer is: plenty.

24. https://www.youtube.com/watch?v=x4BK_2VULCU

25. http://www.youtube.com/watch?v=kEN1oaxDJtA

26. One recent prominent example of this decades-old phenomenon is the 2015 sale of film rights to Garth Risk Hallberg's thousand-plus-page unpublished novel *City on Fire*, a declaration of Hollywood interest that led Jonathan Cape to snap up the publication rights and turbocharged the book's prepublication buzz as the next Great American Novel (Appleyard, 2015).

27. Voigt makes a similar point regarding the book trailer for *It's a Book*, arguing that "book videos are not only marketing elements but that they are in fact an emerging new art form very similar to movies or adaptations" (2013: 677). Later in her article she champions academic investigation of book trailers that she sees proceeding along primarily aesthetic lines "with regards to choice of colours, camera angles, construction of dialogues, common tropes, etc." (685). It thus differs markedly from the sociological perspective on book trailers advocated and enacted in this volume.

28. The significance of digital paratexts for literary culture is explored at greater length in the conclusion to the present volume.

29. For extended discussion of book bloggers' role in changing contemporary literary reviewing culture, see chapter 4.

30. http://www.blogtour.org/

31. http://www.virtualbooktourcafe.com/

32. http://atomrtours.com/

33. http://lbc.typepad.com/

34. https://www.netgalley.com/

35. Interestingly, Gail Pool, a thoughtful and clear-eyed commentator on book review culture, as late as 2007 was able to write idealistically of online literary reviewing: "The Web does allow for the truly independent reviewer: the individual who sets up a personal Web

site for his reviews is, in a literal sense, self-employed and can say precisely what he wants" (98).

36. See, for example, the previously long-running litblog *Bookslut*'s pitch to potential advertisers, which combines several of these motivations: "When you advertise on Bookslut, you are advertising on a highly reputable website. We have been named one of the 50 best websites by *Time* and one of the best literature websites by *The New York Times*. We are a respected tastemaker, and your ad will be shown to some of the savviest readers on the web" (http://www.bookslut.com/advertise/intro.php). Nevertheless, in other writing, *Bookslut*'s founder and chief blogger Jessa Crispin articulated deep-seated ambivalence about her role simultaneously both inside and outside a mainstream book industry of which she is highly critical: "Don't think there weren't nights where I woke up with the thought 'My entire purpose in life is to help people make decisions about which books to buy; I am simply part of someone's marketing strategy' chilling me to the bone" (2016: 63–64). In a fascinating coincidence, Crispin here replicates in almost identical language Jeff Bezos's casting of Amazon as less a retailer than a form of readers' advisory service, though in Crispin's case this thought triggers deep unease.

37. http://www.quirkbooks.com/page/about. The original book trailer for *Pride and Prejudice and Zombies* can be found at https://www.youtube.com/watch?v=FzowFJTApfY.

38. https://www.youtube.com/watch?v=_jZVE5uF24Q

39. Melbourne-based literary periodical *The Lifted Brow*, winner of the Best Original Non-fiction category in the 2015 international Stack Awards for independent publications, has had considerable success with this kind of launch event, bundling annual subscriptions into the ticket price for their author-readings-cum-launch-parties marking release of a new issue. See http://theliftedbrow.com/.

40. Bourdieu's clearest definition of his concept of "social capital" occurs in a 1992 interview: "Social capital is the sum of the resources, actual or virtual, that accrue to an individual or a group by virtue of possessing *a durable network of more or less institutionalized relationships* of mutual acquaintance or recognition" (Bourdieu and Wacquant, 1992: 119; italics added).

41. https://www.goodreads.com/

42. For example, UK newspaper the *Guardian*'s Books section has spawned a lively and well-trafficked website that invites reader comments on its articles (https://www.theguardian.com/books). Reader responses frequently run to hundreds of posts in reply to a single article. By contrast, the online-born *Sydney Review of Books* (established in 2013) offers readers no comments facility (http://sydneyreviewofbooks.com/), inviting readers only to post the SRB's content to their social media accounts.

43. John Parsons's article "The Social Publisher" (2013) includes an interesting table itemizing the optimal social media channels for marketing and publicizing books as classified by genre (21).

Chapter 3 · *Curating the Public Life of Literature*

1. For example, Sydney Writers' Festival: https://www.youtube.com/user/SydWritersFest; Singapore Writers Festival: https://www.youtube.com/user/sgwritersfest; Jaipur Literature Festival: https://www.youtube.com/user/JprLitFest; International Literature Festival Dublin: https://www.youtube.com/user/DWF2014.

2. Casanova has defined her "world republic of letters" as "a parallel territory, relatively

autonomous from the political domain, and dedicated as a result to questions, debates, inventions of a specifically literary nature" (2005: 71–72).

3. http://clunesbooktown.com.au/

4. http://www.booktown.net/

5. http://www.wordalliance.org/

6. http://ifoa.org/international-visitors-programme

7. See, for example, the Sydney Writers' Festival's unambiguous pitch to be the Australasian festival of choice in its three-minute highlight-reel YouTube video, replete with images of its stunning harborside setting, warmly appreciative celebrity authors, and passionately engaged audiences (https://www.youtube.com/user/SydWritersFest). The recurrent images of and spoken references to the balmy weather seem a deliberate lure for northern-hemisphere authors daunted by the long flight (although the May festival actually takes place in the southern hemisphere's late Autumn). In this context, UK novelist Jeanette Winterson's comment that "if there was only one festival in the world I could go to it'd be the Sydney Writers' Festival" is marketing gold, up there with Bill Clinton's much-quoted dubbing of the Hay Festival "the Woodstock of the mind" (McCrum, 2006).

8. The JLF Melbourne website describes the event thus: "Connecting South Asia's and Australia's unique identities, the festival brings 'the greatest literary show on earth' to Australia's City of Literature" (http://mwf.com.au/jlf-melbourne/).

9. See http://en.unesco.org/creative-cities/home; http://www.cityofliterature.com/cities-of-literature/cities-of-literature/.

10. http://www.mwf.com.au/mwf-2015/

11. http://litontour.com/

12. http://www.skynews.com.au/news/national/nsw/2017/01/24/sydney-2nd-most-expensive-city-in-the-world.html

13. http://www.swf.org.au/live/

14. See, for example, http://cityofliterature.com.au/~cityofli/explore/libraries/sydney-writers-festival-live-and-local-frankston-library.

15. Comments by SWF Executive Director Jo Dyer in an email newsletter to subscribers (August 12, 2016).

16. Academic and critic Michael Meehan is also a former Chair of Adelaide Writers' Week.

17. *Mortification: Writers' Stories of Their Public Shame* is an entire anthology made up of writers recalling their greatest professional humiliations, many of which took place at literary festivals, and thus getting some self-deprecatory mileage from the experience (Robertson, 2003).

18. As an illustration of this last point, the Melbourne Writers Festival issues an annual call for nominations for its "Audience Advocates" program. This twelve-person committee, which aims to represent "all kinds of readers with all kinds of ideas," functions as a suggestion pool, draft program sounding board, and debriefing panel for the Festival's professional staff (http://mwf.com.au/become-an-audience-advocate/). In a further display of the Festival's openness and receptivity, the Audience Advocates in turn comb and consider suggestions made by the public at large via the MWF's Digital Suggestion Box (http://mwf.com.au/digital-suggestion-box/). This receptivity to public opinion stands in marked contrast to the French literary festival analyzed by Gisèle Sapiro, Les Correspondances de Manosque, where selection is determined by a board of three literary insiders, who demon-

strate a marked preference for fiction drawn from "the pole of small-scale production" or high art, in Bourdieusian terminology (2016: 16).

19. See this volume's introduction for a discussion of Darnton's influential model of a book's trajectory.

20. "This stunning photo from yesterday afternoon comes courtesy of @Nevendbkshelf on Twitter. We'd love to share your Festival moments with you—simply post using #Sydney WritersFestival" (subscriber newsletter, May 22, 2015).

21. "We're looking back on our 30 year history and want you to share your favourite MWF moment. We are creating an archive of your Festival memories. Want to see your MWF moment on our website? Add it here" (subscriber newsletter, May 29, 2015).

22. Similarly, Martin Robertson and Ian Yeoman, in a slightly odd forecast of how literary festivals may look in 2050, predict a status differential whereby the live trumps the recorded: "Live events have greater social capital than cloud (online) events (although these will still exist and be attractive to those [who] can neither afford the live [n]or liminal consumption choices" (2014: 332).

23. http://twitterfictionfestival.com/about/

24. http://digitalwritersfestival.com/2016/

25. DWF Facebook post (December 18, 2014).

26. "The DWF2016 Program Has Launched!" email to Emerging Writers' Festival subscribers announcing the DWF2016 program (October 18, 2016).

27. Earlier digital literary experiments with live writing include pseudonymous husband and wife crime-writing team Nicci French's real-time-written "Your Place and Mine" for Penguin UK's landmark program of digital storytelling, We Tell Stories (2008). Over the course of five days for a predetermined hour each night the pair wrote live online, with all their drafts, revisions, and pauses viewable by a global internet public (http://www.wetell stories.co.uk/stories/week4/about/).

28. For example, http://digitalwritersfestival.com/2015/event/20-minute-cities-edin burgh/.

29. http://digitalwritersfestival.com/2014/events/irl-literary-collectives-and-place/

30. http://digitalwritersfestival.com/2016/event/art-and-the-suburbs/

31. http://digitalwritersfestival.com/2014/

Chapter 4 · *Consecrating the Literary*

Epigraph: In the liner notes for *Lonely Avenue*, Hornby writes of "A Working Day," "Shortly after this song was finished, I was talking to one of the parents at my kids' school. He's an artist, and I asked him how his day had been. 'Oh, you know,' he said. 'I'm either a genius or a wanker.' Yes, I do know, as does anyone who sits on their own all day making crap up" (n.p.).

1. Slightly earlier in the same chapter, Habermas writes, "The private people for whom the cultural product became available as a commodity profaned it inasmuch as they had to determine its meaning on their own" (1989: 37).

2. For perhaps the earliest academic commentary on Amazon's customer reviews, see Suresh Kotha (1998: 217): "The firm offers space for readers to post their 'own' reviews. It then steps out of the way and lets its customers sell to each other. Thus, a large part of the editorial content on the firm's Website is created by customers themselves (along with the firm's editors)."

3. https://web.archive.org/web/20050207013315/http://books.guardian.co.uk/links /areas_of_interest/general/links/0%2C6135%2C1406190%2C00.html. Or see, for example, David Orr's article in the *New York Times*, "Where to Find Digital Lit" (2004).

4. For example, *Brain Pickings* blogger Maria Popova was a headline guest at the 2014 Melbourne Writers Festival, and the 2015 Sydney Writers' Festival featured the panel "Everyone's a Critic, But Should They Be?" including *Junkee* blogger Steph Harmon (http:// mwf.com.au/mwf-review-maria-popova-brain-pickings/; http://www.swf.org.au/component /option,com_2015/Itemid,416/agid,4298/lang,en/task,view_detail/). Additionally, in March 2017 litblogger and *Bookslut* founder Jessa Crispin was featured speaker at a sold-out event convened by the Wheeler Centre for Books, Writing and Ideas in Melbourne (https://www .wheelercentre.com/broadcasts/podcasts/the-wheeler-centre/jessa-crispin-why-i-am-not-a -feminist).

5. The book-reviewer identity crisis hastened by the rise of Web 2.0 has its exact parallel in the world of film reviewing. Observe, in UK film critic Mark Kermode's book *Hatchet Job: Love Movies, Hate Critics* (2013), the familiar "gnawing anxiety that the profession to which I had devoted my working life was in danger of losing its identity":

> Part of this change has been due to the rise of amateur online reviewers, their growing presence turning what was once an elitist profession into a more all-inclusive pastime. For some this may seem like a positive change; the declining dominance of a few "name" specialists who make their living commentating upon movies in favour of a new democracy in which everyone can be a critic. As the marketplace widened exponentially, so criticism itself seemed to be mutating, transforming from a trade into something more like a hobby, shifting from the ephemeral to the inconsequential—in the sense that reviews could now be published by anyone, without consequence. (28)

Similarly, Alex Ross, classical music critic for the *New Yorker*, recognizes in his article, "The Fate of the Critic in the Clickbait Age" (2017), that the issues raised by amateur online criticism cross art forms: "Classical music is hardly alone in witnessing a dying-off of critics. Colleagues in other disciplines—dance, theatre, visual arts, books, even movies and pop music—report similar struggles."

6. Some of the scant works on book reviewing are in fact memoirs, such as Anthony Curtis's *Lit Ed* (1998), or how-to guides, such as Mayra Calvani and Anne K. Edwards' *The Slippery Art of Book Reviewing* (2008).

7. Kakutani announced her decision to step down from the role of *NYT* chief book critic in July 2017 (see https://www.authorsguild.org/industry-advocacy/legendary-book -critic-michiko-kakutani-steps-new-york-times/).

8. Preface to *Culture and Anarchy* ([1875] 2006: 5). Cf. book reviewing in academic journals where, because of the specialist audience being addressed, the reviewer/reader knowledge differential is less stark.

9. Cf. also research into scholarly book reviewing and its role in discipline formation, though this too is often written by publishing practitioners rather than academics (e.g. Wasserman, M., 1994; Obeng-Odoom, 2014).

10. See Yglesias, 1994; Wasserman, M., 1994; Willis, 1994; Aguilar-San Juan, 1994; Pool, 1994; Barrington, 1994; Rapping, 1994; Seajay, 1994; Weisbard, 1995.

11. http://www.vidaweb.org/

12. http://www.cwila.com/
13. http://thestellaprize.com.au/the-count/2015-stella-count/
14. http://www.womensprizeforfiction.co.uk/
15. http://thestellaprize.com.au/about/
16. Harvey and Lamond make a similar point about the positive professional and academic spillover effect of book reviews (2016).
17. VIDA justifies its selection of publications on the grounds that they are "widely recognized as prominent critical and/or commercial literary venues":

> Publication in these magazines and journals furthers the careers of writers by bolstering applications for grants, residencies, employment (academic and otherwise), graduate programs, awards, and more. Winning/earning/receiving these types of honors affords writers the time and resources needed to continue/advance their careers. . . .
> These journals were chosen based on the following criteria:

- · Consistent editorial staff
- · Not edited by students
- · *Appears in print*
- · All regions represented
- · Multiple genres represented
- · Staying power (year established)
- · Widely accepted as reputable among literary community
- · Likelihood of work appearing in these journals to go on to be nominated for / win a Pushcart and/or appear in Best American Series

See http://www.vidaweb.org/faq/; italics added.

18. Cf. blogger, *Bookslut* founder, and self-declared radical feminist Jessa Crispin's take on seeking admission to the citadels of literary respectability: "I want to tell them [activists such as VIDA]: this world is not for you, you are better without it. Outside the gates, not in. This world was, in fact, in part, designed specifically to keep you out. It does not want you. It will not nourish you" (2016: 61). *Bookslut* announced that its fourteenth edition would be its last and that the blog would cease publishing new content after May 2016 (http://www.bookslut.com/blog/).

19. For further discussion of the democratization of cultural authority catalyzed by the Internet, see chapter 5.

20. The label of polemicist is Keen's own: on the opening page of *The Cult of the Amateur* (2007), the author describes his project as "a polemic about the destructive impact of the digital revolution on our culture, economy, and values" (1).

21. https://www.amazon.com/gp/help/customer/display.html/ref=help_search_1-1?ie=UTF8&nodeId=201930050&qid=1491451723&sr=1-1

22. Such review-the-reviewer features have become common in the Web 2.0 era as online review portals pioneer their own forms of reviewer hierarchy. For example, Mattias Frey notes film review website Rotten Tomatoes' feature whereby "users may . . . sort and filter reviews by whether they are positive or negative or written by a 'Top Critic' or by one of the users' favorite critics, so-called 'My Critics' " (2015: 85).

23. For more on the "Harriet Klausner effect" and the pernicious consequences of Amazon's culture of metrics, see chapter 5.

24. http://www.goodreads.com/review/guidelines. As Goodreads' algorithm is a black box, unable to be examined, this can only be conjectured.

25. For more on litbloggers and litblogger cooperatives, see chapter 2.

26. For example, http://austbookbloggerdirectory.blogspot.com.au/.

27. See chapter 1.

28. See, for example, https://www.youtube.com/watch?v=TA5aWZJSgLI; https://www.youtube.com/watch?v=IxAfi9KlD-0.

29. For more on this point, see chapter 2.

30. The paradigmatic example of the "warring film critics" TV format is, of course, *Siskel & Ebert* in the United States. An equally disputatious on-screen partnership was that of David Stratton and Margaret Pomeranz in Australian TV's *The Movie Show* (Special Broadcasting Service) and later *At the Movies* (Australian Broadcasting Corporation) which, combined, ran for twenty-five years.

31. Ann Steiner, scholar of the contemporary book world, concurs, stating: "In studying criticism on the web, it is clear that a number of critical strategies depend upon earlier forms of professional criticism" (2008).

32. http://sydneyreviewofbooks.com/could-not-put-it-down/

33. http://sydneyreviewofbooks.com/as-one-in-rejecting-the-label-middlebrow/

34. http://www.complete-review.com/main/main.html

35. http://www.complete-review.com/main/editorial.html

36. This was the case at least during the website's first decade, after which Orthofer outed himself as the author of around 95 percent of the website's unattributed content, acknowledging: "I've always tried to stay in the background (and would, of course, prefer disappearing completely unrecognized behind the scenes, an entirely anonymous puppet-master), but despite my best efforts to de-personalize the site it has become futile to avoid the obvious: *complete review*, c'est moi. . . . Hence one minor change: posts and reviews will now be signed 'M. A. Orthofer,' as I might as well lay claim to (and accept blame for) them" (http://www.complete-review.com/saloon/archive/200904a.htm#ll9).

37. The extent to which affective responses to books are perceived as highly gendered infused a 2007 dispute between US litbloggers and the National Book Critics Circle (see below). *The Washington Post*'s books columnist Michael Dirda had chided litbloggers for their "shallow grandstanding and overblown ranting, [undertaken] all too often by kids hoping to be noticed for their sass and vulgarity." This prompted book blogger Colleen Mondor to retaliate: "We [litbloggers] must not think for a moment that we contribute anything beyond serving as accessories to the real literary discussions. . . . Out here on the internet, if you write about books, if you publish the work of new writers, even if you interview a great author then you are apparently only doing it because the real folks who do this work happen to be busy that day. Thinking that the members of the lit blogosphere (kid lit, genre lit, every part and parcel of it) are in any way comparable to the true lords of the book universe would be highest folly on our parts" (http://www.chasingray.com/archives/2007/04/post_7.html; Getlin, 2007, online correction to print article, May 15, 2007; http://articles.latimes.com/2007/may/13/entertainment/ca-bloggers13; http://www.edrants.com/in-which-i-am-misquoted-by-josh-getlin/).

38. http://www.goodreads.com/review/guidelines

39. Lisa Nakamura attributes some of the success of social cataloging sites such as Goodreads to the free availability of their review content, in distinction to the "pay-to-read"

model of literary criticism produced by academic journal publishing (2013: 242). But, even if non-credentialed readers had the financial means to access literary critical journals, it is unlikely they would be motivated to do so because of the terminological barriers academic literary-critical discourse throws up (see Farr, 2005: 50). "Everyday" readers seek a different form of literary-critical discussion altogether.

40. As represented by Patricia Ticineto Clough and Jean Halley's influential collection of the same name (2007) and, in literary studies specifically, by the work of scholars such as Sianne Ngai (2007) and Lauren Berlant (2008).

41. Remark by Colleen Mondor, creator of the *Chasing Ray* book blog, in response to a National Book Critics Circle post criticizing litbloggers for undermining print review culture (see above).

42. http://bookcritics.org/blog/archive/the_shared_solitude_of_reading

43. Commentaries on this issue are legion. See Howard, 1992: 106; Longley, 1998: 217; Pool, 2007: 12; Gillieron and Kilgarriff, 2007: 170–77; Rich, 2007; Birkerts, 2007; Calvani and Edwards, 2008: 124; Teres, 2009: 243; Palattella, 2010; Nolan and Ricketson, 2013; Waters, 2013: 8; Robinson, 2014; Frew, 2014: 6; Delaney, B., 2014: 10, 12; Crispin, 2016: 58.

44. https://literaryminded.com.au/

45. Curiously, though published in 2000, Curran's survey of UK book reviewing is entirely silent on the subject of Amazon customer reviews.

46. These various rituals of distinction traverse disciplines. For example, writing of academic film studies, Mattias Frey notes "the long-term goal of film studies to establish itself as a serious subject of inquiry and maintain an institutional presence at universities and other highbrow cultural institutions has meant that, for generations, scholars have attempted to distance themselves from 'mere reviewers' and to differentiate their profession from journalism" (Frey and Sayad, 2015: 2).

47. https://en.wikipedia.org/wiki/Sockpuppet_(Internet). Similarly, the Urban Dictionary's top-ranking definition for "sock puppet" reads: "An account made on an internet message board, by a person who already has an account, for the purpose of posting more-or-less anonymously" (http://www.urbandictionary.com/define.php?term=sock%20puppet).

48. There is still comparatively little analysis of online reader reviews from the field of literary and media studies (as opposed to business studies) and even less about book blogs (cf. Steiner, 2010; Totanes, 2011).

49. http://www.thesundaytimes.co.uk/sto/news/uk_news/Arts/article1121933.ece

50. For more on Amazon sock puppetry, see Keen, 2007: 20; Ray Murray and Squires, 2013: 16; and Taylor, 2013: 14.

51. http://www.amazon.com/gp/help/customer/display.html?ref=footer_cou?ie=UTF8&nodeId=508088

52. https://www.amazon.com/gp/help/customer/display.html?nodeId=201929730

53. http://www.goodreads.com/review/guidelines

54. https://www.amazon.com/gp/help/customer/display.html?ref=help_search_1–1?ie=UTF8&nodeId=201930050&qid=1491275743&sr=1–1

55. New ways to game online ratings systems emerge, however, as soon as system administrators tinker with the algorithm or site terms of service in an attempt to stamp them out. For example, Kermode reveals "vote washing" of reviews on Amazon, whereby a negatively judged and hence low-ranking review is cut and pasted, given a new title, and

reposted, thereby climbing in the rankings (2013: 214–16). Similarly, Jolie C. Matthews discusses the 2012 gaming of social cataloging site Goodreads by the agent and friends of a debut author attempting to dislodge a negative, one-star review from the front page of reader reviews of her title through a coordinated campaign of "liking" positive reviews (2016: 2307, 2311).

56. "Amazon reserves the right (but not the obligation) to remove or edit such content, but does not regularly review posted content" (https://www.amazon.com/gp/help/customer /display.html/ref=footer_cou?ie=UTF8&nodeId=508088).

57. Amazon has, over the last decade and a half, partially or wholly acquired the three major reader self-cataloging and reviewing sites: Library Thing (a 40 percent stake in 2006), Shelfari (acquired outright in 2008), and Goodreads (purchased in 2013). This is part of a long-evident Amazon operating tactic of "getting big fast" by putting competitors out of business or simply subsuming them (Spector, 2000). For example, in January 2016 Amazon announced that it was "merging" Shelfari with Goodreads and that the smaller social networking site would cease to exist after June 2016 (Shelfari's former URL now automatically redirects to Goodreads). Shelfari enthusiasts publicly interpreted this announcement as Amazon "killing" Shelfari: "Right now I'm wallowing in self-pity and watching my fellow Shelfari members grieve the loss of a site that has become so special to so many of us. So, thanks to Amazon for destroying something that we all love. From what I'm seeing on the discussion threads, it looks like you have sent a lot of potential business to LibraryThing and Leafmarks" (though this latter site itself closed around the same time) (https://thereadersroom.org/2016/01/12/amazon-kills-shelfari/). Amazon executives were likely unperturbed by this threatened consumer boycott: at the time of writing Goodreads' user base was 55 million, compared to Library Thing's 2.1 million subscribers. When it comes to bookish social cataloging sites, Goodreads has, through consolidation and market power, become effectively the only game in town.

Salon writer and shrewd chronicler of digital literary developments Laura Miller wrote presciently in the wake of Amazon's 2013 acquisition of Goodreads: "You could say that the users are not the customers but the product. In buying the company, Amazon purchased both its reviews . . . but also their data, a vast collection of information on what people read and like" (2013).

58. https://www.amazon.com/gp/help/customer/display.html/ref=help_search_1–1?ie =UTF8&nodeId=201930050&qid=1491451723&sr=1–1

59. http://www.goodreads.com/review/guidelines; http://www.librarything.com/er/list

60. https://www.amazon.com/gp/help/customer/display.html/ref=help_search_1–1?ie =UTF8&nodeId=201909000&qid=1491449167&sr=1–1

61. OR Books, a small-sized print-on-demand and e-book publisher based in New York, proudly labels itself on its website a "radical, exciting response to Amazonian hegemony" (http://www.orbooks.com/).

Chapter 5 · *Entering Literary Discussion*

1. Canadian author and editor Drew Nelles is firmly in the latter camp, as the title of his essay "Solitary Reading in an Age of Compulsory Sharing" (2013) makes clear. He concludes his diatribe against the "enforced sociability" of reading online with the imperative: "Learn to be alone again" (47, 52).

2. Giuseppe Arcimboldo's painting "The Librarian" (c. 1566), familiar from its use on the front cover of the Cambridge University Press edition of D. F. McKenzie's landmark *Bibliography and the Sociology of Texts* (1999), is the best-known example of the subgenre.

3. See, for example, https://thereadersroom.org/2016/01/12/amazon-kills-shelfari/.

4. The journal *Annales d'histoire économique et sociale* flourished between the 1930s and 1950s and is associated with the French school of social history whose method was to examine a specific locale over *la longue durée* (the long term) to quantify changes in the material circumstances of daily life and their associated cultural formations or *mentalités*. Its most influential exponents in the book history context were Lucien Febvre and Henri-Jean Martin, whose 1958 book *L'Apparition du Livre* was widely influential on the nascent discipline, especially after its 1976 English translation as *The Coming of the Book*.

5. The phrase was first deployed by Jay David Bolter in *Writing Space* (1990) but was popularized by Ted Striphas, who used it as the title of his 2009 monograph.

6. http://infinitesummer.org/

7. http://www.bookcrossing.com/

8. For more on the way in which digital literary manifestations have slipped through the cracks of humanities and social science disciplines, see the conclusion to the present volume.

9. Darnton (1986).

10. Price (2004).

11. On the origins of book history in the disciplines of history, literature, and bibliography, see Leslie Howsam's useful triangular diagram in *Old Books and New Histories: An Orientation to Studies in Book and Print Culture* (2006: 9–10).

12. http://www.open.ac.uk/Arts/RED/index.html

13. http://www.bsu.edu/libraries/wmr/. This project was named one of the fifty most important National Endowment for the Humanities–funded projects of the last fifty years, an award conferred by then US President Barack Obama upon projects that have "changed the landscape of the humanities" (announced in a post to SHARP-L LISTSERV by Professor Frank Felsenstein of Ball State University, October 1, 2015).

14. Fish's "interpretive community" is akin to Tony Bennett's concept of a "reading formation," which he defines as "a set of discursive and inter-textual determinations which organise and animate the practice of reading, connecting texts and readers in specific relations to one another in constituting readers as reading subjects of particular types and texts as objects-to-be-read in particular ways" (1987: 70).

15. http://www.sharpweb.org/main/

16. Moretti (2013).

17. See chapter 2 for an extended discussion of Marcus's critique.

18. Klausner, who died in 2015, posted numerous book reviews daily, invariably awarding titles four or five stars, fueling speculation that she did not actually read the works and/ or that she was paid for positive reviews. Klausner lost her top ranking only when Amazon changed its algorithm to rank reviews according to those readers found most helpful, effectively demoting Klausner's blandly positive, effusively brief reviews in the reviewer hierarchy. See Kaplan (2015).

19. See chapter 4's discussion of affect as commercial asset in the context of online book reviewing.

20. http://www.goodreads.com/group

21. http://blog.erratasec.com/2010/05/popular-highlights-on-amazon-kindle.html# .VfuDkUow-Uk

22. https://kindle.amazon.com/

23. https://www.amazon.com/gp/help/customer/display.html?nodeId=201241990

24. http://www.goodreads.com/blog/show/677-share-your-kindle-notes-and-high lights-with-your-friends-beta

25. Ted Striphas (2010a: 300) and Yung-Hsing Wu (2013) have both noted the highly designed paratextual wrappings of Amazon's Kindle e-reading device, as well as its optional protective case and original box.

26. https://www.kobo.com/readinglife#ereaders

27. https://www.kobo.com/readinglife#ereaders

28. Drew Nelles similarly asks, in light of Facebook's "frictionless sharing" with online friends of whatever an account holder is reading: "If you read something and don't share it, did you really read it at all?" (2013: 45–46).

29. There are obvious parallels here with companies such as Amazon claiming intellectual property in voluntarily created customer reviews, including the right to sell these to third parties, as explored in chapter 4.

30. Infinite Summer participant "a.m.kelly" posted in the first week of proceedings: "It's a great thing to feel really deeply involved in some project and goddamn I love a good novel so I'm psyched to read this one with all of you fine people here on the Internet. I'm tempted even to say something like this [and woe am I to use such lame neologisim.] [*sic*] BOOK CLUB 2.0" (http://infinitesummer.org/archives/320).

31. http://infinitesummer.org/about. Long reports in her research into online book clubs that this "no spoilers" rule is typical because reading often takes place asynchronously, even if members are supposed to have completed the book by a pre-arranged date for the opening of discussion (2003: 212–13; see also Chelton, 2001: 32).

32. http://infinitesummer.org/about

33. Michael Pietsch stated, "It's the kind of thing I always hoped could happen for *Infinite Jest*" (Peltz, 2009: L2).

34. http://infinitesummer.org/about

35. http://infinitesummer.org/archives/498

36. http://infinitesummer.org/archives/920#en39

37. For example, guest Marcus Sakey wrote in week one: "Last year, David Foster Wallace hung himself. I'd never met the man, but it threw me into a funk. After a week of moping about, I picked up *Infinite Jest* again as a sort of personal tribute, and read it for the third time. Read it trusting him, read it feeling the sorrow and the joy and the sheer intellectual pleasure" (http://infinitesummer.org/archives/396). For more in this vein, see: http://infinitesummer.org/archives/920#en39. Fellow IS guest Kathleen Fitzpatrick (2012), in a rare academic consideration of this experiment in "social reading in the network age," also notes parallels with the mass outpouring of fannish grief in the wake of Cobain's 1994 suicide (201, 185).

38. http://infinitesummer.org/archives/920

39. The post is titled "Waving the White Flag: Reading as Rehabilitation": "Wallace's judgments on addicts and addictions fell upon me with great force, and something about

the ferocity of his critique, coupled with his profound compassion and humaneness toward the subject, compelled me to waste absolutely zero time in booting the pills and Getting My Shit Together" (http://infinitesummer.org/archives/959).

40. Timothy Aubry's monograph *Reading as Therapy: What Contemporary Fiction Does for Middle-Class Americans* considers Wallace's representation of addiction and therapy in *Infinite Jest*, but does not mention Infinite Summer, despite Aubry's book being published in 2011.

41. http://infinitesummer.org/archives/354

42. For its 2016 iteration, the Australian-organized Digital Writers' Festival chose [Stella] Miles Franklin's classic novel *My Brilliant Career* (1901) as the subject of its online reading group, positively inviting contrarian readings: "We will be posting the text of *My Brilliant Career*, in full, on our website. Using the genius.com interface, you can annotate the book to your heart's content. Be critical, be celebratory, be analytical, be irreverent. Discover what, exactly, Franklin's iconic novel has to teach us about the Australia of today" (http://digitalwritersfestival.com/2016/event/brilliant-bookclub/).

43. Cultural studies scholar Martin Barker, in his editorial to a special issue of the online audience studies journal *Participations* (2008), also notes how this disciplinary divide between cultural studies' valorization of popular media and the inherited cultural cachet of the book characterizing literary studies has been bridged by few scholars, notably Janice Radway. He concludes that "the two traditions really need to talk more with each other. A sharing of questions, theories, concepts and methods is what we are looking for."

44. http://www.bookcrossing.com/

45. http://www.bookcrossing.com/labels

46. http://www.bookcrossing.com/about

47. http://www.bookcrossing.com/about

48. http://www.bookcrossing.com/bookstats/mosttraveled

49. http://www.bookcrossing.com/about

50. http://www.bookcrossing.com/memberstats

51. Such face-to-face interaction may be rare on mass online bookish communities such as Amazon and Goodreads; however, online book clubs with a more focused geographic ambit frequently sponsor in-person events. For example, Joachim Vlieghe, Jaël Muls, and Kris Rutten note that the Flemish-language reading-promotion website and affiliated Facebook group, ledereenleest.be, sponsored an in-person social event in Belgium (2016: 31).

52. http://www.bookcrossing.com/convention

53. http://www.amazon.co.uk/gp/customer-reviews/R1GY0YZ5S5I8W5/ref=cm_cr_pr_rvw_ttl?ie=UTF8&ASIN=0099555174

54. http://www.amazon.co.uk/gp/customer-reviews/R2CI2J0FTIIYO3/ref=cm_cr_pr_rvw_ttl?ie=UTF8&ASIN=0099555174

55. http://www.amazon.com/gp/cdp/member-reviews/AM16USVV5TJEJ/ref=pdp_new_read_full_review_link?ie=UTF8&page=1&sort_by=MostRecentReview#RRY76E0BBIDNZ

56. http://dovegreyreader.typepad.com/dovegreyreader_scribbles/. Though Padmini Ray Murray and Claire Squires note that the site's creator, Lynne Hatwell, is invited to literary festivals and courted by publishers, so these claims should not be taken at face value (2013: 15). The website contains a section devoted to the blogger's tent at the 2014 Port

Eliot Festival (her fifth appearance there) in Cornwall, UK, although this is, as contemporary writers' festivals go, a pretty grassroots affair (see Murray and Weber, 2017).

57. Rehberg Sedo observes, "Because they function as a social communications network, primed to spread the word, book clubs represent a tempting new target market for publishers" (2011a: 19). Her chapter in the same collection investigates how the cultural spheres of book prize selection, publishers' advance marketing strategies, and teacher and librarian professional identities coalesce in a particular young adult book club (2011b). Similarly, Fuller, Rehberg Sedo, and Squires write (2011: 187): "Publishers—and to a lesser extent booksellers—are using reading groups as a marketing resource."

58. BookMovement's fine print assures corporate clients: "With these pages, Book-Movement is able to track what clubs are reading nationwide and provide a ranked list of Top Book Club Picks, based on the book selections and recommendations of our members. Our rankings are updated every Monday."

59. Steven Johnson (2010), "Yes, People Still Read, but Now It's Social," *New York Times*. http://www.nytimes.com/2010/06/20/business/20unbox.html.

Conclusion · *Accounting for Digital Paratext*

1. http://nickm.com/vox/golden_age.html

2. I say "outlier" because the relationship between mainstream literary studies and electronic literature is frequently a distant one. As Electronic Literature Organization founder Scott Rettberg has noted, "electronic literature . . . does not necessarily function as a subfield of literature," with electronic literature enthusiasts as often located in fine arts, computer science, film, and communication programs as in literary departments (2016: 128).

3. Genette, 1997: 357.

4. The website of book history's leading scholarly association, the Society for the History of Authorship, Reading and Publishing (SHARP), encapsulates the group's interests as "the composition, mediation, reception, survival, and transformation of written communication in material forms from marks on stone to new media" (http://www.sharpweb .org/main/).

5. See chapter 5 for a summary of how historians of reading have used traces left by readers in individual book copies to draw inferences about the usage and esteem of books in a given time and place.

6. http://www.sharpweb.org/main/purpose-history/

7. https://archive.org/

8. https://www.reading.ac.uk/special-collections/collections/archives/sc-publishers .aspx

9. Paul Erickson made a similar observation in a 2003 volume arising from the Media in Transition conference convened at MIT, noting that the presence of the word "history" in book history inhibited study of contemporary bookish phenomena: "Many scholars in a field as archive-centred as this are likely not comfortable doing research involving subjects that are still alive, and in fact may tend to view such work as not being 'real history'" (111).

10. http://library-cafe.blogspot.com.au/2014/05/may-28–2014-historian-elizabeth .html

11. Tellingly, literary scholar and book historian Geraint Evans contributed the chapter "Elizabeth Eisenstein and the Idea of Media History" to a volume titled *Recharting Media*

Studies: Essays on Neglected Media Critics (2008), edited by Philip Bounds and Mala Jagmohan.

12. For example, Ted Striphas, one of the few cultural studies scholars to place the contemporary book at the center of their work, admits worrying that his proposed undergraduate course on "The Cultures of Books and Reading" would be undersubscribed by students: "Would a class about book culture, offered not in a literature but in a communication department, spark their interest? Or would it seem too out of touch, too frumpy, too analog?" (2009: xxiii).

13. Stuart Lee observes a similar problem in relation to assessing undergraduate learning outcomes via his Oxford University course's requirement to build a website rather than write an essay of a certain word count: "In short our answer reflected the nebulous natures of web sites and we could only give rough estimates of guidance: namely, fifteen pages for the site" (2006: 65).

14. For more on "the Gutenberg parenthesis" see chapter 5.

15. "Book Culture from Below" was the theme of SHARP's 2010 annual conference in Helsinki, Finland (http://web.archive.org/web/20110819173312/http://www.helsinki.fi/sharp2010/index.htm).

16. Again, on both these points see chapter 5.

17. The neologism "produser" was a portmanteau term coined by Axel Bruns (2008: 23) to denote the merging of "producer" and "consumer" roles facilitated by networked digital technologies. It was designed to disrupt media studies' traditional tripartite division of its subject into "sender" (producer), "message" (text), and "receiver" (consumer) categories.

18. http://www.wiscprintdigital.org/conferences/

Adsett, Alex. 2012. "Self-publishing in the Digital Age." *Island* 128, Autumn: 132–39.

Aguilar-San Juan, Karin. 1994. "Forced Choices." *The Women's Review of Books* 11.9, June: 19–20.

Allen, Katie. 2009. "Coming Attractions." *Bookseller,* March 12, 2009. http://www.thebook seller.com/feature/coming-attractions.

Allington, Daniel. 2016. " 'Power to the Reader' or 'Degradation of Literary Taste?' Professional Critics and Amazon Customers as Reviewers of *The Inheritance of Loss.*" *Language and Literature* 25.3: 254–78.

Allington, Daniel, and Stephen Pihlaja. 2016. "Reading in the Age of the Internet." *Language and Literature* 25.3: 201–10.

Alsever, Jennifer. 2006. "The Author as Über-Marketer." *Business 2.0,* May: 56.

Alter, Alexandra. 2012. "Your E-Book Is Reading You." *Wall Street Journal,* July 19, 2012. http://www.wsj.com/articles/SB100014240527023048703045774900950051438304.

———. 2014. "John Green and His Nerdfighters Are Upending the Summer Blockbuster Model." *Wall Street Journal,* May 14, 2014. http://www.wsj.com/articles/john-green-and -his-nerdfighters-are-upending-the-summer-blockbuster-model-1400088712.

Altick, Richard. 1998. *The English Common Reader: A Social History of the Mass Reading Public, 1800–1900.* 2nd ed. Columbus: Ohio State UP.

Anderson, Benedict. 1983. *Imagined Communities: Reflections on the Origin and Spread of Nationalism.* London: Verso.

Anderson, Chris. 2006. *The Long Tail: Why the Future of Business is Selling Less of More.* New York: Hyperion.

Appleyard, Bryan. 2015. "Fairy Tale of New York." *Sunday Times* (UK), October 11, 2015: Magazine.

Arnold, Matthew. (1875) 2006. *Culture and Anarchy.* Oxford World's Classics. Oxford: Oxford UP.

Arons, Rachel. 2013. "The Awkward Art of Book Trailers." *New Yorker,* December 19, 2013. http://www.newyorker.com/books/page-turner/the-awkward-art-of-book-trailers.

Atwood, Margaret. 2006. "The Ballad of the LongPen™." *Guardian,* September 30, 2006. http://www.theguardian.com/books/2006/sep/30/margaretatwood.

———. 2010. "Atwood in the Twittersphere." *The New York Review Daily,* March 29, 2010. http://www.nybooks.com/daily/2010/03/29/atwood-in-the-twittersphere/.

Aubry, Timothy. 2011. *Reading as Therapy: What Contemporary Fiction Does for Middle-Class Americans.* Iowa City: U of Iowa P.

Auslander, Philip. 2008. *Liveness: Performance in a Mediatized Culture.* 2nd ed. London: Routledge.

"Author Atwood Invents 'Magic' Pen." 2006. *BBC News,* March 6, 2006. http://news.bbc .co.uk/2/hi/entertainment/4778962.stm.

Baddeley, Anna. 2013. "Margaret Atwood: Doyenne of Digital-savvy Authors." *Observer* (UK), June 9, 2013. http://www.theguardian.com/books/2013/jun/09/margaret-atwood -positron-online-publishing.

Barker, Martin. 2008. "Editorial Introduction." *Participations* 5.2, November. http://www .participations.org/Volume%205/Issue%202/5_02_editorial.htm.

Barnes, Helen. 2010. "Festivals Are All about Insecurity—Will I Get a Seat?" *Australian Author* 42.1, April: 11.

Barnes, Renee. 2018. *Uncovering Online Commenting Culture: Trolls, Fanboys and Lurkers.* London: Palgrave Macmillan.

Barnett, Tully. 2014. "Social Reading: The Kindle's Social Highlighting Function and Emerging Reading Practices." *Australian Humanities Review* 56: 141–62.

———. 2015. "Platforms for Social Reading: The Material Book's Return." *Scholarly and Research Communication* 6.4. http://src-online.ca/src/index.php/src/article/view/211.

Baron, Naomi S. 2015. *Words Onscreen: The Fate of Reading in a Digital World.* New York: Oxford UP.

Baron, Sabrina Alcorn, Eric N. Lindquist, and Eleanor F. Shevlin, eds. 2007. *Agent of Change: Print Culture Studies after Elizabeth L. Eisenstein.* Studies in Print Culture and the History of the Book. Amherst: U of Massachusetts P.

Barrington, Judith. 1994. "Mightier than the Bullet." *The Women's Review of Books* 12.1, October: 19–20.

Barry, Peter. 2011. *I Hate Martin Amis et al.* Melbourne: Transit Lounge.

Barthes, Roland. (1957) 1972. *Mythologies.* Translated by Annette Lavers. London: Paladin.

———. (1968) 1986. "The Death of the Author." In *The Rustle of Language.* Translated by Richard Howard. Oxford: Blackwell. 49–55.

Basaraba, Nicole. 2016. "Creating Persuasive Book Trailers as a New Media Marketing Tool." *Logos* 27.3: 34–51.

Battershill, Claire. 2014. "Writers' Rooms: Theories of Contemporary Authorship in Portraits of Creative Spaces." *Authorship* 3.2. http://www.authorship.ugent.be/article/view/1087.

Baum, Caroline. 2012. "Leading by Trailing." *Australian Author* 44.4, December: 16–18.

Baverstock, Alison. 2008. *How to Market Books.* 4th ed. London: Kogan Page.

———. 2015. *How to Market Books.* 5th ed. London: Routledge.

Belfiore, Eleonora, and Oliver Bennett. 2009. "Researching the Social Impact of the Arts: Literature, Fiction and the Novel." *International Journal of Cultural Policy* 15.1: 17–33.

Belieu, Erin, and Kevin Prufer. 2016. "VIDA: An Interview with Erin Belieu." In *Literary Publishing in the Twenty-first Century.* Edited by Travis Kurowski, Wayne Miller, and Kevin Prufer. Minneapolis, MN: Milkweed Editions. 101–19.

Bell, Alice. 2010. *The Possible Worlds of Hypertext Fiction.* Houndmills, UK: Palgrave Macmillan.

Bell, Alice, Astrid Ensslin, and Hans Rustad, eds. 2014. *Analyzing Digital Fiction.* Routledge Studies in Rhetoric and Stylistics. New York: Routledge.

Bennett, Andy, Jodie Taylor, and Ian Woodward, eds. 2014. *The Festivalization of Culture.* Farnham, UK: Ashgate.

Bennett, Andy, and Ian Woodward. 2014. "Festival Spaces, Identity, Experience and Belonging." In *The Festivalization of Culture.* Edited by Andy Bennett, Jodie Taylor, and Ian Woodward. Farnham, UK: Ashgate. 11–25.

Bennett, Nicola. 1999. *Speaking Volumes: A History of the Cheltenham Festival of Literature.* Cheltenham, UK: Sutton Publishing.

Bennett, Tony. 1987. "Texts in History: The Determinations of Readings and Their Texts." In *Post-Structuralism and the Question of History.* Edited by Derek Attridge, Geoff Bennington, and Robert Young. Cambridge: Cambridge UP. 63–81.

Bennett, Tony, Michael Emmison, and John Frow. 1999. *Accounting for Tastes*. Cambridge: Cambridge UP.

Berensmeyer, Ingo, Gert Buelens, and Marysa Demoor. 2012. "Authorship as Cultural Performance: New Perspectives in Authorship Studies." *Zeitschrift für Anglistik und Amerikanistik* 60.1: 5–29.

Berlant, Lauren. 2008. *The Female Complaint: The Unfinished Business of Sentimentality in American Culture*. Durham, NC: Duke UP.

Bérubé, Michael, ed. 2005. *The Aesthetics of Cultural Studies*. Malden, MA: Blackwell.

Bérubé, Michael, Hester Blum, Christopher Castiglia, and Julia Spicher Kasdorf. 2010. "Community Reading and Social Imagination." *PMLA* 125: 418–25.

Bidisha. 2014. "The Literary Cultures of the Future." *Wasafiri* 29.3: 48–51.

Biriotti, Maurice, and Nicola Miller, eds. 1993. *What is an Author?* Manchester, UK: Manchester UP.

Birkerts, Sven. 2007. "Lost in the Blogosphere: Why Literary Blogging Won't Save Our Literary Culture." *Boston Globe*, July 29, 2007. http://www.boston.com/news/globe/ideas /articles/2007/07/29/lost_in_the_blogosphere/?page=full.

Birmingham, John. 2010. "How to Pull a Crowd." *Australian Author* 42.1, April: 12–15.

Bode, Katherine, and Robert Dixon. 2009. *Resourceful Reading: The New Empiricism, eResearch, and Australian Literary Culture*. Sydney: Sydney UP.

Bolter, Jay David. 1990. *Writing Space: The Computer, Hypertext, and the History of Writing*. Mahwah, NJ: Lawrence Erlbaum Associates.

———. 2001. *Writing Space: Computers, Hypertext, and the Remediation of Print*. 2nd ed. New York: Routledge.

Booth, Paul. 2015. "Crowdfunding: A Spimatic Application of Digital Fandom." *New Media and Society* 17.2: 149–66.

Bourdieu, Pierre. 1993. *The Field of Cultural Production*. Edited by Randal Johnson. Cambridge, UK: Polity.

———. 1996. *The Rules of Art: Genesis and Structure of the Literary Field*. Translated by Susan Emanuel. Stanford, CA: Stanford UP.

Bourdieu, Pierre, and Loïc J. D. Wacquant. 1992. *An Invitation to Reflexive Sociology*. Chicago: U of Chicago P.

Bradley, Jana, Bruce Fulton, Marlene Helm, and Katherine A. Pittner. 2011. "Non-Traditional Book Publishing." *First Monday* 16.8, August 2011. http://firstmonday.org/ojs/index .php/fm/article/view/3353/3030.

Briggs, Asa, and Peter Burke. 2009. *A Social History of the Media: From Gutenberg to the Internet*. 3rd ed. Cambridge, UK: Polity.

Brockes, Emma. 2014. "John Green: Teenager, Aged 36." *Intelligent Life*, May/June. http:// www.intelligentlifemagazine.com/content/features/emma-brockes/john-green.

Brouillette, Sarah. 2007. *Postcolonial Writers in the Global Literary Marketplace*. Houndmills, UK: Palgrave Macmillan.

———. 2014. *Literature and the Creative Economy*. Stanford, CA: Stanford UP.

Brown, Stephen, ed. 2006. *Consuming Books: The Marketing and Consumption of Literature*. London: Routledge.

Bruns, Axel. 2008. *Blogs, Wikipedia, Second Life, and Beyond: From Production to Produsage*. New York: Peter Lang.

Buckridge, Patrick, Pamela Murray, and Jock Macleod. 1995. *Reading Professional Identities*. Brisbane, AU: ICPS.

Burdick, Anne, Johanna Drucker, Peter Lunenfeld, Todd Presner, and Jeffrey Schnapp. 2012. *Digital_Humanities*. Cambridge, MA: MIT P.

Burke, Seán. 1998. *The Death and Return of the Author: Criticism and Subjectivity in Barthes, Foucault and Derrida*. 2nd ed. Edinburgh: Edinburgh UP.

Burkeman, Oliver. 2006. "Atwood Sign of the Times Draws Blank." *Guardian*, March 6, 2006. http://www.theguardian.com/world/2006/mar/06/topstories3.books.

Busse, Kristina. 2013. "The Return of the Author: Ethos and Identity Politics." In *A Companion to Media Authorship*. Edited by Jonathan Gray and Derek Johnson. Malden, MA: Wiley. 48–68.

Byle, Ann. 2012. "Building Buzz with Social Media." *Publishers Weekly*, February 13, 2012: 7–8.

Cain, Sian. 2014. "#Twitterfiction Festival 2014: What You Are (and Are Not) Missing." *Guardian*, Books blog. https://www.theguardian.com/books/2014/mar/14/twitter-fiction -festival-2014.

Calvani, Mayra, and Anne K. Edwards. 2008. *The Slippery Art of Book Reviewing*. Kingsport, TN: Twilight Times Books.

Cannold, Leslie. 2011. "The Tweeting Truth." *Australian Author* 43.3, September: 13–15.

"Can Writers Just Be Writers in This Digital World?" 2014. *Books and Arts, ABC Radio National*, October 3, 2014. http://www.abc.net.au/radionational/programs/booksandarts /the-author-in-the-digital-age/5781270.

Carpenter, Susan. 2012. "John Green's [*sic*] Adds to His Fanbase with 'The Fault in Our Stars.'" *Los Angeles Times*, January 21, 2012. http://articles.latimes.com/2012/jan/21 /entertainment/la-et-john-green-20120121.

Carter, David. 1999. "Good Readers and Good Citizens: Literature, Media and the Nation." *Australian Literary Studies* 19.2: 136–51.

Carter, David, and Kay Ferres. 2001. "The Public Life of Literature." In *Culture in Australia: Policies, Publics and Programs*. Edited by Tony Bennett and David Carter. Cambridge: Cambridge UP. 140–60.

Casanova, Pascale. 2004. *The World Republic of Letters*. Translated by M. B. DeBevoise. Cambridge, MA: Harvard UP.

Cassin, Ray. 2008. "Rushdie Beamed into Festival." *The Age* (Melbourne), July 17, 2008: Magazine. http://www.theage.com.au/articles/2008/07/16/1216162958422.html.

Cavallo, Guglielmo, and Roger Chartier, eds. (1995) 1999. *A History of Reading in the West*. Translated by Lydia G. Cochrane. Studies in Print Culture and the History of the Book. Amherst: U of Massachusetts P.

Cawelti, John G. 1977. "The Writer as a Celebrity: Some Aspects of American Literature as Popular Culture." *Studies in American Fiction* 5.1: 161–74.

Chartier, Roger. (1992) 1994. *The Order of Books: Readers, Authors, and Libraries in Europe between the Fourteenth and Eighteenth Centuries*. Translated by Lydia G. Cochrane. Cambridge, UK: Polity.

Chelton, Mary K. 2001. "When Oprah Meets E-mail: Virtual Book Clubs." *Reference and User Services Quarterly* 41.1: 31–36.

Clark, Giles, and Angus Phillips. 2008. *Inside Book Publishing*. 4th ed. Abingdon, UK: Routledge.

Clifton, Peter. 2010. "Teach Them to Fish: Empowering Authors to Market Themselves Online." *Publishing Research Quarterly* 26: 106–09.

Clough, Patricia Ticineto, and Jean Halley, eds. 2007. *The Affective Turn: Theorizing the Social.* Durham, NC: Duke UP.

Coll, Steve. 2014. "Citizen Bezos." *New York Review of Books,* review of *The Everything Store: Jeff Bezos and the Age of Amazon* by Brad Stone, July 10, 2014. http://www.nybooks.com /articles/archives/2014/jul/10/citizen-bezos-amazon/.

Collins, Jim, ed. 2002. *High-Pop: Making Culture into Popular Entertainment.* Oxford: Blackwell.

———. 2010. *Bring on the Books for Everybody: How Literary Culture Became Popular Culture.* Durham, NC: Duke UP.

———. 2013. "Reading, in a Digital Archive of One's Own." *PMLA* 128.1: 207–12.

Compagnon, Antoine. 2005. "A World without Authors." In *Re-Imagining Language and Literature for the 21st Century.* Edited by Suthira Duangsamosorn. Amsterdam: Rodopi. 217–32.

Conner, Lynne. 2013. *Audience Engagement and the Role of Arts Talk in the Digital Era.* New York: Palgrave Macmillan.

Coombe, Rosemary. 1998. *The Cultural Life of Intellectual Properties: Authorship, Appropriation, and the Law.* Durham, NC: Duke UP.

———. (1998) 2006. "Author(iz)ing the Celebrity: Engendering Alternative Identities." In *The Celebrity Culture Reader.* Edited by P. David Marshall. New York: Routledge. 721–69.

Coover, Robert. 1992. "The End of Books." *New York Times Book Review,* June 21, 1992. http://www.nytimes.com/books/98/09/27/specials/coover-end.html.

———. 1993. "Hyperfiction: Novels for the Computer." *New York Times Book Review,* August 29, 1993. http://www.nytimes.com/books/98/09/27/specials/coover-hyperfiction.html.

———. 1999. "Literary Hypertext: The Passing of the Golden Age." Keynote address to Digital Arts and Culture conference, Atlanta, GA. October 29, 1999. http://nickm.com /vox/golden_age.html.

Coscarelli, Joe. 2009. "David Foster Wallace Lives On for an 'Infinite Summer.'" *Salon,* July 14, 2009. http://www.salon.com/2009/07/14/infinite_summer/.

Couldry, Nick. 2003. *Media Rituals: A Critical Approach.* London: Routledge.

Crispin, Jessa. 2016. "The Self-Hating Book Critic." In *Literary Publishing in the Twenty-First Century.* Edited by Travis Kurowski, Wayne Miller, and Kevin Prufer. Minneapolis, MN: Milkweed Editions. 58–65.

Crompton, Ben. 2013. "The Rise of the Book Trailer." *New York Press,* January 28, 2013. http://www.nypress.com/the-rise-of-the-book-trailer/n.

Crone, Rosalind, and Shafquat Towheed, eds. 2011. *The History of Reading, Volume 3: Methods, Strategies, Tactics.* Houndmills, UK: Palgrave Macmillan.

Cunningham, Stuart, ed. 2008. *The Cultural Economy.* Cultures and Globalization series. Thousand Oaks, CA: Sage.

Curran, James. 2000. "Literary Editors, Social Networks and Cultural Tradition." In *Media Organisations in Society.* Edited by James Curran. London: Arnold. 215–39.

Curtis, Anthony. 1998. *Lit Ed: On Reviewing and Reviewers.* Manchester, UK: Carcanet.

Darnton, Robert. (1982) 1990. "What Is the History of Books?" In *The Kiss of Lamourette.* London: Faber. 107–35.

———. 1986. "First Steps toward a History of Reading." *Australian Journal of French Studies* 23: 5–30.

———. 2009. *The Case for Books: Past, Present, and Future.* New York: Public Affairs.

Davila, Denise. 2010. "Not So Innocent: Book Trailers as Promotional Text and Anticipatory Stories." *ALAN Review* 38.1: 32–42.

Davis, Mark. 2008. "Literature, Small Publishers and the Market in Culture." *Overland* 190, Autumn: 4–11.

———. 2015. "E-books in the Global Information Economy." *European Journal of Cultural Studies* 18.4–5: 514–29.

Deahl, Rachel. 2007. "Production Companies Jockey for Publishers' Business." *Publishers Weekly*, September 10, 2007:13–14.

Dean, Jodi. 2003. "Why the Net Is Not a Public Sphere." *Constellations* 10.1: 95–112.

Dean, Michelle. 2014. "An Open Letter to Joyce Carol Oates: Delete Your Twitter Account." *Gawker*, May 13, 2014. http://gawker.com/an-open-letter-to-joyce-carol-oates-delete-your -twitte-1575788660.

Delaney, Brigid. 2014. "You Call That a Review?" *Australian Author* 46.1, June: 9–12.

Delany, Paul. 2002. *Literature, Money and the Market: From Trollope to Amis.* Basingstoke, UK: Palgrave Macmillan.

Delany, Paul, and George P. Landow. 1994. *Hypermedia and Literary Studies.* Cambridge, MA: MIT P.

Dempster, Lisa. 2012. "Literary Participation at the Digital Frontier." *Island* 128, Autumn: 116–29.

———. 2013. "The Problem with Literary Festivals?" *Wheeler Centre Dailies*, November 6, 2013. http://www.wheelercentre.com/notes/5e591f618053.

Denham, Jess. 2015. "Amazon to Sell Books the Old-Fashioned Way with First Physical Book Shop." *Independent* (UK), November 3, 2015.

Dennys, Harriet. 2006. "Dealers in Literary Crack." *Bookseller,* October 13, 2006: 26–27.

De Valck, Marijke. 2007. *Film Festivals: From European Geopolitics to Global Cinephilia.* Amsterdam: Amsterdam UP.

Diamond, Jason. 2014. "Tweeting While Literary: Joyce Carol Oates, Stephen King, and the Dangers of Being an Author on Twitter." *Flavorwire*, February 10, 2014. http://flavorwire .com/437967/tweeting-while-literary-joyce-carol-oates-stephen-king-and-the-dangers -of-being-an-author-on-twitter.

Dietz, Laura. 2015. "Who Are You Calling an Author? Changing Definitions of Career Legitimacy for Novelists in the Digital Era." In *Literary Careers in the Modern Era.* Edited by Guy Davidson and Nicola Evans. London: Palgrave Macmillan. 196–214.

Di Leo, Jeffrey R. 2012. "Data Mining Fiction." *American Book Review* 33.4: 2, 30.

Dobby, Christine. 2012. "Atwood, Wattpad a 'Natural Fit.'" *National Post* (Canada), June 26, 2012: 3.

Dodd, Mike. 2010. "Historian Pays Damages for Fake Amazon Reviews." *Press Association.* July 17, 2010.

Donadio, Rachel. 2005. "She'd Be Great on TV." *New York Times,* June 26, 2005.

———. 2008. "You're an Author? Me Too!" *New York Times Book Review,* April 27, 2008. http://www.nytimes.com/2008/04/27/books/review/Donadio-t.html?pagewanted=all&_r=0.

Douglas, J. Yellowlees. 2000. *The End of Books—or Books without End? Reading Interactive Narratives.* Ann Arbor: U of Michigan P.

Douglas, Kate. 2001. "'Blurbing' Biographical: Authorship and Autobiography." *Biography* 24.4: 806–26.

Driscoll, Beth. 2013. "Twitter, Literary Prizes and the Circulation of Capital." In *By the Book? Contemporary Publishing in Australia*. Edited by Emmett Stinson. Melbourne: Monash UP. 103–19.

———. 2014. *The New Literary Middlebrow: Tastemakers and Reading in the Twenty-First Century*. Houndmills, UK: Palgrave Macmillan.

———. 2015. "Sentiment Analysis and the Literary Festival Audience." *Continuum: Journal of Media and Cultural Studies*. http://www.tandfonline.com/doi/full/10.1080/10304 312.2015.1040729.

———. 2016. "Local Places and Cultural Distinction: The Booktown Model." *European Journal of Cultural Studies*, July 21, 2016.

Eakin, Emily. 2001. "Jonathan Franzen's Big Book." *New York Times*, September 2, 2001. http://www.nytimes.com/2001/09/02/magazine/jonathan-franzen-s-big-book.html? pagewanted=all.

Earhart, Amy E. 2015. *Traces of the Old, Uses of the New: The Emergence of Digital Literary Studies*. Editorial Theory and Literary Criticism series. Ann Arbor: U of Michigan P.

Egan, Jennifer. 2012. "Black Box." *New Yorker*, June 4 and 11, 2012: 84–97.

Eisenstein, Elizabeth L. 1979. *The Printing Press as an Agent of Change*. Cambridge: Cambridge UP.

———. 2014. Interview. *The Library Café*, May 28, 2014. http://library-cafe.blogspot.com .au/2014/05/may-28–2014-historian-elizabeth.html.

El-Hai, Jack. 2014. "A New Way of Looking at the Video Book Trailer." *Quill*, January–February: 25.

Eliot, Simon, and Jonathan Rose, eds. 2007. *A Companion to the History of the Book*. Malden, MA: Blackwell.

Engelhardt, Tom. 1997. "Gutenberg Unbound." *Nation*, March 17, 1997: 18–21, 29.

English, James F. 2005. *The Economy of Prestige*. Cambridge, MA: Harvard UP.

———. 2010. "Everywhere and Nowhere: The Sociology of Literature After 'the Sociology of Literature.'" *NLH* 41: v–xxiii.

———. 2011. "Festivals and the Geography of Culture: African Cinema in the 'World Space' of its Public." In *Festivals and the Cultural Public Sphere*. Edited by Liana Giorgi, Monica Sassatelli, and Gerard Delanty. Routledge Advances in Sociology. London: Routledge. 63–78.

———. 2012. *The Global Future of English Studies*. Hoboken, NJ: Wiley.

English, James F., and John Frow. 2006. "Literary Authorship and Celebrity Culture." In *A Concise Companion to Contemporary British Fiction*. Edited by James F. English. Malden, MA: Blackwell. 39–57.

Ensslin, Astrid. 2006. "Hypermedia and the Question of Canonicity." *dichtung-digital* 36. http://www.dichtung-digital.de/2006/01/Ensslin/index.htm.

Epstein, Jason. 2001. *Book Business: Publishing Past Present and Future*. New York: Norton.

Erickson, Paul. 2003. "Help or Hindrance? The History of the Book and Electronic Media." In *Rethinking Media Change: The Aesthetics of Transition*. Edited by David Thorburn and Henry Jenkins. Cambridge, MA: MIT P. 95–116.

Evans, Geraint. 2008. "Elizabeth Eisenstein and the Idea of Media History." In *Recharting Media Studies: Essays on Neglected Media Critics*. Edited by Philip Bounds and Mala Jagmohan. Bern, Switzerland: Peter Lang. 173–94.

Ewen, Paul. 2014. *Francis Plug: How to Be a Public Author*. Melbourne: Text Publishing.

Fagge, Nick. 2010. "Women Writers at War over Fake Book Reviews on Amazon." *Daily Mail* (UK), November 30, 2010. http://www.dailymail.co.uk/news/article-1333885/Amazons-amateur-book-reviewing-vicious-free-readers-victims.html.

Farr, Cecilia Konchar. 2005. *Reading Oprah: How Oprah's Book Club Changed the Way America Reads*. Albany: SUNY P.

Farr, Cecilia Konchar, and Jaime Harker, eds. 2008. *The Oprah Affect: Critical Essays on Oprah's Book Club*. Albany: SUNY P.

Febvre, Lucien, and Henri-Jean Martin. (1958) 1976. *The Coming of the Book: The Impact of Printing, 1450–1800*. Translated by David Gerard. London: N.L.B.

Ferguson, Will. 2002. *Happiness™*. Edinburgh, UK: Canongate.

Finkelstein, David, and Alistair McCleery, eds. 2006. *The Book History Reader*. 2nd ed. Abingdon, UK: Routledge.

Finkelstein, David, and Alistair McCleery. 2013. *An Introduction to Book History*. 2nd ed. New York: Routledge.

Finn, Ed. 2012. "New Literary Cultures: Mapping the Digital Networks of Toni Morrison." In *From Codex to Hypertext: Reading at the Turn of the Twenty-First Century*. Edited by Anouk Lang. Amherst: U of Massachusetts P. 177–202.

———. 2013. "Revenge of the Nerd: Junot Díaz and the Networks of American Literary Imagination." *Digital Humanities Quarterly* 7.1. http://www.digitalhumanities.org/dhq/vol/7/1/000148/000148.html.

Fish, Stanley. 1980. *Is There a Text in This Class? The Authority of Interpretive Communities*. Cambridge, MA: Harvard UP.

———. (1980) 2011a. "What Makes an Interpretation Acceptable?" In *The History of Reading: A Reader*. Edited by Shafquat Towheed, Rosalind Crone, and Katie Halsey. Routledge Literature Readers. London: Routledge. 99–108.

———. 2011b. "The Old Order Changeth." *New York Times*, December 26, 2011. http://opinionator.blogs.nytimes.com/2011/12/26/the-old-order-changeth/.

Fister, Barbara. 2005. " 'Reading as a Contact Sport': Online Book Groups and the Social Dimensions of Reading." *Reference and User Services Quarterly* 44.4: 303–09.

Fitzpatrick, Kathleen. 2011a. *Planned Obsolescence: Publishing, Technology, and the Future of the Academy*. New York: New York UP.

———. 2011b. "The Digital Future of Authorship: Rethinking Originality." *Culture Machine* 12. http://www.culturemachine.net/index.php/cm/issue/view/23.

———. 2012. "Infinite Summer: Reading, Empathy, and the Social Network." In *The Legacy of David Foster Wallace*. Edited by Samuel Cohen and Lee Konstantinou. New American Canon. Iowa City: U of Iowa P. 182–207.

Flood, Alison. 2012. "RJ Ellory's Secret Amazon Reviews Anger Rivals." *Guardian*, September 3, 2012. https://www.theguardian.com/books/2012/sep/03/rj-ellory-secret-amazon-reviews.

Florida, Richard. 2002. *The Rise of the Creative Class*. New York: Basic Books.

Foasberg, Nancy M. 2012. "Online Reading Communities: From Book Clubs to Book Blogs." *The Journal of Social Media in Society* 1.1: 30–53. http://thejsms.org/index.php/TSMRI/article/view/3.

Forsyth, Patrick, with Robin Birn. 1997. *Marketing in Publishing*. London: Routledge.

Foucault, Michel. (1969) 2006. "What Is an Author?" In *The Book History Reader*. 2nd ed. Edited by David Finkelstein and Alistair McCleery. Abingdon, UK: Routledge. 281–91.

Fowler, Geoffrey A., and Jeffrey A. Trachtenberg. 2010. "Vanity Press Goes Digital." *Wall Street Journal*, June 3, 2010. http://online.wsj.com/news/articles/SB20001424052748704912004575253132121412028#articleTabs%3Darticle.

Franzen, Jonathan. 1996. "Perchance to Dream: In the Age of Images, A Reason to Write Novels." *Harper's*, April: 35–54.

———. 2001. "Meet Me in St Louis." *New Yorker*, December 24, 2001. http://www.newyorker.com/archive/2001/12/24/011224fa_FACT1.

———. 2013. "What's Wrong with the Modern World." *Guardian*, September 13, 2013. http://www.theguardian.com/books/2013/sep/13/jonathan-franzen-wrong-modern-world.

Freeth, Kate. 2007. *A Lovely Kind of Madness: Small and Independent Publishing in Australia*. Melbourne: Small Press Underground Networking Community.

Frew, Wendy. 2014. "And the Winner Is . . ." *Australian Author* 46.1, June: 5–8.

Frey, Mattias. 2015. "The New Democracy? Rotten Tomatoes, Metacritic, Twitter, and IMDb." In *Film Criticism in the Digital Age*. Edited by Mattias Frey and Cecilia Sayad. New Brunswick, NJ: Rutgers UP. 81–98.

Frey, Mattias, and Cecilia Sayad, eds. 2015. *Film Criticism in the Digital Age*. New Brunswick, NJ: Rutgers UP.

Friedman, Jane. 2016. "The Future Value of a Literary Publisher." In *Literary Publishing in the Twenty-First Century*. Edited by Travis Kurowski, Wayne Miller, and Kevin Prufer. Minneapolis, MN: Milkweed Editions. 277–86.

Fuller, Danielle, and DeNel Rehberg Sedo. 2012. "Mixing it Up: Using Mixed Methods Research to Investigate Contemporary Cultures of Reading." In *From Codex to Hypertext: Reading at the Turn of the Twenty-First Century*. Edited by Anouk Lang. Amherst: U of Massachusetts P. 234–51.

———. 2013. *Reading beyond the Book: The Social Practices of Contemporary Literary Culture*. Routledge Research in Cultural and Media Studies. New York: Routledge.

———. 2014. " 'And Then We Went to the Brewery': Reading as a Social Activity in a Digital Era." *World Literature Today* 88.3–4, May/August: 14–18.

Fuller, Danielle, DeNel Rehberg Sedo, and Claire Squires. 2011. "Marionettes and Puppeteers? The Relationship between Book Club Readers and Publishers." In *Reading Communities from Salons to Cyberspace*. Edited by DeNel Rehberg Sedo. Houndmills, UK: Palgrave Macmillan. 181–99.

Gaiman, Neil, and the Twitterverse. 2010. *Hearts, Keys, and Puppetry*. Ashland, OR: Blackstone Audio.

Gapper, John. 2017. "Books Are Back Because Amazon Likes Them." *Financial Times* (UK), February 8, 2017. https://www.ft.com/content/f8bd3938-ed4d-11e6-ba01-119a44939bb6.

Gardiner, Juliet. 2000a. "Recuperating the Author: Consuming Fictions of the 1990s." *PBSA* 94.2: 255–74.

———. 2000b. " 'What Is an Author?' Contemporary Publishing Discourse and the Author Figure." *PRQ* 16.1: 63–76.

———. 2002. "Reformulating the Reader: Internet Bookselling and Its Impact on the Construction of Reading Practices." *Changing English* 9.2: 161–68.

Genette, Gérard. (1987) 1997. *Paratexts: Thresholds of Interpretation*. Translated by Jane E. Lewin. Cambridge: Cambridge UP.

Getlin, Josh. 2007. "Battle of the Book Reviews." *Los Angeles Times,* May 13, 2007. http://articles.latimes.com/2007/may/13/entertainment/ca-bloggers13.

Gibson, Chris, and John Connell, eds. 2011. *Festival Places: Revitalising Rural Australia.* Tourism and Cultural Change series. Bristol, UK: Channel View.

Gillan, Jennifer. 2015. *Television Broadcasting: The Return of the Content-Promotion Hybrid.* New York: Routledge.

Gillieron, Rebecca, and Catheryn Kilgarriff. 2007. *The Bookaholics' Guide to Book Blogs.* London: Marion Boyars Publishers.

Gillies, Mary Ann. 2007. *The Professional Literary Agent in Britain, 1880–1920.* Toronto: U of Toronto P.

Giorgi, Liana. 2009. "Literature Festivals and the Sociology of Literature." *The International Journal of the Arts in Society* 4.4: 317–26.

———. 2011. "Between Tradition, Vision and Imagination: The Public Sphere of Literature Festivals." In *Festivals and the Cultural Public Sphere.* Edited by Liana Giorgi, Monica Sassatelli, and Gerard Delanty. Routledge Advances in Sociology. London: Routledge. 29–44.

Giorgi, Liana, Monica Sassatelli, and Gerard Delanty, eds. 2011. *Festivals and the Cultural Public Sphere.* Routledge Advances in Sociology. London: Routledge.

Gitelman, Lisa. 2014. *Paper Knowledge: Toward a Media History of Documents.* Sign, Storage, Transmission series. Durham, NC: Duke UP.

Glass, Loren. 2004. *Authors Inc.: Literary Celebrity in the Modern United States, 1880–1980.* New York: NYU P.

Gleick, James. 2011. *The Information: A History, A Theory, A Flood.* New York: Pantheon Books.

Goldstone, Andrew, and Ted Underwood. 2014. "The Quiet Transformations of Literary Studies: What Thirteen Thousand Scholars Could Tell Us." *New Literary History* 45.3: 359–84.

Gomez, Jeff. 2005. "Thinking outside the Blog: Navigating the Literary Blogosphere." *Publishing Research Quarterly* 21.3: 3–11.

———. 2008. *Print Is Dead: Books in Our Digital Age.* New York: St. Martin's Press.

Grainge, Paul, and Catherine Johnson. 2015. *Promotional Screen Industries.* London: Routledge.

Gray, Jonathan. 2010. *Show Sold Separately: Promos, Spoilers, and Other Media Paratexts.* New York: NYU P.

Greene, Fred, Keith Johnston, and Ed Vollans. 2014. "Would I Lie to You? Researching Audience Attitudes to, and Uses of, the Promotional Trailer Format." *International Journal of Media and Cultural Politics* 10.1: 113–20.

Groskop, Viv. 2010a. "How to Stalk Your Favourite Author." *Daily Telegraph* (UK), April 24, 2010: 25.

———. 2010b. "Literary Luvvies Come Over all aTwitter about Tweeting." *Observer* (UK), December 19, 2010: 41.

Gruzd, Anatoliy, and DeNel Rehberg Sedo. 2012. "#1b1t: Investigating Reading Practices at the Turn of the Twenty-First Century." *Mémoires du Livre / Studies in Book Culture* 3.2. http://www.erudit.org/revue/memoires/2012/v3/n2/1009347ar.html.

Guthrie, Meredith. 2013. "Whatever You Do, Don't Call It 'Mommy Porn': *Fifty Shades of*

Grey, Fan Culture, and the Limits of Intellectual Property Rights." *Infinite Earths.* http://79.170.40.240/infiniteearths.co.uk/?p=993.

Gutjahr, Paul C. (2002) 2011. "No Longer Left Behind: Amazon.com, Reader-Response, and the Changing Fortunes of the Christian Novel in America." In *The History of Reading: A Reader.* Edited by Shafquat Towheed, Rosalind Crone, and Katie Halsey. Abingdon, UK: Routledge. 389–401.

Habermas, Jürgen. (1962) 1989. *The Structural Transformation of the Public Sphere: An Inquiry into a Category of Bourgeois Society.* Translated by Thomas Burger. Cambridge, UK: Polity.

Haigh, Gideon. 2006. "Information Idol." *The Monthly*, February: 25–33.

———. 2010. "Feeding the Hand That Bites: The Demise of Australian Literary Reviewing." *Kill Your Darlings* 1. http://www.killyourdarlingsjournal.com/?post_type=article&p=1472.

Hallinan, Blake, and Ted Striphas. 2016. "Recommended for You: The Netflix Prize and the Production of Algorithmic Culture." *New Media and Society* 18.1: 117–37.

Halzack, Sarah. 2015. "Amazon Opening a Brick-and-Mortar Bookstore." *Washington Post*, November 3, 2015.

Hamilton, Caroline. 2012. "The New Networking." *Island* 128, Autumn: 71–80.

Hamilton, Caroline, and Kirsten Seale. 2014. "Great Expectations—Making a City of Literature." *Meanjin* 73.1: 142–51.

Hanke, Andrea. 2015. "On the Virtual Road." *Australian Author Online* 6, October: 18–19.

Hanrahan, Michael, and Deborah L. Madsen, eds. 2006. *Teaching, Technology, Textuality: Approaches to New Media.* Teaching the New English series. Houndmills, UK: Palgrave Macmillan.

Harmon, Amy. 2004. "Amazon Glitch Unmasks War of Reviewers." *New York Times*, February 14, 2004. http://www.nytimes.com/2004/02/14/us/amazon-glitch-unmasks-war-of-reviewers.html?scp=6&sq=amazon+book+reviews&st=nyt.

Harrad, Kate. 2012. "Twitter—the Virtual Literary Salon." *Guardian*, Books Blog, January 11, 2012. http://www.theguardian.com/books/booksblog/2012/jan/11/twitter-virtual-literary-salon.

Hartley, Jenny. 2001. *Reading Groups.* Oxford: Oxford UP.

Hartley, John, ed. 2005. *Creative Industries.* Oxford: Blackwell.

Hartling, Florian. 2007. "Hypertext and Collective Authors: The Influence of the Internet on the Formation of New Concepts of Authorship." In *Literatures in the Digital Era: Theory and Praxis.* Edited by Amelia Sanz and Dolores Romero. Newcastle, UK: Cambridge Scholars Publishing. 289–96.

Harvey, Ellen. 2013. "Building a Social Hive." *Book Business*, December: 22–25.

Harvey, Melinda, and Julieanne Lamond. 2016. "Taking the Measure of Gender Disparity in Australian Book Reviewing as a Field, 1985 and 2013." *Australian Humanities Review* 60. http://australianhumanitiesreview.org/2016/11/15/taking-the-measure-of-gender-disparity-in-australian-book-reviewing-as-a-field-1985-and-2013/.

Hawker, Philippa. 2014. "The Fault in Our Stars: Interview with Bestselling YA Author John Green on the Move from Page to Screen." *Sydney Morning Herald*, July 3, 2014. http://www.smh.com.au/entertainment/movies/the-fault-in-our-stars-interview-with-bestselling-ya-author-john-green-on-the-move-from-page-to-screen-20140528-zrka9.html.

Hayles, N. Katherine. 2002. *Writing Machines*. Mediaworks pamphlets. Cambridge, MA: MIT P.

———. 2004. "Print Is Flat, Code Is Deep: The Importance of Media-Specific Analysis." *Poetics Today* 25.1: 67–90.

———. 2005. *My Mother Was a Computer: Digital Subjects and Literary Texts*. Chicago: U of Chicago P.

———. 2008. *Electronic Literature: New Horizons for the Literary*. Notre Dame, IN: U of Notre Dame P.

———. 2012. *How We Think: Digital Media and Contemporary Technogenesis*. Chicago: U of Chicago P.

Hayles, N. Katherine, and Jessica Pressman, eds. 2013. *Comparative Textual Media: Transforming the Humanities in the Postprint Era*. Electronic Mediations series. Minneapolis: U of Minnesota P.

Heiss, Anita M. 2003. *Dhuuluu-Yala—To Talk Straight: Publishing Indigenous Literature*. Canberra, AU: Aboriginal Studies Press.

Hely, Steve. 2009. *How I Became a Famous Novelist*. Melbourne: Black Inc.

Henly, Susan Gough. 2011. "Meet the Bloggers." *The Age* (Melbourne), January 28, 2011: Melbourne Magazine, 34.

Hepburn, James. 1968. *The Author's Empty Purse and the Rise of the Literary Agent*. London: Oxford UP.

Hesmondhalgh, David. 2007. *The Cultural Industries*. 2nd ed. London: Sage.

Holson, Laura M. 2012. "From Exile to Everywhere." *New York Times*, March 25, 2012: L1.

"Honoring—and Poking Fun at—Book Trailers." 2011. *All Things Considered*, National Public Radio, June 2, 2011. http://www.npr.org/2011/06/02/136897396/moby-awards-honors-book-trailers.

Hornby, Nick. 2010. "A Working Day." *Lonely Avenue*. Music by Ben Folds. Nonesuch Records / Warner Music.

Horton, Donald, and R. Richard Wohl. 1956. "Mass Communication and Para-Social Interaction: Observations on Intimacy at a Distance." *Psychiatry* 19: 215–29.

Howard, Gerald. 1992. "The Cultural Ecology of Book Reviewing." *Media Studies Journal* 6: 90–110.

Howsam, Leslie. 2006. *Old Books and New Histories: An Orientation to Studies in Book and Print Culture*. Studies in Book and Print Culture. Toronto: U of Toronto P.

Hungerford, Amy. 2012. "McSweeney's and the School of Life." *Contemporary Literature* 53.4: 646–80.

Indyk, Ivor. 1997. "Literary Authority." *Australian Book Review* 196, November: 36–40.

Ingleton, Pamela. 2012. "How Do You Solve a Problem Like Twitterature? Reading and Theorizing 'Print' Technologies in an Age of Social Media." *Technoculture: An Online Journal of Technology in Society* 2. https://tcjournal.org/drupal/vol2/ingleton.

Innis, Harold A. (1950) 2007. *Empire and Communications*. Lanham, MD: Rowman and Littlefield.

Iordanova, Dina, and Ragan Rhyne, eds. 2009. *The Festival Circuit*. Film Festival Yearbook 1. St. Andrews, UK: St. Andrew's Film Studies / College Gate Press.

Iser, Wolfgang. 1974. *The Implied Reader*. Baltimore, MD: Johns Hopkins UP.

———. 1978. *The Act of Reading: A Theory of Aesthetic Response*. London: Routledge and Kegan Paul.

Jaffe, Meredith. 2015. "Middlebrow? What's So Shameful about Writing a Book and Hoping It Sells?" *Guardian,* November 5, 2015. https://www.theguardian.com/books/2015/nov/05/middlebrow-whats-so-shameful-about-writing-a-book-and-hoping-it-sells-well.

Jameson, Julietta. 2012. "I'm Not Doing This for Nothing." *Australian Author* 44.3, September: 6–9.

Janssen, Susanne. 1997. "Reviewing as Social Practice: Institutional Constraints on Critics' Attention for Contemporary Fiction." *Poetics* 24: 275–97.

Jenkins, Henry. 2006. *Convergence Culture: Where Old and New Media Collide.* New York: NYU P.

Jockers, Matthew. 2013. *Macroanalysis: Digital Methods and Literary History.* Topics in the Digital Humanities. Urbana: U of Illinois P.

Jockers, Matthew L., and Daniela M. Witten. 2010. "A Comparative Study of Machine Learning Methods for Authorship Attribution." *Literary and Linguistic Computing* 25.2: 215–23.

Johanson, Katya, and Robin Freeman. 2012. "The Reader as Audience: The Appeal of the Writers' Festival to the Contemporary Audience." *Continuum: Journal of Media and Cultural Studies* 26.2: 303–14.

Johnson, Stephanie. 2015. *The Writers' Festival.* Auckland, NZ: Vintage.

Johnson, Steven. 2010. "Yes, People Still Read, but Now It's Social." *New York Times,* June 19, 2010. http://www.nytimes.com/2010/06/20/business/20unbox.html.

"Jonathan Franzen Falls Foul of Twitterati after Scorning Social Media." 2013. *Guardian,* October 4, 2013. http://www.theguardian.com/books/2013/oct/03/jonathan-franzen-twitter-social-media-today.

Kachka, Boris. 2008. "The End." *New York Magazine,* September 14, 2008. http://nymag.com/news/media/50279/.

Kaiser, Kevin. 2012. "Rewriting the Rules of Marketing." *Writer's Digest,* July/August: 32–35.

Kammen, Michael. 1999. *American Culture, American Tastes: Social Change and the 20th Century.* New York: Knopf.

Kaplan, Sarah. 2015. "The Woman Who Wrote 31,014 Amazon Book Reviews and Upended the Internet, Dead at 63." *Washington Post,* October 29, 2015. https://www.washingtonpost.com/news/morning-mix/wp/2015/10/29/the-woman-who-wrote-31014-amazon-book-reviews-and-upended-the-internet-dead-at-63-2/.

Katz, Christina. 2010. "Elements of a Successful Fiction Platform." *Writer's Digest,* November/December: 46–51.

Kaufman, Leslie. 2013. "Read Any Good Web Sites Lately? Book Lovers Talk Online." *New York Times,* February 13, 2013: C1.

Keating, Sara. 2013. "What Does Wattpad Offer Established Authors like Atwood?" *Irish Times,* November 16, 2013: 13.

Keen, Andrew. 2007. *The Cult of the Amateur: How Today's Internet Is Killing Our Culture.* New York: Doubleday.

Keep, Elmo. 2014. "Nobody Cares about Your Personal Brand." *Australian Author.* March 6, 2014. http://australian-author.org/online/nobody-cares-about-your-personal-brand.

Kermode, Mark. 2013. *Hatchet Job: Love Movies, Hate Critics.* London: Picador.

Khanna, Sundeep. 2013. "Salman Rushdie vs. Jonathan Franzen: Twitter Wars of the Literary Kind." *Livemint,* September 17, 2013. http://www.livemint.com/Opinion/pfiUAaTOU7bDHCzUaxSWNI/Salman-Rushdie-Vs-Jonathan-Franzen-Twitter-wars-of-the-lite.html.

Kiley, Dean. 1998. "So Then I Said to Helen." *Meanjin* 57.4: 799–808.

Killick, Ruth. 2013. "Meet the Publicist." *The Author* 124.2, Summer: 63–64.

Kirschenbaum, Matthew G. 2008. *Mechanisms: New Media and the Forensic Imagination.* Cambridge, MA: MIT P.

———. 2009. "Where Computer Science and Cultural Studies Collide." *Chronicle of Higher Education,* January 23, 2009. http://www.chronicle.com/article/where-computer-science-and/14806.

Knausgaard, Karl Ove. (2009) 2014. *A Man in Love. My Struggle*: Book 2. Translated by Don Bartlett. London: Vintage.

Knox, Malcolm. 2005. "The Ex Factor: BookScan and the Death of the Australian Novelist." *The Monthly*, May: 51–55.

Kotha, Suresh. 1998. "Competing on the Internet: The Case of Amazon.com." *European Management Journal* 16.2: 212–22.

Kumar, Nanda, and Izak Benbasat. 2002. "Para-Social Presence and Communication Capabilities of a Web Site." *E-Service Journal* 1.3: 5–24.

Kurowski, Travis, Wayne Miller, and Kevin Prufer, eds. 2016. *Literary Publishing in the Twenty-First Century.* Minneapolis, MN: Milkweed Editions.

Landow, George P. 1992. *Hypertext: The Convergence of Contemporary Critical Theory and Technology.* Baltimore, MD: Johns Hopkins UP.

———, ed. 1994. *Hyper/Text/Theory.* Baltimore, MD: Johns Hopkins UP.

———. 1997. *Hypertext 2.0.* rev. ed. Baltimore, MD: Johns Hopkins UP.

———. 2006. *Hypertext 3.0: Critical Theory and New Media in an Era of Globalization.* 3rd ed. Baltimore, MD: Johns Hopkins UP.

Landry, Charles. 1996. *The Art of Regeneration: Urban Renewal through Cultural Activity.* London: Comedia.

Lang, Anouk, ed. 2012. *From Codex to Hypertext: Reading at the Turn of the Twenty-First Century.* Amherst: U of Massachusetts P.

Larson, Mia. 2009. "Festival Innovation: Complex and Dynamic Network Interaction." *Scandinavian Journal of Hospitality and Tourism* 9.2–3: 288–307.

La Salle, Peter. 1997. "No Ventriloquism: The Idea of Voice in Book Reviewing." *AGNI* 45: 163–77.

Lea, Richard, and Matthew Taylor. 2010. "Historian Orlando Figes Admits Posting Amazon Reviews that Trashed Rivals." *Guardian*, April 23, 2010. https://www.theguardian.com/books/2010/apr/23/historian-orlando-figes-amazon-reviews-rivals.

Leadbeater, Charles. 1999. *Living on Thin Air: The New Economy.* London: Viking.

Leavis, Q. D. (1932) 1979. *Fiction and the Reading Public.* Harmondsworth, UK: Penguin.

Lee, Stuart. 2006. "Putting IT into the English Syllabus: A Case of Square Pegs and Round Holes?" In *Teaching, Technology, Textuality: Approaches to New Media.* Edited by Michael Hanrahan and Deborah L. Madsen. Houndmills, UK: Palgrave Macmillan. 57–68.

Lejeune, Philippe. 2009. "Diaries on the Internet." In *On Diary.* Edited by Jeremy D. Popkin and Julie Rak. Translated by Katherine Durnin. Honolulu: U of Hawaii P. 280–316.

"Literary Festivals: Who Are They For?" 2010. *The Book Show*, ABC Radio National, April 23, 2010. http://www.abc.net.au/radionational/programs/bookshow/literary-festivals-who-are-they-for/3106890.

Littau, Karin. 2006. *Theories of Reading: Books, Bodies, and Bibliomania.* Cambridge, UK: Polity.

Liu, Alan. 2006. "The Humanities: A Technical Profession." In *Teaching, Technology, Textuality: Approaches to New Media*. Edited by Michael Hanrahan and Deborah L. Madsen. Houndmills, UK: Palgrave Macmillan. 11–26.

Llewellyn, Caro. 2005. "The Hunger for Ideas." *Text*. "Literature and Public Culture" special issue 4, October. http://www.textjournal.com.au/speciss/issue4/llewellyn.htm.

Lodge, David. 2015. "Oxford Literary Festival: The Rise of Literary Festivals." *Financial Times* (UK), March 6, 2015. http://www.ft.com/cms/s/2/cc65e1ba-c2ab-11e4-ad89-00144feab7de.html.

Long, Elizabeth. 1985–1986. "The Cultural Meaning of Concentration in Publishing." *Book Research Quarterly* 1.4: 3–27.

———. 2003. *Book Clubs: Women and the Uses of Reading in Everyday Life*. Chicago: U of Chicago P.

Longley, Edna. 1998. "'Between the Saxon Smile and Yankee Yawp': Problems and Contexts of Literary Reviewing in Ireland." In *Grub Street and the Ivory Tower: Literary Journalism and Literary Scholarship from Fielding to the Internet*. Edited by Jeremy Treglown and Bridget Bennet. Oxford: Clarendon Press. 201–23.

Look, Hugh. 1999. "The Author as Star." *Publishing Research Quarterly* 15.3: 12–29.

Loten, Angus, Adam Janofsky, and Reed Albergotti. 2014. "New Facebook Rules Will Sting Entrepreneurs." *Wall Street Journal*, November 27, 2014. http://www.wsj.com/articles/new-facebook-rules-will-sting-entrepreneurs-1417133694.

Luckerson, Victor. 2014. "The Free-Marketing Gravy Train Is Over on Facebook." *Time*, March 22, 2014. http://time.com/34025/the-free-marketing-gravy-train-is-over-on-facebook/.

Lurie, Caroline. 2004. "Festival, Inc." *Australian Author* 36.2, August: 8–12.

Lynch, Clifford. 2001. "The Battle to Define the Future of the Book in a Digital World." *First Monday* 6.6, June. http://firstmonday.org/ojs/index.php/fm/article/view/864/773.

Lyons, Martyn, and Lucy Taksa. 1992. *Australian Readers Remember: An Oral History of Reading 1890–1930*. Melbourne: Oxford UP.

Mackrell, Alice. 1993. *Coco Chanel*. Fashion Designers series. New York: Holmes and Meier.

Maclaran, Pauline, and Rosalind Masterson. 2006. "You Can't Tell a Book by Its Cover: Bookworms, Bookcases and Bookcrossing." In *Consuming Books: The Marketing and Consumption of Literature*. Edited by Stephen Brown. London: Routledge. 126–37.

Mahajan, Karan. 2016. "One Man's Impossible Quest to Read—and Review—the World." *New Yorker*, February 16, 2016. http://www.newyorker.com/books/page-turner/one-mans-impossible-quest-to-read-and-review-the-world.

Manovich, Lev. 2001. *The Language of New Media*. Cambridge, MA: MIT P.

———. (2008) 2013. *Software Takes Command: Extending the Language of New Media*. New York: Bloomsbury Academic.

Marcus, James. 2004. *Amazonia*. New York: New Press.

———. 2013. "The Mercenary Position." *Harpers*, December: 99–102.

Marino, Mark C. 2006. "Critical Code Studies." *Electronic Book Review*, December 4, 2006. http://www.electronicbookreview.com/thread/electropoetics/codology.

Marshall, P. David, ed. 2006. *The Celebrity Culture Reader*. New York: Routledge.

Martens, Marianne. 2016. *Publishers, Readers, and Digital Engagement*. New Directions in Book History. London: Palgrave Macmillan.

Marwick, Alice, and danah boyd. 2011. "To See and Be Seen: Celebrity Practice on Twitter."

Convergence: The International Journal of Research into New Media Technologies 17.2: 139–58.

Mason, Bruce, and Sue Thomas. 2008. *A Million Penguins Research Report*. Institute of Creative Technologies, De Montfort University, UK. http://www.ioct.dmu.ac.uk/documents /amillionpenguinsreport.pdf.

Masson, Sophie. 2011. "Slices of the Literary Industry." *Quadrant* 55.9: 90–93.

———. 2014. *The Adaptable Author: Coping with Change in the Digital Age*. Sydney: Keesing Press / Australian Society of Authors.

Matthews, Jolie C. 2016. "Professionals and Nonprofessionals on Goodreads: Behavior Standards for Authors, Reviewers, and Readers." *New Media and Society* 18.10: 2305–22.

Mayo, Kat. 2016. "Won't Somebody Please Think of the Readers." *The Best of Australian Author Online* 7, March: 3–4.

McCrum, Robert. 2006. "Has the Novel Lost Its Way?" *Observer*, May 28, 2006. http://www .guardian.co.uk/books/2006/may/28/fiction.features.

McDonald, Peter D. 1997. *British Literary Culture and Publishing Practice 1880–1914*. Cambridge: Cambridge UP.

McGann, Jerome. 1991. *The Textual Condition*. Princeton, NJ: Princeton UP.

———. 2001. *Radiant Textuality: Literature after the World Wide Web*. Houndmills, UK: Palgrave Macmillan.

———. 2004. "A Note on the Current State of Humanities Scholarship." *Critical Inquiry* 30:2: 409–13. http://www.uchicago.edu/research/jnl-crit-inq/issues/v30/30n2.McGann .html.

McGurl, Mark. 2016. "Everything and Less: Fiction in the Age of Amazon." *Modern Language Quarterly* 77.3: 447–71.

McKenzie, D. F. (1986) 1999. *Bibliography and the Sociology of Texts*. Cambridge: Cambridge UP.

McLuhan, Marshall. 1962. *The Gutenberg Galaxy: The Making of Typographic Man*. London: Routledge and Kegan Paul.

McLuhan, Marshall, and David Carson. 2011. *The Book of Probes*. Berkeley, CA: Gingko Press.

McNeill, Lynne. 2007. "Portable Places: Serial Collaboration and the Creation of a New Sense of Place." *Western Folklore* 66.3–4: 281–99.

———. 2012. "Real Virtuality: Enhancing Locality by Enacting the Small World Theory." In *Folk Culture in the Digital Age: The Emergent Dynamics of Human Interaction*. Edited by Trevor J. Blank. Logan: Utah State UP. 85–97.

McPhee, Hilary. 2001. *Other People's Words*. Sydney: Picador.

Meehan, Michael. 2005. "The Word Made Flesh: Festival, Carnality and Literary Consumption." *Text*. "Literature and Public Culture" special issue 4, October. http://www.text journal.com.au/speciss/issue4/meehan.htm.

Metropolitan. 1990. Directed by Whit Stillman. New Line Cinema.

Metz, Nina. 2012. "Super Sad Book Trailers: The Conundrum of Online Book Advertisements—and Why They Usually Fail." *Chicago Tribune*, July 6, 2012. http://articles.chi cagotribune.com/2012-07-06/features/ct-prj-0708-book-trailers-20120706_1_book -trailers-publishers-videos.

Michell, Lynn. 2015. "The Bad Giant: An Independent Publisher's View of Amazon." *The Author* 126.2, Summer: 46–47.

Miller, Laura. 2010. "When Anyone Can Be a Published Author." *Salon,* June 23, 2010. http://www.salon.com/2010/06/23/slush_3/.

———. 2011. "Just Write It! A Fantasy Author and His Impatient Fans." *New Yorker,* April 11, 2011. http://www.newyorker.com/reporting/2011/04/11/110411fa_fact_miller.

———. 2013. "How Amazon and Goodreads Could Lose Their Best Readers." *Salon,* October 24, 2013. http://www.salon.com/2013/10/23/how_amazon_and_goodreads_could_lose_their_best_readers/.

Miller, Laura J. 1999. "Cultural Authority and the Use of New Technology in the Book Trade." *Journal of Arts Management, Law, and Society* 28.4: 297–313.

———. 2006. *Reluctant Capitalists: Bookselling and the Culture of Consumption.* Chicago: U of Chicago P.

———. 2009. "Selling the Product." In *A History of the Book in America: Volume 5—The Enduring Book: Print Culture in Postwar America.* Edited by David Paul Nord, Joan Shelley Rubin, and Michael Schudson. Chapel Hill: U of North Carolina P. 91–106.

———. 2011. "Perpetual Turmoil: Book Retailing in the Twenty-First Century United States." *Logos* 22.3: 16–25.

Miller, Mark Crispin. 1997. "The Crushing Power of Big Publishing." *The Nation,* March 17, 1997: 11–18.

Miller, Peter. 2013. "Building an Author Brand in Today's Digital World—Literary Manager Peter Miller." Interview with Jeff Rivera, May 10, 2013. YouTube. http://www.youtube.com/watch?v=_vj5eenUQqk.

Moeran, Brian. 2011. "The Book Fair as a Tournament of Values." In *Negotiating Values in the Creative Industries: Fairs, Festivals and Competitive Events.* Edited by Brian Moeran and Jesper Strandgaard Pedersen. Cambridge: Cambridge UP. 119–44.

Moeran, Brian, and Jesper Strandgaard Pedersen, eds. 2011. *Negotiating Values in the Creative Industries: Fairs, Festivals and Competitive Events.* Cambridge: Cambridge UP.

Monfort, Nick, and Noah Wardrip-Fruin. 2004. "Acid-free Bits: Recommendations for Long-lasting Electronic Literature." *Electronic Literature Organization* 1.0. http://www.eliterature.org/pad/afb.html#sec2.

Montenegro, Dolores. 2013. "The Problem with Literary Festivals." *New Statesman,* October 14, 2013. http://www.newstatesman.com/books/2013/10/problem-literary-festivals.

Moody, Nickianne. 2011. "Entertainment Media, Risk and the Experience Commodity." In *The Richard and Judy Book Club Reader: Popular Texts and the Practices of Reading.* Edited by Jenni Ramone and Helen Cousins. Farnham, UK: Ashgate. 43–58.

Moran, Joe. 2000. *Star Authors: Literary Celebrity in America.* London: Pluto Press.

Moretti, Franco. 2005. *Graphs, Maps, Trees: Abstract Models for Literary History.* London: Verso.

———. 2013. *Distant Reading.* London: Verso.

Morey, Yvette, Andrew Bengry-Howell, Christine Griffin, Isabelle Szmigin, and Sarah Riley. 2014. "Festivals 2.0: Consuming, Producing and Participating in the Extended Festival Experience." In *The Festivalization of Culture.* Edited by Andy Bennett, Jodie Taylor, and Ian Woodward. Farnham, UK: Ashgate. 251–68.

Morris, Keiko. 2017. "Amazon to Open First Manhattan Bookstore." *Wall Street Journal,* January 4, 2017. https://www.wsj.com/articles/amazon-to-open-first-manhattan-bookstore-1483580781.

Morrison, Aimée. 2007. "Blogs and Blogging: Text and Practice." In *A Companion to Digital Literary Studies*. Edited by Ray Siemens and Susan Schriebman. Oxford: Blackwell. 369–87.

Morrison, Kimberlee. 2014. "How John Green Built an Engaged Fandom for *The Fault in Our Stars*." *Adweek*, June 9, 2014. http://www.adweek.com/socialtimes/john-green-built -engaged-fandom-fault-stars/199323.

Moss, Tara. 2013. "The Only Way Forward." *Australian Author* 45.1, April: 23–25.

Moulthrop, Stuart, and Dene Grigar. 2017. *Traversals: The Use of Preservation for Early Electronic Writing*. Cambridge, MA: MIT P.

Murphy, Priscilla Coit. 2005. *What a Book Can Do: The Publication and Reception of "Silent Spring."* Studies in Print Culture and the History of the Book. Amherst: U of Massachusetts P.

Murray, Simone. 2004a. *Mixed Media: Feminist Presses and Publishing Politics*. London: Pluto Press.

———. 2004b. "'Celebrating the Story the Way It Is': Cultural Studies, Corporate Media and the Contested Utility of Fandom." *Continuum: Journal of Media & Cultural Studies* 18.1: 7–25.

———. 2006. "Content Streaming." In *Paper Empires: A History of the Book in Australia, Volume 3—1946–2005*. Edited by Craig Munro, Robyn Sheahan-Bright, and John Curtain. Brisbane, AU: U of Queensland P. 126–31.

———. 2007. "Generating Content: Book Publishing as a Component Media Industry." In *Making Books: Contemporary Australian Publishing*. Edited by David Carter and Anne Galligan. Brisbane, AU: U of Queensland P. 51–67.

———. 2012. *The Adaptation Industry: The Cultural Economy of Contemporary Literary Adaptation*. Routledge Research in Cultural and Media Studies. New York: Routledge.

———. 2016a. "'Selling' Literature: The Cultivation of Book Buzz in the Digital Literary Sphere." *Logos*. "Independent Publishing Conference" special issue 27.1: 11–21.

———. 2016b. "Literary Studies." In *International Encyclopedia of Communication Theory and Philosophy*. Edited by Klaus Bruhn Jensen, Robert T. Craig, Jeff Pooley, and Eric Rothenbuhler. Malden, MA: Wiley. 1–12. DOI: 10.1002/9781118766804.wbiect184.

———. Forthcoming. "Authorship." In *The Oxford Handbook of Publishing Studies*. Edited by Angus Phillips and Michael Bhaskar. Oxford: Oxford UP.

Murray, Simone, and Millicent Weber. 2017. "'Live and Local?': The Significance of Digital Media for Writers' Festivals." *Convergence: The International Journal of Research into New Media Technologies*. "Writing Digital" special issue 23.1: 61–78.

Muzaffar, Maroosha. 2013. "Where Are You Going, Where Have You Been?" *New York Times*, April 4, 2013. http://www.nytimes.com/interactive/2013/04/14/education/edlife /20130414.html?_r=0.

Myler, Kerry. 2011. "You Can't Judge a Book by Its Coverage: The Body That Writes and the Television Book Club." In *The Richard and Judy Book Club Reader: Popular Texts and the Practices of Reading*. Edited by Jenni Ramone and Helen Cousins. Farnham, UK: Ashgate. 85–107.

Nafisi, Azar. 2014. *The Republic of Imagination: A Case for Fiction*. London: Windmill Books.

Nakamura, Lisa. 2013. "'Words with Friends': Socially Networked Reading on *Goodreads*." *PMLA* 128.1: 238–43.

"Neil Gaiman: Top Ten Most Prolific Authors on Twitter." n.d. *Telegraph* (UK), Picture Gal-

lery. http://www.telegraph.co.uk/culture/books/9957341/Top-ten-most-prolific-authors
-on-Twitter.html?frame=2521143.

Nelles, Drew. 2013. "Solitary Reading in an Age of Compulsory Sharing." In *The Edge of the
Precipice: Why Read Literature in the Digital Age?* Edited by Paul Socken. Montreal and
Kingston: McGill-Queen's UP. 42–52.

Nelson, Meredith. 2006. "The Blog Phenomenon and the Book Publishing Industry." *Publishing Research Quarterly* 22.2: 3–26.

Newman, Richard. 2008. "LibraryThing: The Book Club You Can 'Win.'" *Australian Journal
of Communication* 35.3: 15–27.

Ngai, Sianne. 2007. *Ugly Feelings.* Cambridge, MA: Harvard UP.

Nolan, Sybil, and Matthew Ricketson. 2013. "Unintended Consequences: The Impact of
Structural Reform in the Newspaper Industry on the Marketing of Books." In *By the
Book? Contemporary Publishing in Australia.* Edited by Emmett Stinson. Melbourne:
Monash UP. 29–39.

Nowra, Louis. 2010. "Eleven Things You Should Know About Writers' Festivals." *Australian
Author* 42.1, April: 6–10.

Nunberg, Geoffrey, ed. 1996. *The Future of the Book.* Berkeley: U of California P.

Obeng-Odoom, Franklin. 2014. "Why Write Book Reviews?" *Australian Universities' Review*
56.1: 78–82.

O'Brien, Connor Tomas. 2013. "World's First Exclusively Online Writers' Festival Announced
for 2014." Interview via Twitter. *Concrete Playground*, December 4, 2013. http://concrete
playground.com/brisbane/interviews/worlds-first-exclusively-online-writers-festival
-announced-for-2014/.

Ohlsson, Anders, Torbjörn Forslid, and Ann Steiner. 2014. "Literary Celebrity Reconsid-
ered." *Celebrity Studies* 5.1–2: 32–44.

Olson, David R. 1994. *The World on Paper.* Cambridge: Cambridge UP.

Ommundsen, Wenche. 1999. "The Circus Is in Town: Literary Festivals and the Mapping
of Cultural Heritage." *Australian Writing and the City.* Proceedings of the Association
for the Study of Australian Literature (ASAL) annual conference. Edited by Fran de
Groen and Ken Stewart. Sydney: ASAL. 173–79.

———. 2004. "Sex, Soap and Sainthood: Beginning to Theorise Literary Celebrity." *JASAL*
3: 45–56.

———. 2007. "From the Altar to the Market-Place and Back Again: Understanding Literary
Celebrity." In *Stardom and Celebrity: A Reader.* Edited by Sean Redmond and Su Holmes.
London: Sage. 244–55.

———. 2009. "Literary Festivals and Cultural Consumption." *Australian Literary Studies*
24.1: 19–34.

Ong, Walter J. 1982. *Orality and Literacy: The Technologizing of the Word.* London: Methuen.

Orr, David. 2004. "Where to Find Digital Lit." *New York Times*, October 3, 2004. http://www
.nytimes.com/2004/10/03/books/review/where-to-find-digital-lit.html.

Orthofer, M. A. 2010. *The Complete Review: Eleven Years, 2500 Reviews—A Site History with
Commentary on Diverse and Sundry Related Matters.* N.p.: Aesthetics of Resistance Press.

Orwell, George. (1946) 2003. "Confessions of a Book Reviewer." *The Complete Works of
George Orwell.* http://www.george-orwell.org/Confessions_of_a_Book_Reviewer/0.html.

Ouellette, Laurie, and Jonathan Gray, eds. 2017. *Keywords for Media Studies.* New York:
NYU P.

Packer, George. 2014. "Cheap Words." *New Yorker,* February 17, 2014. http://www.new yorker.com/reporting/2014/02/17/140217fa_fact_packer?currentPage=all.

Page, Ruth, and Bronwen Thomas, eds. 2011. *New Narratives: Stories and Storytelling in the Digital Age.* Lincoln: U of Nebraska P.

Palattella, John. 2010. "The Death and Life of the Book Review." *The Nation,* June 3, 2010. https://www.thenation.com/article/death-and-life-book-review/.

Parsons, John. 2013. "The Social Publisher." *Book Business* 16.5, October: 18–22.

Paskin, Willa. 2016. "*Game of Thrones* Finally Breaks Free of George R. R. Martin's Books, and It's Kind of Thrilling." *Slate,* April 25, 2016. http://www.slate.com/blogs/browbeat /2016/04/25/game_of_thrones_season_6_premiere_the_red_woman_reviewed.html.

Patrick, Bethanne. 2016. "I Am Jessa Crispin's Problem with Publishing." *Literary Hub,* May 13, 2016. http://lithub.com/i-am-jessa-crispins-problem-with-publishing/.

Paul, Pamela. 2010. "The Author Takes a Star Turn." *New York Times,* July 11, 2010: L1.

Pavia, Will. 2013. "Jonathan Franzen: Would Charlotte Bronte Have Tweeted? I Don't Think So." *Times* (UK), October 10, 2013: 4–5.

Pedersen, Sarah. 2008. "Now Read This: Male and Female Bloggers' Recommendations for Further Reading." *Participations* 5.2. http://www.participations.org/Volume%205/Issue %202/5_02_pedersen.htm.

Peltz, Jennifer. 2009. "3,000-Person Book Club v. 1,000-Page Hardly Read Classic." *Globe and Mail* (Toronto), June 22, 2009: L2.

Pettitt, Tom. 2007. "Before the Gutenberg Parenthesis: Elizabethan-American Compatibilities." Plenary presentation to Media in Transition 5 conference, MIT. http://web.mit .edu/comm-forum/mit5/papers/pettitt_plenary_gutenberg.pdf.

Peyre. Henri. 1963. "What Is Wrong with American Book-Reviewing?" *Daedalus.* "The American Reading Public" special issue 92.1: 128–44.

Pinder, Julian. 2012. "Online Literary Communities: A Case Study of Library Thing." In *From Codex to Hypertext: Reading at the Turn of the Twenty-First Century.* Edited by Anouk Lang. Amherst: U of Massachusetts P. 68–87.

Piper, Andrew. 2015. "Novel Devotions: Conversional Reading, Computational Modeling, and the Modern Novel." *New Literary History* 46: 63–98.

Plato. 2005. *Phaedrus.* Translated by C. J. Rowe. Penguin Classics. London: Penguin.

Poland, Louise. 1999. "Independent Australian Publishers and the Acquisition of Books." *Journal of Australian Studies* 63: 110–18.

Pool, Gail. 1994. "Eliminate the Negative?" *The Women's Review of Books* 11.12, September: 15–16.

———. 2007. *Faint Praise: The Plight of Book Reviewing in America.* Columbia: U of Missouri P.

———. 2008. "Book Reviewing: Do It Yourself." *The Women's Review of Books* 25.2: 9.

Popescu, Adam. 2014. "Can Twitter Help Publishers Reinvent Books?" *Fast Company,* March 12, 2014. http://www.fastcolabs.com/3027644/can-twitter-help-publishers-re invent-books.

Porton, Richard, ed. 2009. *On Film Festivals.* Dekalog series. London: Wallflower Press.

Poster, Mark. 2001. *What's the Matter with the Internet?* Electronic mediations series. Minneapolis: U of Minnesota P.

Powell, Julie. (2005) 2009. *Julie and Julia: My Year of Cooking Dangerously.* Boston: Little, Brown.

Power, Liza. 2015. "Tales from the Bored Zone." *The Age* (Melbourne), January 10, 2015: Spectrum, 14–15.

Pressman, Jessica. 2007. "Navigating Electronic Literature." *Electronic Literature*, March 2007. http://newhorizons.eliterature.org/essay.php@id=14.html.

———. 2009. "The Aesthetic of Bookishness in Twenty-First-Century Literature." *Michigan Quarterly Review* 48.4. http://hdl.handle.net/2027/spo.act2080.0048.402.

Pressman, Jessica, and Lisa Swanstrom, eds. 2013. "The Literary And/As the Digital Humanities." *Digital Humanities Quarterly* 7.1. http://www.digitalhumanities.org/dhq/vol /7/1/000154/000154.html.

Price, Leah. 2004. "Reading: The State of the Discipline." *Book History* 7: 303–20.

Prothero, Stephen. 2010. "Fear and Trembling before the iPad." *Publishers Weekly,* May 10, 2010: 48.

Pugh, Sheenagh. 2005. *The Democratic Genre: Fan Fiction in a Literary Context.* Bridgend, UK: Seren Books.

Rabkin, Eric S. 2006. "Audience, Purpose, and Medium: How Digital Media Extend Humanities Education." In *Teaching, Technology, Textuality: Approaches to New Media.* Edited by Michael Hanrahan and Deborah L. Madsen. Houndmills, UK: Palgrave Macmillan. 135–47.

Radford, Ceri. 2012. "How Twitter Is Changing the Literary World." *Telegraph*, March 12, 2012. http://www.telegraph.co.uk/culture/books/9137910/How-Twitter-is-changing-the -literary-world.html.

Radway, Janice A. 1984. *Reading the Romance: Women, Patriarchy, and Popular Literature.* Chapel Hill: U of North Carolina P.

———. 1997. *A Feeling for Books: The Book-of-the-Month Club, Literary Taste, and Middle-Class Desire.* Chapel Hill: U of North Carolina P.

Ramone, Jenni, and Helen Cousins, eds. 2011. *The Richard and Judy Book Club Reader: Popular Texts and the Practices of Reading.* Farnham, UK: Ashgate.

Rapping, Elayne. 1994. "Growing Pains." *The Women's Review of Books* 12.2, November: 25–26.

Ray Murray, Padmini, and Claire Squires. 2013. "The Digital Publishing Communications Circuit." *Book 2.0* 3.1: 3–23.

Reagle, Joseph M. 2015. *Reading the Comments: Likers, Haters, and Manipulators at the Bottom of the Web.* Cambridge, MA: MIT P.

Rehberg Sedo, DeNel. 2002. "Predictions of Life After Oprah: A Glimpse at the Power of Book Club Readers." *Publishing Research Quarterly* 18.3: 11–22.

———. 2003. "Readers in Reading Groups: An Online Survey of Face-to-Face and Virtual Book Clubs." *Convergence: The Journal of Research into New Media Technologies* 9.1: 66–90.

———, ed. 2011a. *Reading Communities from Salons to Cyberspace.* Houndmills, UK: Palgrave Macmillan.

———. 2011b. "'I Used to Read Anything That Caught My Eye, But . . .': Cultural Authority and Intermediaries in a Virtual Young Adult Book Club." In *Reading Communities from Salons to Cyberspace.* Edited by DeNel Rehberg Sedo. Houndmills, UK: Palgrave Macmillan. 101–22.

Rettberg, Jill Walker. 2014. *Blogging.* 2nd ed. Digital Media and Society series. Cambridge, UK: Polity.

Rettberg, Scott. 2016. "Electronic Literature as Digital Humanities." In *A New Companion to Digital Humanities*. Edited by Susan Schreibman, Ray Siemens, and John Unsworth. Chichester, UK: Wiley. 127–36.

Rich, Motoko. 2007. "Are Book Reviewers Out of Print?" *New York Times,* May 2, 2007. http://www.nytimes.com/2007/05/02/books/02revi.html.

Rickett, Joel. 2007. "Film 'Trailers' for Books." *Bookseller,* November 30, 2007: 8.

Robertson, Martin, and Ian Yeoman. 2014. "Signals and Signposts of the Future: Literary Festival Consumption in 2050." *Tourism Recreation Research* 39.3: 321–42.

Robertson, Robin, ed. 2003. *Mortification: Writers' Stories of their Public Shame*. Toronto: HarperCollins.

Robinson, Colin. 2010. "The Trouble with Amazon." *The Nation,* July 14, 2010. http://www.thenation.com/article/37484/trouble-amazon.

———. 2014. "The Loneliness of the Long-Distance Reader." *New York Times,* January 4, 2014. https://www.nytimes.com/2014/01/05/opinion/sunday/the-loneliness-of-the-long-distance-reader.html?_r=0.

Rombes, Nicholas. 2005. "The Rebirth of the Author." *CTheory.net* 10, June 2005. http://www.ctheory.net/articles.aspx?id=480.

Rommel, Thomas. 2004. "Literary Studies." In *A Companion to Digital Humanities*. Edited by Susan Schreibman, Ray Siemens, and John Unsworth. Malden, MA: Blackwell. 88–96.

Ronai, Francesca. 2010. "Coming Attractions." *Bookseller,* September 10, 2010: 22–23.

Rooney, Brigid. 2009. *Literary Activists: Writer-Intellectuals and Australian Public Life*. Brisbane, AU: U of Queensland P.

Rose, Jonathan. 1992. "Rereading the English Common Reader: A Preface to a History of Audiences." *Journal of the History of Ideas* 53.1: 47–70.

———. 2001. *The Intellectual Life of the British Working Classes*. New Haven, CT: Yale UP.

Rose, Mark. 1993. *Authors and Owners: The Invention of Copyright*. Cambridge, MA: Harvard UP.

Ross, Alex. 2017. "The Fate of the Critic in the Clickbait Age." *New Yorker,* March 13, 2017. http://www.newyorker.com/culture/cultural-comment/the-fate-of-the-critic-in-the-clickbait-age.

Rowberry, Simon Peter. 2016. "Commonplacing the Public Domain: Reading the Classics Socially on the Kindle." *Language and Literature* 25.3: 211–25.

———. 2017. "Ebookness." *Convergence* 23.3: 289–305.

Rubin, Joan Shelley. 2009. "The Enduring Reader." In *A History of the Book in America: Volume 5—The Enduring Book: Print Culture in Postwar America*. Edited by David Paul Nord, Joan Shelley Rubin, and Michael Schudson. Chapel Hill: U of North Carolina P. 412–31.

Ruddick, Graham. 2015. "Amazon Begins a New Chapter with Opening of First Physical Bookstore." *Guardian,* November 4, 2015.

Ruffel, Lionel. 2014. "The Public Spaces of Contemporary Literature." Translated by Matthew H. Evans. *Qui Parle* 22.2: 101–22.

Russo, Richard. 2014. "Letter from Richard Russo on the Amazon-Hachette Dispute." *Authors Guild.* July 10, 2014. http://www.authorsguild.org/general/letter-from-richard-russo-on-the-amazon-hachette-dispute/.

Sage, Lorna. 1998. "Living on Writing." In *Grub Street and the Ivory Tower: Literary Journal-*

ism and Literary Scholarship from Fielding to the Internet. Edited by Jeremy Treglown and Bridget Bennet. Oxford: Clarendon Press. 262–76.

Sapiro, Gisèle. 2016. "The Metamorphosis of Modes of Consecration in the Literary Field: Academies, Literary Prizes, Festivals." *Poetics* 59: 5–19.

Schiffrin, André. 2001. *The Business of Books: How International Conglomerates Took Over Publishing and Changed the Way We Read.* London: Verso.

Schnittman, Evan. 2008. "Discoverability and Access in Book Publishing: Longtail Marketing and Content Access Models Explored." *Publishing Research Quarterly* 24: 139–42.

Scott, Allen J. 2006. "Creative Cities: Conceptual Issues and Policy Questions." *Journal of Urban Affairs* 28.1: 1–17.

Seajay, Carol. 1994. "The Backlash and the Backlist." *The Women's Review of Books* 12.3, December: 18–19.

Seaton, A. V. 1996. "Hay on Wye, The Mouse That Roared: Book Towns and Rural Tourism." *Tourism Management* 17.5: 379–82.

———. 1999. "Book Towns as Tourism Developments in Peripheral Areas." *International Journal of Tourism Research* 1.5: 389–99.

Self, Will. 2013. Review of *Hatchet Job* by Mark Kermode. *Guardian,* October 9, 2013. http://www.theguardian.com/books/2013/oct/09/hatchet-job-mark-kermode-review.

Sheff, David. 2000. "Jeff Bezos." *David Sheff,* February 2000. http://davidsheff.com/article /jeff-bezos/.

Siemens, Ray, and Susan Schreibman, eds. 2007. *A Companion to Digital Literary Studies.* Malden, MA: Wiley.

Silverman, Jacob. 2012. "Against Enthusiasm." *Slate,* August 2012. http://www.slate.com /articles/arts/books/2012/08/writers_and_readers_on_twitter_and_tumblr_we_need _more_criticism_less_liking_.html.

Simons, Judy, and Kate Fullbrook, eds. 1998. *Writing: A Woman's Business—Women, Writing and the Marketplace.* Manchester, UK: Manchester UP.

Skains, R. Lyle. 2010. "The Shifting Author-Reader Dynamic: Online Novel Communities as a Bridge from Print to Digital Literature." *Convergence* 16:1: 95–111.

Smith, Sidonie, and Julia Watson. 2014. "Virtually Me: A Toolbox about Online Self-Presentation." In *Identity Technologies: Constructing the Self Online.* Edited by Anna Poletti and Julie Rak. Madison: U of Wisconsin P. 70–95.

Spector, Robert. 2000. *Amazon.com: Get Big Fast.* New York: HarperBusiness.

Spender, Dale. 1995. *Nattering on the Net: Women, Power and Cyberspace.* Melbourne: Spinifex Press.

Spender, Lynne. 2004. *Between the Lines: A Legal Guide for Writers and Illustrators.* Sydney: Keesing Press / Australian Society of Authors.

Squires, Claire. 2007. *Marketing Literature: The Making of Contemporary Writing in Britain.* Houndmills, UK: Palgrave Macmillan.

Stadler, Matthew. 2016. "The Ends of the Book: Reading, Economies, & Publics." In *Literary Publishing in the Twenty-First Century.* Edited by Travis Kurowski, Wayne Miller, and Kevin Prufer. Minneapolis, MN: Milkweed Editions. 14–31.

Starke, Ruth. 2006. "Festival Big Top." In *Paper Empires: A History of the Book in Australia, Volume 3—1946–2005.* Edited by Craig Munro, Robyn Sheahan-Bright, and John Curtain. Brisbane, AU: U of Queensland P. 156–59.

Starkey, Neal. 2005. "Online Book-Clubbing Made Easy." *American Libraries* 36.8, September: 50–51.

Staskiewicz, Keith. 2011. "Like the Trailer? Buy the Book." *Entertainment Weekly,* August 5, 2011: 77.

St Clair, William. 2004. *The Reading Nation in the Romantic Period.* Cambridge: Cambridge UP.

Steger, Jason. 2014. "Bookmarks." *Saturday Age* (Melbourne), June 21, 2014: Spectrum, 37.

Steiner, Ann. 2008. "Private Criticism in the Public Space: Personal Writing on Literature in Readers' Reviews on Amazon." *Participations* 5.2. http://www.participations.org/Volume%205/Issue%202/5_02_steiner.htm.

———. 2010. "Personal Readings and Public Texts: Book Blogs and Online Writing about Literature." *Culture Unbound* 2: 471–94. http://www.cultureunbound.ep.liu.se/article.asp?doi=10.3384/cu.2000.1525.10228471.

Stewart, Cori. 2010a. *The Culture of Contemporary Writers' Festivals.* Saarbrücken, Germany: Verlag Dr. Müller.

———. 2010b. "We Call Upon the Author to Explain: Theorising Writers' Festivals as Sites of Contemporary Public Culture." *Journal of the Association for the Study of Australian Literature.* "Common Readers and Cultural Critics" special issue. http://openjournals.library.usyd.edu.au/index.php/JASAL/issue/view/751/showToc:.

———. 2013. "The Rise and Rise of Writers' Festivals." In *A Companion to Creative Writing.* Edited by Graeme Harper. Chichester, UK: Wiley. 263–77.

Stinson, Emmett. 2017. "The Ethics of Evaluation." *Sydney Review of Books,* May 23, 2017. http://sydneyreviewofbooks.com/ethics-evaluation-consumer-recommendations-literary-value/.

Stokes, Jane. 2013. *How to Do Media and Cultural Studies.* 2nd ed. London: Sage.

Stone, Brad. 2013. *The Everything Store: Jeff Bezos and the Age of Amazon.* New York: Little, Brown.

Stone, Brad, and Motoko Rich. 2010. "Amazon Removes Macmillan Books." *New York Times,* January 30, 2010. http://www.nytimes.com/2010/01/30/technology/30amazon.html.

Streitfeld, David. 2015. "Amazon Adds New Perks for Workers and Opens a Bookstore." *New York Times,* November 3, 2015.

Striphas, Ted. 2009. *The Late Age of Print: Everyday Book Culture from Consumerism to Control.* New York: Columbia UP.

———. 2010a. "The Abuses of Literacy: Amazon Kindle and the Right to Read." *Communication and Critical/Cultural Studies* 7.3: 297–317.

———. 2010b. "How to Have Culture in an Algorithmic Age." *The Late Age of Print,* June 14, 2010. http://www.thelateageofprint.org/2010/06/14/how-to-have-culture-in-an-algorithmic-age/.

———. 2012. "What Is an Algorithm?" *Culture Digitally,* February 1, 2012. http://culturedigitally.org/2012/02/what-is-an-algorithm/.

———. 2015. "Algorithmic Culture." *European Journal of Cultural Studies* 18.4–5: 395–412.

Sullivan, Jane. 2013a. "A Suggested Trail through the Online Maze." *Saturday Age* (Melbourne), March 29, 2013: Life and Style, 27.

———. 2013b. "Bookworms on the Web." *Saturday Age* (Melbourne), April 20, 2013: Life and Style, 30.

Sullivan, J. Courtney. 2009. "See the Web Site, Buy the Book." *New York Times Book Review*, January 25, 2009: 23.

Sutherland, J. A. 1978. *Fiction and the Fiction Industry*. London: Athlone Press.

Talbot, Margaret. 2014. "The Teen Whisperer." *New Yorker*, June 9, 2014. http://www.new yorker.com/magazine/2014/06/09/the-teen-whisperer.

Taylor, Martin. 2013. "How Book Marketing Changes When It's Digital." *News on Bookselling*, November. http://issuu.com/newsonbookselling/docs/nov_nob.

Teres, Harvey. 2009. "The Critical Climate." In *A History of the Book in America: Volume 5—The Enduring Book: Print Culture in Postwar America*. Edited by David Paul Nord, Joan Shelley Rubin, and Michael Schudson. Chapel Hill: U of North Carolina P. 233–45.

Thomas, Bronwen. 2011a. "'Update Soon!': Harry Potter Fanfiction and Narrative as a Participatory Process." In *New Narratives: Stories and Storytelling in the Digital Age*. Edited by Ruth Page and Bronwen Thomas. Lincoln: U of Nebraska P. 205–19.

———. 2011b. "What Is Fanfiction and Why Are People Saying Such Nice Things about It?" *StoryWorlds: A Journal of Narrative Studies* 3: 1–24.

———. 2014. "140 Characters in Search of a Story: Twitterfiction as an Emerging Narrative Form." In *Analyzing Digital Fiction*. Edited by Alice Bell, Astrid Ensslin, and Hans Kristian Rustad. London: Routledge. 94–108.

Thompson, John B. 2005. *Books in the Digital Age: The Transformation of Academic and Higher Education Publishing in Britain and the United States*. Cambridge, UK: Polity.

———. 2010. *Merchants of Culture: The Publishing Business in the Twenty-First Century*. Cambridge, UK: Polity.

Thompson, Rachel. 2013. "Why Blogging Is Key for Authors." *BookPromotion.com*, n.d. http://www.bookpromotion.com/authors-need-blog/.

Tian, Xuemei, and Bill Martin. 2010. "Digital Technologies for Book Marketing." *Publishing Research Quarterly* 26.3: 151–67.

Timberg, Scott. 2015. "Five Reasons to Wish Amazon an Unhappy Birthday." *Salon*, July 11, 2015.http://www.salon.com/2015/07/10/5_reasons_to_wish_amazon_an_unhappy _birthday/.

Tokars, Mike. 2015. "Why Amazon.com Opened a Bookstore." *Christian Science Monitor*, November 3, 2015.

Topping, Alexandra. 2010. "Historian Orlando Figes Agrees to Pay Damages for Fake Reviews." *Guardian*, July 17, 2010. https://www.theguardian.com/books/2010/jul/16 /orlando-figes-fake-amazon-reviews.

Tosca, Susana, and Helle Nina Pedersen. 2015. "Is There a Text in This Tablet?" In *The Tablet Book*. Edited by C. Bassett, R. Burns, R. Glasson, and K. O'Riordan. Falmer, UK: Reframe Books. 180–205. http://reframe.sussex.ac.uk/wp-content/uploads/2015/03/7 _Is-There-a-Text-in-this-tablet_FINAL.pdf.

Totanes, Vernon R. 2011. "Filipino Blogs as Evidence of Reading and Reception." In *The History of Reading, volume 3: Methods, Strategies, Tactics*. Edited by Rosalind Crone and Shafquat Towheed. Houndmills, UK: Palgrave Macmillan. 177–95.

Towheed, Shafquat, Rosalind Crone, and Katie Halsey, eds. 2011. *The History of Reading: A Reader*. Routledge Literature Readers. London: Routledge.

Travis, Trysh. 2003. "Divine Secrets of the Cultural Studies Sisterhood: Women Reading Rebecca Wells." *American Literary History* 15.1: 134–61.

Tucker, Joshua. 2010. "Making Sense of the Kindle's Highlighting Feature." *Salon*, August 10, 2010. http://www.salon.com/2010/08/09/kindle_social_highlighting/.

Turner, Graeme. 2004. *Understanding Celebrity*. London: Sage.

Tushnet, Rebecca. 1996. "Legal Fictions." *Loyola of Los Angeles Entertainment Law Review* 17: 651.

———. 2007. "Payment in Credit: Copyright Law and Subcultural Creativity." *Law and Contemporary Problems* 70.

Twyford-Moore, Sam. 2012. "Twitter>The Novel? @tejucole> Teju Cole?" *Meanjin* 71.4: 34–42.

van der Weel, Adriaan. 2015. "Appropriation: Towards a Sociotechnical History of Authorship." *Authorship* 4.2. http://www.authorship.ugent.be/article/view/1438.

Vinjamuri, David. 2012. "Do Customer Reviews Have a Future? Why Amazon's Sock Puppet Scandal Is Bigger Than It Appears." *Forbes*, December 9, 2012. http://www.forbes.com/sites/davidvinjamuri/2012/09/12/do-consumer-reviews-have-a-future-why-ama zons-sock-puppet-scandal-is-bigger-than-it-appears/.

Vlieghe, Joachim, Jaël Muls, and Kris Rutten. 2016. "Everybody Reads: Reader Engagement with Literature in Social Media Environments." *Poetics* 54: 25–37.

Vlieghe, Joachim, Kelly Page, and Kris Rutten. 2016. " 'Twitter, the Most Brilliant Tough Love Editor You'll Ever Have.' Reading and Writing Socially During the Twitter Fiction Festival." *First Monday* 21.4. http://firstmonday.org/ojs/index.php/fm/article/view /6334/5326.

Vlieghe, Joachim, and Kris Rutten. 2013. "Rhetorical Analysis of Literary Culture in Social Reading Platforms." *CLCWeb: Comparative Literature and Culture* 15.3. http://dx.doi .org/10.7771/1481-4374.2244.

Voigt, Kati. 2013. "Becoming Trivial: The Book Trailer." *Culture Unbound* 5: 671–89. http:// www.cultureunbound.ep.liu.se/article.asp?doi=10.3384/cu.2000.1525.135671.

Walker, Tim. 2012. "Coming Soon to a Shelf near You: The Publishing Industry Has Gone Mad for Film-Style Trailers." *Independent* (UK), February 16, 2012. http://www.inde pendent.co.uk/arts-entertainment/books/features/coming-soon-to-a-shelf-near-you -the-publishing-industry-has-gone-mad-for-film-style-trailers-6945653.html.

Wallace, David Foster. 1996. *Infinite Jest*. London: Abacus.

Walmsley, Ben. 2016. "From Arts Marketing to Audience Enrichment: How Digital Engagement Can Deepen and Democratize Artistic Exchange with Audiences." *Poetics* 58: 66–78.

Ward, Peter. 2016. "Touring Westeros by Bus, 'Game of Thrones' Fans Seek Sights and Spoilers." *Newsweek*, April 9, 2016. http://www.newsweek.com/2016/04/22/northern -ireland-westeros-bus-tour-hbo-game-thrones-george-rr-martin-445737.html.

Wark, McKenzie. 2004. *A Hacker Manifesto*. Cambridge, MA: Harvard UP.

———. 2007. *Gamer Theory*. Cambridge, MA: Harvard UP.

Wasserman, Marlie. 1994. "In the Food Chain." *The Women's Review of Books* 11.7, April: 15–16.

Wasserman, Steve. 2012. "The Amazon Effect." *Nation*, June 18, 2012. http://www.thena tion.com/article/168125/amazon-effect#.

Waters, Juliet. 2013. "The Code of Life." *New York Times*, December 15, 2013: 8.

Weber, Millicent. 2015. "Conceptualizing Audience Experience at the Literary Festival." *Continuum: Journal of Media and Cultural Studies* 29.1: 84–96.

———. 2016. "Audience in the Spotlight: Investigating Literary Festival Engagement." PhD dissertation, Monash University, Melbourne.

Weedon, Alexis. 2007. "In Real Life: Book Covers in the Internet Bookstore." In *Judging a Book by Its Cover: Fans, Publishers, Designers, and the Marketing of Fiction.* Edited by Nicole Matthews and Nickianne Moody. Aldershot, UK: Ashgate. 117–25.

Weiner, Jennifer. 2013. "What Jonathan Franzen Misunderstands about Me." *New Republic,* September 18, 2013. https://newrepublic.com/article/114762/jennifer-weiner-re sponds-jonathan-franzen.

Weinman, Sarah. 2008. "Book Trailers." *Poets and Writers,* November/December: 95–98.

Weisbard, Phyllis Holman. 1995. "Reviews and Their Afterlife." *The Women's Review of Books* 12.4, January: 16–17.

West, James L. W., III. 1988. *American Authors and the Literary Marketplace since 1900.* Philadelphia: U of Pennsylvania P.

Whitlock, Gillian. 2007. "Arablish: The Baghdad Blogger." *Soft Weapons: Autobiography in Transit.* Chicago: U of Chicago P. 24–44.

"Who's Writing Literary Reviews?" 2011. *The Book Show,* ABC Radio National, February 22, 2011. http://www.abc.net.au/radionational/programs/bookshow/whos-writing-literary -reviews/2995094.

Wilcockson, Nigel. 2012. "Self-Publish and Be Damned." *The Author* 123.4, Winter: 125–27.

Wilkens, Matthew. 2012. "Canons, Close Reading, and the Evolution of Method." In *Debates in the Digital Humanities.* Edited by Matthew K. Gold. Minneapolis: U of Minnesota P. 249–58.

———. 2015. "Digital Humanities and Its Application in the Study of Literature and Culture." *Comparative Literature* 67.1: 11–20.

Wilkins, Kim. 2014. "Creativity in the Age of Distraction." *Writing Queensland* 244, September: 6–7. https://search.informit.com.au/fullText;dn=623096375480073;res=IELAPA.

Williams, David. 2012. "The Indiscriminate Tide." *The Author* 123.4, Winter: 128–29.

Willis, Ellen. 1994. "Great Expectations." *The Women's Review of Books* 11.8, May: 14–15.

Wind, Lee. 2014. "Your Web Presence: 3 Keys to Connecting with Young Readers Online." *Writer's Digest* 94.4, May/June: 32–35.

Wirtén, Eva Hemmungs. 2004. *No Trespassing.* Toronto: U of Toronto P.

Women in Publishing. 1987. *Reviewing the Reviews: A Woman's Place on the Book Page.* London: Journeyman Press.

" 'Women Reviewing/Reviewing Women.' " 1994. *The Women's Review of Books* 11.6, March: 13.

Woodmansee, Martha. 1984. "The Genius and the Copyright: Economic and Legal Conditions of the Emergence of the 'Author.' " *Eighteenth-Century Studies* 17.4: 425–48.

———. 1994. *The Author, Art, and the Market: Rereading the History of Aesthetics.* New York: Columbia UP.

Woodmansee, Martha, and Peter Jaszi, eds. 1993. *The Construction of Authorship.* Durham, NC: Duke UP.

Woodward, Richard B. 1999. "Reading in the Dark: Has American Lit Crit Burned Out?" *Village Voice,* October 26, 1999: Literary Supplement, 92–94, 131.

Wright, David. 2012. "Literary Taste and List Culture in a Time of 'Endless Choice.' " In *From Codex to Hypertext: Reading at the Turn of the Twenty-First Century.* Edited by Anouk Lang. Amherst: U of Massachusetts P. 108–23.

Wu, Yung-Hsing. 2013. "Kindling, Disappearing, Reading." *Digital Humanities Quarterly* 7.1. http://www.digitalhumanities.org/dhq/vol/7/1/000115/000115.html.

Yagoda, Ben. 2006. "Michiko Kakutani: A Critic with a Fixation." *Slate,* April 10, 2006. http://www.slate.com/articles/arts/culturebox/2006/04/michiko_kakutani.html.

Yglesias, Helen. 1994. "Through the Back Door." *The Women's Review of Books* 11.6, March: 13.

York, Lorraine. 2000. " 'He Should Do Well on the American Talk Shows': Celebrity, Publishing, and the Future of Canadian Literature." *Essays on Canadian Writing* 71: 96–105.

———. 2007. *Literary Celebrity in Canada.* Toronto: U of Toronto P.

———. 2013a. *Margaret Atwood and the Labour of Literary Celebrity.* Toronto: U of Toronto P.

———. 2013b. " 'How a Girl from Canada Break the Bigtime': Esi Edugyan and the Next Generation of Literary Celebrity in Canada." *Canadian Literature* 217: 18–33, 204.

Young, Damon. 2015. "Words Aren't All I Have." *Saturday Age* (Melbourne), May 16, 2015: Spectrum, 21.